Salvation Manual

Topical Exegesis of the Book of Genesis - Volume 2

Johnny, Nsikan Effiong

Grosvenor House
Publishing Limited

This book is published by
Grosvenor House Publishing Ltd
Link House
140 The Broadway, Tolworth, Surrey, KT6 7HT.
www.grosvenorhousepublishing.co.uk

This book is a commentary on the Bible and non-Biblical illustrations
used are fiction. Any resemblance to
people or events, past or present, is purely coincidental.

A CIP record for this book
is available from the British Library

Paperback ISBN 978-1-80381-047-8
Hardback ISBN 978-1-80381-112-3
eBook ISBN 978-1-80381-085-0

www.smni.org

TABLE OF CONTENTS

FOREWORD

The purpose of God to reach humanity with the message of salvation has not diminished across generations. He entrusts that eternal assignment to men who are willing and available. The author of *Salvation Manual: Topical Exegesis*, Nsikan E. Johnny, was challenged in a service at which his pastor demanded to know how many times members of the congregation had read the whole Bible. One person answered, saying "twenty-plus". That incident planted in him the hunger for the word of God, which led him to design ways to read and understand the Bible. The Lord, several times, kept pointing him to these facts: the primary purpose of the Bible is to unfold the salvation of humanity through Christ; the doctrine of salvation is foundational to every subject in the word of God; and each subject must be interpreted in the light of salvation through Christ. The author's unwavering dislike of wrong biblical teachings, either deliberately for selfish motives or out of ignorance, is unparalleled.

It has been my pleasure to know Nsikan E. Johnny for quite some time in a friendship that has gone from mere acquaintance to being co-labourers in ministry. His vision to reach out to people with the truth relating to salvation led him to organise Bible studies which he taught at his office. Later, he sponsored a Bible quiz programme on radio in Akwa Ibom State, Nigeria. In 2015, the vision expanded to a national level through the Bible *Answer And Win* programme on social media and its accompanying blog site, which he presided over to transform lives. However, the vision has not stopped; it keeps growing, which is evident in this book, all in a bid to promote the message of salvation to the ends of the earth.

The subject of salvation resonates through the book's pages. The book is eternally valuable, scripturally based, doctrinally sound and reflects God's will about salvation, which is beneficial for all ages. It is given with prayers to positively change the erroneous trend concerning Bible truth and salvation. This remarkable work instructs and illustrates the importance of the Bible as a manual for our lives. It helps unlock salvation principles that will benefit both preachers and teachers of the word and all who would live a Christlike life. It is shaped with one thought in mind: to help people understand God's word with an *emphasis on salvation*. The book is well written, informative and an eye-opener for Christians who want to know God for themselves. It implores Christians to study the Bible from the angle of salvation, which will protect them from possible errors of wrong teachings.

A big thanks to the author for writing this much-needed manual. Through the help of the Holy Spirit, I believe this piece of work will help people return to the narrow path now that the door of mercy is still open. I recommend this book to you, fellow pilgrims; it shall serve as a guide through this world back to our heavenly home.

Revd B. Agbor Anayo
Bristol, UK.

PREFACE

Precious things in the world are hard to come by, and sometimes when found they are highly priced. Salvation is more precious than anything else and is not without a cost or price. Christ paid the price through His death and He admonishes us to carry our cross and follow Him. This entails responsibility on our part to obtain this gift of salvation. If a man finds a jewel of inestimable value, will he not sell all he has to enable him to purchase it? The gift of salvation is something we should go all out to obtain, with all that is in us and all we have.

This book is written and published chiefly with a view to enlightening many. In defence of that which is true and with a desire to correct the many erroneous teachings spreading through the church, I think of this book as a valuable companion for all genuine seekers journeying through life. My soul's salvation and the salvation of others have always driven me to create avenues and systems to spread the gospel. Lying deep in my heart, the great commission demanded by the Saviour has become not only a purpose but a passion for continuing my Master's work and making known to the world the burden placed in my heart by the Holy Spirit.

The scripture says that faith comes by hearing and hearing by the word of God (Romans 10:17). But what happens when the word is not correctly taught, or correctly taught but not completely broken down and hence not properly understood? So much has gone wrong among sincere seekers of God due to a lack of understanding of the scriptures. That is why we have preachers, called and empowered by the Holy Spirit, to teach the word and ensure mankind find their way back to God. However, many still teach wrongly due to many factors. As such, souls are endangered and instead of being saved they proceed to hell. Against this backdrop, *Salvation Manual: Topical Exegesis* is born – it is a series of topical commentaries on each book of the Bible that explains vital biblical subjects with the emphasis on salvation.

Knowledge is power, but nothing is as powerful as the right knowledge of the word of God. All those who find the Bible hard to understand or who have questions should try reading this book. Assuredly, all your doubts and confusion will be cleared. If you are ready to make sacrifices towards the salvation of your soul, *Salvation Manual: Topical Exegesis* is for you. If you desire to understand God and His works by following His word, *Salvation Manual: Topical Exegesis* is the guide. With this book, the messages in the Bible are explained with their right application. The Bible contains the word of God and this book details the right and practical application of the word to ensure the salvation of our souls.

INTRODUCTION

Much of man's foremost quest in life has revolved around the needs that affect his survival and ensure his relevance. From a tender age to the winter of his life he devises plans and spares no effort in attaining these goals. However, man often ignores attention to matters with eternal value in his ephemeral pursuits.

Ask a man without eyes about his greatest need and he will most likely tell you he wants to see. Quiz some people who have had to endure penury what they desire most and they will most certainly tell you they want riches. While these desires in and of themselves are not wrong, they do not rank as man's prime need or what is most essential for us. Man's greatest need has never been the food that satiates his hunger, the building that gives him shelter, the status that makes him relevant or anything that caters to his physical needs. Our souls' salvation constitutes the greatest need that should occupy the top echelon of our priorities. The words of Jesus, "seek first the kingdom of God", strike at the core of what should be our life's goal; it entails prioritising the salvation of our soul over anything else in the world. It is what we should long for, strive for and live for. The words in this book have been written down to help you achieve such a precious and priceless gift – salvation – that would make your existence in this world a meaningful one.

Salvation Manual: Topical Exegesis of the Book of Genesis (Vol. 2) is a continuation of *Salvation Manual: Topical Exegesis of the Book of Genesis (Vol. 1)*. This volume expounds on the lessons from Genesis Chapter 26 to 50. It started with the close dealing of God with Isaac after the death of Abraham, his father. It introduces us to the faithfulness of God in keeping to His covenant relationship established with Abraham. The narrative concentrates on the life of the family of Isaac, Jacob and his son Joseph. As God continued His relationship with the family of Isaac, we saw the interaction between Jacob and Esau – the twin brothers – their crises of birthright, Jacob's flight to Paddan Aram and the reconciliation after years. Relevant lessons on actions and decisions by the two brothers were drawn, which are useful for us today as Christians.

In this book, you will encounter personalities with different characters. The book highlights areas of their strength worthy of emulation, weaknesses to avoid and God's position regarding the decisions they took and the attending consequences. These actions are analysed based on Christ's teaching, and the book assesses their relevance to us today. As you take a tour through the book, several ethical lessons are taught on industriousness, resilience, integrity and wisdom in planning. Scripturally balanced counsels are offered on how conflicts should be handled, the importance of forgiveness and reconciliation, the individuality of our walk with God, the effect of a Christian's presence in any place, and how a request should be directed to God. Social issues ranging from handling sexual seduction, adultery and rape to moderation in burial ceremonies are extensively discussed. Also, appropriate relationships within the family, which is the bedrock of society, are lessons you will find as you go through.

Deep spiritual thoughts and practical applications are presented using the word of God as the basis. You will see God providing a road map as He reacts to issues, and His dislike for injustice and wickedness. In all, you could behold the interest of God in the details of our lives. In several instances, using the background of the scriptures and relevant references from other books of the Bible, spiritual lessons are drawn from the express commands of God and from the lives and experiences of biblical characters. These lessons are intended to provide practical ways to handle moral, social and spiritual issues without compromising the welfare and salvation of your soul.

While this volume tells stories about several other people and their roles in fulfilling God's whole agenda and purpose, we see God focusing on three people – Isaac, Jacob and Joseph. We also see Him showing concern for His people, judging and punishing those who do wrong, converting what seems to be human manipulations to fit into His plan and purpose, and helping His people by shaping their history to achieve the promise He made to Abraham.

Several lessons are drawn from the life of Jacob's family: the dreams of Joseph, the hatred of his brothers, the selling of Joseph to slavery. The exemplary godly life of Joseph in Egypt will challenge you and help you understand that godliness is possible even in difficult situations. You will also learn how a life of obedience could attract God's presence. The elevation of Joseph and the eventual relocation of Jacob and his sons to Egypt is one event that was wrought by the hand of God for a greater purpose. Joseph's forgiveness of his brothers and his understanding of the hand of God in all that happened is a timeless spiritual lesson that is X-rayed. In reality, God worked out His eternal purpose, defying all malevolent human interventions.

As you read carefully, you will see that the book connects all the happenings with God's ultimate plan for the salvation of mankind, the nurturing of the nation He will bring the promised Messiah from. God was working as a master weaver to fulfil the promise He made to Abraham. "The nations of the world will be blessed through him."

The phrase *"emphasis on salvation"* reverberates through the pages of this book. This concept portrays how we are to approach the study of God's word – focusing our minds on how the word of God will help us grow intimately in our relationship with God, a relationship that will culminate in a glorious eternal destination with God.

As you read this concluding volume of *Salvation Manual: Topical Exegesis of the Book of Genesis*, you will come across the last topic, Going Back Home. In Genesis 50:24, Joseph made a declaration of faith: ***"Joseph said to his brothers, 'I am dying, but God will surely*** *visit you, and bring you up out of this land to the land which he swore to Abraham, to Isaac, and to Jacob.'"* (NHEB.) This topic presses home the point that believers should walk in this world with the consciousness that there is a promised eternal home at the end of this life.

This book is loaded with salvation messages and practical ways to have an unbroken relationship with Christ. The paramount objective of this work is to encourage all readers to seek their souls' salvation through obedience to the word of God.

CHAPTER 1

TOPIC 1: INDUSTRIOUSNESS: OUR ROLE

GENESIS 26:1–6, 12–33

To be industrious is to be hardworking, diligent and productive. Success is never a product of an accident; instead, it is the upshot of discipline, resilience and industriousness. Many things have been freely given to us by God, yet playing individual roles to actualise them is requisite. The Lord has provided the fishes abundantly in the waters but the fishermen have to go to the river to catch them. The arable lands have been provided but the farmers have to cultivate them at the appropriate time. Therefore, there is the place of individual responsibility in every success story, and there is the place of God. When we faithfully and diligently play our roles, God's role is guaranteed in whatever we do. Deuteronomy 28:12 says: *"The LORD will open to you his good treasure in the sky, to give the rain of your land in its season, and to bless all the work of your hand..."* (NHEB.) But when we do nothing, God will multiply nothing. God's blessing does not give room for laziness.

When Isaac arrived at Gerar the Lord appeared to him and instructed him not to go down to Egypt but to dwell in that land; He said that He would be with him and would bless him. God also reaffirmed to him the promise He made to his father, Abraham, to give him and his descendants the land he sojourned at and to bless all nations of the earth through his offspring because Abraham had obeyed Him and kept His commandments. Isaac obeyed the Lord and stayed in Gerar.

1

Note that God had already assured Isaac that He would bless him in that land. This assurance was enough to make Isaac relaxed and complacent about life, in anticipation of the promise made to him by God. However, Isaac understood that even if God had assured him of His blessing, he still had a part to play in the fulfilment of God's will. This is why he worked, notwithstanding this: *"Isaac sowed in that land, and reaped in the same year one hundred times what he planted. The LORD blessed him."* (Genesis 26:12 NHEB.)

Isaac's success began with his obedience. God commanded him to stay in Gerar, he obeyed, and the land of Gerar became his location for viable farming. God blessed him and he became extremely wealthy in a foreign land, so much so that the Philistines began to envy him. By God's favour upon his life, Isaac's land benefited hundredfold, but there would have been nothing for him to reap had he not sown.

God's will is for His children to prosper. The Lord delights in the prosperity of His children. Nevertheless, God does not rain down money from heaven for anyone; He blesses the works of our hands. It is what we are engaged in that He blesses and multiplies. God rewards hard work and diligence. In contemporary times, industriousness can mean diligence in pursuing a good education, skill(s) or business(es). When we play our part, God blesses the works of our hands. Spiritual exercises such as praying and fasting are honourable. Giving is also good, but nothing can replace industriousness. The Christian who refuses to be industrious will live as though it is not God's will for him to prosper. He will live as though he does not have the same privileges and opportunities as the successful, not realising that all that is missing in his success equation is the role he ought to have played. Success is the reward for diligence and hard work; in the same manner, laziness leads to failure. When we choose to be lazy or passive towards life, we are, by implication, inviting poverty to our lives, and our needs will come upon us like an armed man: *"A little sleep, a little slumber, a little folding of the hands to sleep: [11] so your poverty will come as a robber, and your scarcity as an armed man."* (Proverbs 6:10–11 NHEB.)

The word of God is filled with wisdom for a purposeful life. One may wonder what one could ever learn from the insects. Though tiny and seemingly insignificant, the Bible instructs the slothful to study the ways of the ants to apply the lessons learnt to his life. *"Go to the ant, you sluggard. Consider her ways, and be wise. ⁷which having no chief, overseer, or ruler, ⁸provides her bread in the summer, and gathers her food in the harvest."* (Proverbs 6:6–8 NHEB.) By these verses, we understand that God instructs us by His word and by nature. None is lazy or idle in the world of ants; they are constantly engaged in one purposeful activity or another. They are industrious, resourceful, brilliant miners and creative architects. They have no rulers or instructors yet are purpose driven. Each member is committed to its responsibility for achieving a common goal. Despite their tiny size and feebleness – which they make up for in hard work, tenacity and utmost dedication – they perform tremendous feats.

Note that there is no need for losing our head over what we do not have; what we have is enough for our growth. We should not be discouraged by what others throw at us. If they throw stones at us, we should not throw them back; we can use them as stepping-stones to greater heights. Isaac did not mourn over closed wells or dwell on the continual crises from the Philistines about what he knew was his right; he simply moved forward, and God rewarded him. His industriousness and resilience made him stand out in the society in which he lived. We must never forget that even in our dedication to honourable work we will encounter opposition as long as we are in this world, but we must live carefully like strangers just passing through and not do anything against the word of God in our industriousness. Our focus must always be on the salvation of our souls.

God's role is to release the blessing; our role is to apply ourselves to honest work. For a child of God, one side without the other would not produce a good yield. God is not lazy, and He will not encourage laziness from any of His children. Though a devoted servant of God, Apostle Paul exemplified diligence and instructed the believers in Thessalonica to do the same. *"⁷For you know how you ought to imitate us. For we did not behave ourselves rebelliously among you,* *⁸neither did we eat bread from anyone's hand without paying for it, but in labor and travail worked night and day, that we might not burden any of you; ¹⁰For even when we were with you, we commanded you this: 'If anyone will not work, neither let him eat.' ¹¹For we hear of some who walk among you in rebellion, who do not work at all, but are busybodies. ¹²Now those who are that way, we command and exhort in the Lord Jesus Christ, that with quietness they work, and eat their own bread."* (2 Thessalonians 3:7–8, 10–12 NHEB.) God did not create anybody to be lackadaisical or slothful about life. After He formed Adam, before Adam sinned, God put him in charge of the Garden of Eden, to tend to it. Sin only made working difficult, but indolence was never God's plan for man. Not only is diligence the will of God, but it also brings a man to a place of great honour among men: *"Do you see a man skilled in his work? He will serve kings. He won't serve obscure men."* (Proverbs 22:29 NHEB.)

No one becomes successful suddenly: it takes persistent effort for one to become successful. Success begins with a positive attitude towards life, an attitude of diligence and industriousness. In our pursuit of success in life we ought not to forget that God must be the principal object of the affections of our hearts and that nothing should take His place. All our endeavours should be towards the glory of God and the advancement of His cause.

TOPIC 2: ISAAC'S LIE

GENESIS 26:1–11

When people consciously mislead or deceive others they choose the path of cunning strategy at the expense of truth, without considering that the span of lies can never be greater than the truth. This path sometimes seems clever. What an exhilarating feeling they have if they succeed in their attempt to conceal the truth. Such actions sometimes emanate from attempts to cover wrongs done, fear of uncertainty or trying to run from the consequences of the truth.

4

Often, even with their momentary feeling of success, they still find themselves falling deep into the mess they then try to run from.

When the men of Gerar inquired from Isaac concerning his wife Rebekah, he told them that Rebekah was his sister; this was not true. He did this to protect himself because he feared that, as a beautiful woman, they might take Rebekah from him and kill him. Isaac repeated what his father had done in Egypt and Gerar (see Genesis Chapter 12:10–20 and Genesis Chapter 20:1–3). In Abraham's case, Sarah had twice been taken from him but God intervened. It is unclear as to whether Isaac was aware of his father's experience but supposing he was he should have learnt that God protected his father in both cases. Thus, God would have been able to save him as well. If he was unaware, he should have trusted God irrespective of the consequences.

Isaac misleading Abimelech into believing that Rebekah was his sister was wrong. If he was right, Isaac would not have tried to find a soft landing when the truth came to light. Although it took a while, the truth did show up and Isaac's lie was uncovered. Many who tell lies fail to acknowledge that truth will eventually prevail over lies, whether in this life or in the life to come. Truly, lies might be hidden from men but not from God.

Some people lie to protect themselves or their loved ones from physical harm or punishment. Others lie to cover what they consider shameful or out of greed, and would lie again to cover their initial lie, as did Gehazi, Elisha's servant, in 2 Kings chapter 5, deceptively receiving Naaman's gifts contrary to his master's wish.

Eventually liars get caught in the web of dishonesty and, over time, lose consciousness of their guilt. At this point, truth is strange on their lips and lying becomes easy, like speaking one's native language. Whenever we decide to lie and sacrifice truth because of fear, we directly remove our dependency on God and put it on what we think will keep us secure, thereby leaving God outside the calculation.

Proverbs 3:5–6 says: *"Trust in the LORD with all your heart, and do not lean on your own understanding. ⁶In all your ways acknowledge him, and he will make your paths straight."* (NHEB.)

There are moments when the damage caused by lies are irreparable. They are like arrows shot into the skin; pulling them out by way of apologies does not remove the scar. If a false testimony sends an innocent man to the gallows and after a while the false accuser and his accomplice decide to confess and apologise, does that undo the damage done to the dead man's family? Repentance may bring forgiveness, apologies may bring reconciliation, but none of these will revive the dead man nor wipe away the memories. Therefore, we must avoid lying and deception at all costs.

Lies have become so commonplace that you do not need to search far to find them. Ranging from lying under oath in court to falsification of documents, and from deceiving spouses and relatives to lying impulsively for the slightest reason, all fit into the psalmist's description: *"For there is nothing reliable in their mouth. Their heart is destruction. Their throat is an open tomb; with their tongues they flatter."* (Psalm 5:9 NHEB.)

We need to understand that no circumstance can justify a lie before God. We must never lie, not even to save our lives nor, as some would do, to exaggerate a testimony with the excuse that it is all to give glory to God. As Paul noted, some people might say, *"For if the truth of God through my lie abounded to his glory, why am I also still judged as a sinner?"* (Romans 3:7 NHEB.) What a perverse way of reasoning. The concept of "the end justifies the means" does not hold when the means is a lie. No sinful means can be glorifying to God. Our faithfulness must be unto death. Lying is a sin against God and all unrepentant liars will have their place in the lake of fire.

It is also important to note that lying is not limited to making statements to deceive. Whether it is deception, hypocrisy, misrepresentation of the truth or what people call professional or white lies, every form of misleading people with words and actions falls into the family of lies, and, as Jesus puts it, those who practice this have Satan as their father.

Irrespective of the cause or motive behind lying, one thing is common to all lies: it is processed in the heart before it manifests itself. Jesus, in Mark 7:21–23, teaches us that deceit, among other evil actions, proceeds from the heart. *"For from within, out of a person's heart, proceed evil thoughts, adulteries, sexual sins, murders, thefts, ^{22}covetings, wickedness, deceit, lustful desires, an evil eye, blasphemy, pride, and foolishness. ^{23}All these evil things come from within, and defile the person."* (NHEB.) To overcome lies one must tackle them from the root – the heart. The beginning of living a life of truth is to invite Jesus into your heart, for He is the way, the truth and the life. For believers who still find themselves trapped in the sin of lying, daily heart-renewing with the word of God and living in the consciousness that God hates lies is paramount. Transformation comes only through the renewal of heart: *"And do not be conformed to this world, but be transformed by the renewing of your mind, so that you may prove what is the good, well-pleasing, and perfect will of God."* (Romans 12:2 NHEB.)

TOPIC 3: RESILIENCE

GENESIS 26:12–22

Life on earth is like travelling along a road replete with bumps, gaping potholes, muddy highways, a foggy atmosphere and whatnot. The ability to keep going till you reach your destination despite a series of unpleasant experiences is an attitude that borders on resilience. To be resilient is to remain undaunted in the face of challenges; it is also the ability to bounce back after defeat.

Isaac exhibited a dogged character in handling challenges that life threw at him. Having been prospered by God, he found himself the object of envy from the Philistines. He was resilient and had hope that someday the Philistines would let him be. For this, Isaac dug well after well. He was envied at Gerar. In the valley of Gerar the Philistines claimed his well, so he named the well Esek. Isaac did not get tired; he dug another well, which was also claimed, so he called it Sitnah. Isaac did not give up; he must have believed that someday he would get settled and have wells that no one would take from him. So he went further to dig another well which no one tried to take from him, and he called the place of the well Rehoboth: *"For now the LORD has made room for us, and we will be fruitful in the land."* (Genesis 26:22 NHEB.)

Isaac was a peaceable person who did not struggle with the Philistines when they demanded the wells. He avoided any confrontation and tried to live at peace with them despite the rejection. Experiencing circumstances such as Isaac's may seem challenging, but we need to depend on God's wisdom that is pure and peaceable. Note that in confronting challenges by the wisdom of God we may suffer loss, but let us be assured that God will recompense us for all we have lost, either in this life or in the life to come.

Isaac's response represents the sort of behaviour we are to exhibit as Christians, for we are strangers on transit in this world. Whenever we are cheated out of our rights we are required to take the high road by not engaging in acts that will bring the name of God into disrepute. Understanding and peaceful negotiation are the high road believers must tread when faced with similar challenges. Romans 12:18 says: *"If it is possible, as much as it is up to you, be at peace with all people."* (NHEB.)

Challenges constitute one of the inescapable realities in our day-to-day lives and in our Christian journey. Our response to challenges is often not of the right attitude required to overcome them. When faced with a challenging situation, many people in self-pity or despair, allow the challenge to dictate the course of their lives. Some blame others and, by so doing, give up their pursuit. Proverbs 24:10 says: *"If you falter in the time of trouble, your strength is small."* (NHEB.)

We must grow to a point at which we face squarely those things aimed at slowing us down in the journey of life.

Resilience requires reacting positively to challenges or misfortune. For example, in our secular activities, someone who ventures into a new business despite previous setbacks exemplifies an individual with a resilient attitude. Similarly, students who do not give up their pursuits despite previous failures demonstrate resilience. We are to remain undaunted in the face of challenges in life. Apostle Paul wrote: *"Five times from the Jews I received forty stripes minus one. 25 Three times I was beaten with rods. Once I was stoned. Three times I suffered shipwreck. I have been a night and a day in the deep. 26 I have been in travels often, perils of rivers, perils of robbers, perils from my countrymen, perils from the Gentiles, perils in the city, perils in the wilderness, perils in the sea, perils among false brothers; 27 in labor and travail, in watchings often, in hunger and thirst, in fastings often, and in cold and nakedness."* (2 Corinthians 11:24–27 NHEB.) In all these challenges Paul remained steadfast. His resilience is revealed in his persistence in preaching the gospel despite his challenges. He also wrote in Philippians 3:13–14: *"but one thing I do. Forgetting the things which are behind, and reaching forward to the things which are ahead, 14 I press on toward the goal for the prize of the high calling of God in Christ Jesus."* (NHEB.)

In the Christian journey we are like football players taking part in a match. The opponents tackle, pull down and sometimes purposely want to injure us in a bid to prevent us from achieving our goal. The opponent's primary concern is to stop us from achieving the ultimate goal of life, our souls' salvation. They do this by attempting to distract us with the cares of life. The enemy may oppose us through challenges or adversities and if believers are not resilient they may look back at the things they lost, the pains suffered and the heartaches that live with them. And then, their attention is diverted from their goal because of setbacks. Resilience will get a believer back on their feet to shake off the dust released by adversity. Resilience will also make a believer trust and rely on God for help when it seems that the enemy is winning with his discouragement strategy. Nothing is as helpful at this time as our coach's voice – the word of God – pushing us on and encouraging us. Psalm 37:23–24 says, *"The steps of a man are established by the LORD, and he delights in his way. [24] Though he stumble, he shall not fall, for the LORD holds him up with his hand."* (NHEB.) The ability to remain strong and steadfast in the face of challenges will enable us to build our character. Once resilience is part of our lives we will not be easily fazed by challenges. *"Not only this, but we also rejoice in our sufferings, knowing that suffering works perseverance; [4] and perseverance, proven character; and proven character, hope"* (Romans 5:3–4 NHEB).

Isaac's resilience paid off. He dug a well that the enemies did not contend with and named it Rehoboth. In our spiritual walk, before arriving at our place of rest, there will be hindrances. We must earnestly strive to ensure that no matter how much we are stretched or challenged with adversity on our Christian journey we must not give up the salvation of our souls.

We will always be faced with challenges as long as the earth remains and we still breathe. Jesus says in John 16:33: *"In the world you have oppression..."* (NHEB.) To be resilient, we must have in mind the inescapable reality of difficulties in this life. By accepting this fact, we will be more prepared to confront them. In the same vein, accepting the reality of difficulties also helps us deal with challenges, be it in our secular lives or our Christian race, *"For this momentary light affliction is working for us a far more exceeding and everlasting weight of glory"* (2 Corinthians 4:17 NHEB).

TOPIC 4: AFFINAL RELATIONSHIP

GENESIS 26:34–35

An African folktale is told of a woman who went to a wise old man to seek counsel on taming her "difficult" mother-in-law and gaining her

10

love. The old man demanded three strands of hair from a live lion's mane. After her initial "impossibility" thought she set out on her mission. She knew of a mountain site where a lion visited regularly so she decided to pay the lion a visit. Every day she would go to the mountain site with a goat. When the lion appeared, she made sure that the lion saw her and, just as the lion contemplated his attack, she released the goat. As the lion attacked the goat she walked away. Soon she decided to stay as the lion devoured its prey and after a while sensed that the lion had come to recognise her as its meal supplier. A day came when she summoned the courage to pat the lion's mane; she plucked three strands of the lion's hair in the process. The old man, impressed at how a feeble woman could tame a lion, asked how she had succeeded. After narrating her experience the man said "You could tame a lion, certainly your mother-in-law is not as wild as that lion. Go and do likewise with her." The lesson here is that it is possible to relate with everyone, even with so-called "difficult" people. We have what it takes to turn every unpleasant relationship around. That same measure can prevent a good relationship from becoming sour.

One of the essential characteristics of humanity is relationships. It is what connects two or more people together. There are various forms of relationship, such as parent–child, friendships, marriages and affinal. An affinal relationship is a relationship that exists between a person and his spouse's blood relations. Marriage relationships do not just end with the couple; they involve families of both spouses. When relationships with in-laws are like the relationship between Esau's wives and his parents, as described in the context under consideration, comfort and peace become scarce commodities. ***"When Esau was forty years old, he took as wife Judith, the daughter of Beeri the Hittite, and Basemath, the daughter of Elon the Hittite. ³⁵ They grieved Isaac's and Rebekah's spirits."*** (Genesis 26:34–35 NHEB.)

Compare the arrival of Rebekah to Abraham's family with the arrival of Esau's wives to Isaac's family. While one brought comfort the other brought grief. A closer look at the two reveals further differences. Everything about the choice of Rebekah showed that God was involved – from Abraham's counsel to Eliezer's prayers at the well and even to Rebekah's family's farewell blessings. Everything showed God's involvement (Genesis chapter 24).

Fast-forward to Esau's marriage: in one statement it is recorded that Esau got two Hittite women as wives, and the most notable thing recorded about them is that they made life bitter for Isaac and Rebekah. That certainly meant Esau's choice of wives from Canaan was wrong, and that his choice resulted in tension and bitterness in the family. In contrast to the behaviour expected of spouses towards their in-laws, Esau's wives, Judith and Basemath, rather than serving as sources of joy and affection, became sources of grief. Their behaviour was such that Isaac agreed to Rebekah's suggestion not to allow Jacob to marry from among the Canaanites due to witnessing first-hand how women from the land could be ill-mannered. Though the kind of grief Esau's wives caused was not stated, it was unbearable. Esau's wrong choice could not be unmade; the most responsible thing to have done would have been for Esau and his wives to work on the stormy relationship to bring about positive results. If they had played their part, their parents would have reciprocated the gesture.

Before we look at how to work on sour relationships let us look at the causes of tension in affinal relationships. Unwholesome interference of parents is one of the significant causes of problems in marriages and relationships with in-laws. Although a parent could deliberately set out to cause tension in their child's marriage for the mere reason that they do not like their child's partner, most parents do not fall into that category. Many find themselves interfering out of sincere and genuine concern, even though their interferences sometimes get out of hand due to ignorance. It takes discipline for parents to resist the urge to interfere in a child's home, especially when they think they are right. However, with God's wisdom and equal love for the couple, parents can play their role as guardians and counsellors without constituting hindrances to their children's happiness.

Another cause of tension in affinal relationships is upbringing. A spouse who was not brought up to respect other people's ways of life and opinions will undoubtedly clash with their in-laws. Relationships between in-laws and spouses are often susceptible to friction when the husband or wife treats their spouse's parents with disregard.

Sour affinal relationships do not only arise from interactions between spouses and in-laws. Sometimes, interactions between couples can result in problems that spill over to the parents. Many times, parents unwisely allow themselves to be pulled into taking sides in a couple's misunderstanding.

For there to be a cordial relationship between spouses and their in-laws or to turn already-soured relationships around, spouses need to view their partner's parents and siblings as theirs. When this is done, it is easier to treat them well. We must endeavour to take care of our in-laws just as we would our parents and siblings. The same divine injunction that instructs us to honour our parents should be seen as urging us to do the same for our in-laws: *"Children, obey your parents in the Lord, for this is right. ²"Honor your father and mother," which is the first commandment with a promise: ³"that it may be well with you, and that you may live long in the land.""* (Ephesians 6:1–3 NHEB.)

Since spouses owe their parents-in-law the kind of honour due to their biological parents, they should initiate reconciliation in instances of disagreement or disunity. On the part of parents, they should respond to their children-in-law with the love of Christ and, where the need arises, be willing to go the extra mile in initiating reconciliation for the sake of their salvation.

One of the most significant examples of affinal relationships in the Bible occurred between Ruth and Naomi in the book of Ruth. Ruth expressed towards Naomi, her mother-in-law, the kind of love she would typically show her parents. Ruth's love for Naomi was such that people regarded her as better than seven sons to Naomi: *"The women said to Naomi, "Blessed be the LORD, who has not left you this day without a redeemer; and let his name be famous in Israel. ¹⁵ He shall be to you a restorer of life, and sustain you in your old age, for your daughter-in-law, who loves you, who is better to you than seven sons, has borne him.""* (Ruth 4:14–15 NHEB.) This was evidenced in how both of them essentially transcended their relationship to a mother–daughter level. Afterwards, Ruth, the Moabite, became part of the ancestry of King David and our Lord Jesus.

Continually exhibiting friendly, respectful, tolerant and Christlike attitudes towards in-laws is another way to revamp soured affinal relationships and probably sweeten bitter ones. Christian couples should not wait until their in-laws demonstrate love to them before they accord them respect. We should live in such a way that people outside have an interest in Christ. Likewise, Christian parents-in-law should understand that not everyone has the opportunity to be properly brought up in fear of the Lord and should learn to accommodate such people. Godly attitudes warm relationships and can make in-laws who had not known Christ turn to God.

CHAPTER 2

TOPIC 1: MISPLACEMENT OF FEAR

GENESIS 27:1–13

To fear God is the whole duty of man. *"Fear God, and keep his commandments; for this is the whole duty of man."* (Ecclesiastes 12:13 NHEB.) Reverential fear is not dread: it is borne out of love and respect for God; it is the kind of fear required of every believer. This type of fear leads to abstinence from sin for God's sake and not for fear of others or of our actions' physical consequences.

When Rebekah presented Jacob with the plot of tricking his father into blessing him over his brother, Jacob objected to the proposal. *"Jacob said to Rebekah his mother, "Look, Esau my brother is a hairy man, and I am a smooth man. ¹²What if my father touches me? I will seem to him as a deceiver, and I would bring a curse on myself, and not a blessing.""* (Genesis 27:11–12 NHEB.) Jacob's objection was not because he acknowledged that the deceitful act was evil in the sight of God but because of his fear of being caught and cursed. Jacob's stance towards doing wrong highlights an issue most of us struggle with. Sometimes, we decide against doing what is wrong not because it is wrong but for fear of being caught in the process. When we do not resist sin because we fear God but because we fear the physical consequences of getting caught, how easy it will be for the devil to trick us with such a stance. He will conveniently place in our hearts assurances, suggestions or reasons why we should carry out the act. Jacob yielded to his mother when she addressed every area of his fears. She also said to him, *"Let your curse be on me..."* (Genesis 27:13 NHEB.)

If a person's priority is the fear of being caught or the physical consequences of their actions, they will be more motivated to sin when assured they will not be caught. Several times we are faced with similar situations to that of Jacob. Imagine being alone with a member of the opposite sex who is not your spouse and who appeals to your sexual desire. Rather than fearing God's word you fear pregnancy or sexually transmitted disease. How easy it is for the person to dissuade you from your flimsy objections with the option of preventive measures? In another instance, if someone fears imprisonment above displeasing God, will they not refuse the suggestion to engage in a fraudulent act because they could go to jail if caught? Give them the assurance that the action will be adequately concealed, and that even if it is revealed no one will arrest them because they will be covered, and the person will most likely commit the fraudulent act. The questions for us are: Where does our fear lie? Is it in the consequences of being found out? Or is it bound to God who destroys not only the body but also the soul that sins? *"I tell you, my friends, do not be afraid of those who kill the body, and after that have no more that they can do. ⁵But I will warn you whom you should fear. Fear him, who after he has killed, has power to cast into hell. Yes, I tell you, fear him."* (Luke 12:4–5 NHEB.)

Only the fear of God will keep someone from sin even when they know they will not be caught. *"The fear of the LORD is to hate evil..."* (Proverbs 8:13 NHEB.) Joseph's life is a classic illustration of a person who had fear for God rather than men or the physical consequences of sin, and it served him well. His master's wife was attracted to him and approached him with sexual advances, attempting to lie with him. Joseph could have simply asked her, "What if we are caught?" She could have assured him of a way they would go about it without being caught. But Joseph feared God, and his resolution not to go against God was unshaken when he ended his reply to her with,

"How then can I do this great wickedness, and sin against God?" (Genesis 39:9 NHEB.) Potiphar's wife kept on with her sexual advances day after day, but Joseph never budged; he feared going against the word of God and, therefore, his master's wife could not manoeuvre her way into sleeping with him.

As Christians, we should not have the same fear as those of the world. Our fear should not be for the physical consequences of sin or man. Instead, it should be for God, who holds the essence of our lives in His hands. When we place our fears on something else, as Jacob did, the devil finds a loophole through which to lure us to sin; we become defenceless against the attack of the evil one. James 4:7 says: *"resist the devil, and he will flee from you."* (NHEB.) We resist the devil using God's word, as Jesus did. His responses to His three temptations from the devil were consistent: "It is written." Satan can take advantage of our fear of physical consequences but he cannot mislead us when we have the right knowledge of God's word and truly fear God.

Many today relegate the fear of God to the background because God is merciful. They assume they will be spared by the mercy of God for their misdeeds and as such they trivialise sin. We should never forget that we are tempted to disregard God's word whenever we are tempted to sin and, by implication, disregard His authority. A believer who loves God will not violate God's authority: *"One who says, "I know him," and does not keep his commandments, is a liar, and the truth is not in him. ⁵But whoever keeps his word, God's love has truly been perfected in him. This is how we know that we are in him"* (1 John 2:4–5 NHEB). We can see how love for God and reverential fear is intertwined. Love entails us obeying in everything; fear of God requires a departure from evil for the sake of God and the love we have for Him.

The reason for our stance at any moment during which we are lured to sin really matters. May we fear God rather than the physical consequences of sin.

TOPIC 2: DECEPTION

GENESIS 27:1–46

As he gravitated his way purposefully to the open country, Esau revelled in a whirlwind of ecstasy at what he had just heard. The day, this special day, had finally come for him to be bestowed with his father's blessings. This day was no ordinary day, nor was this hunting regular hunting for him. This was the most significant among the catalogue of hunting exercises he had ever embarked on. As he returned with his game his joyful trip home soon turned to misery. His father broke the news to him. It was not what he had expected. Unbeknown to him, his mother, Rebekah, and brother Jacob, had jointly hatched and successfully executed a plan to usurp his blessing. The pain. The tears. The regret. The betrayal. The deception. They all coursed through his body like a bolt of lightning permeating through the sky. Reality dawned on him: he had lost his blessing.

Deception is the act of misleading someone into believing what is untrue; it could be by using words, actions or silence. More often than not, deception leaves in its wake unpleasant effects on the victim. The one who practises deception is selfish – thinking of themselves and what they stand to benefit without considering the victim. Deception usually stems from a dishonest or disobedient heart.

In Genesis 27, within a very short period, Isaac's family experienced what could be described as a deception masterminded by a family member, favouring one family member over another. It started out by a father's natural desire to bless his favourite son with no mention of blessing the other; one would wonder why he did not call the two sons together and pronounce a blessing on each at the same time, just as Jacob did before his death. It was followed by a mother's natural desire to thwart that blessing to favour her favourite son, not minding what happened to the other.

The way Jacob responded and mentioned God in the deception is concerning. When Isaac asked him how he made a kill so quickly, without fear, he said: *"Because the LORD your God gave me success."* (Genesis 27:20 NHEB.) What did he mean by God giving him success? Presenting cooked sheep to his father as venison? That was deceit and can never be called success from God. How often do we define deceit as success today and link God to it? Many have risen to offices, gained employment, gained admission to schools, won favour and money on the wings of deception. If we succeed in covering up the act and attribute it to God and even offer thanksgiving in the church concerning it, it is against the will of God; we will face the eternal consequence of our ill actions unless we repent and restitute where necessary.

Rebekah was skilled enough to make goat meat taste like venison and goat hair feel like human hair and was the mastermind behind the whole deception. She was aware of the prophecy that Jacob would be superior to Esau. She could not stand by and watch the fulfilment of this prophecy being thwarted. She stepped in to mastermind the blessing of Jacob instead of Esau through deception. It is possible that the prophecy Rebekah heard during her pregnancy propelled her actions. However, the prophecy did not spell out the "how" nor give her the responsibility to bring it to pass. She acted in error and Jacob followed. She seemed not to have understood that God did not need her effort or scheme to bring the prophecy to fulfilment. Never should God's children copy Rebekah's action; we should trust God that He can bring His word to fulfilment. God did not rebuke them, but that was not an approval of their actions.

Rebekah's deception continued: *"I am weary of my life because of the daughters of Heth. If Jacob takes a wife of the daughters of Heth, such as these, of the daughters of the land, what good will my life do me?"* (Genesis 27:46 NHEB.) By stating this, Rebekah put an idea into Isaac's mind to send Jacob away to Mesopotamia. Rebekah did this by using sets of factual statements. Esau's wives were indeed a headache; it is also true that the situation may have been worse had Jacob married a Hittite. However, Rebekah's set of factual statements hid her heart's actual intent, which was to send

Jacob away to safety because of Esau's plan to kill him. Before man's courts you would not be able to convict her of lying, but in God's court, she would be judged by her motives. God judges the intent of our hearts. *"For man does not see as God sees, for man looks at the outward appearance, but the LORD looks at the heart."* (1 Samuel 16:7 NHEB.)

Some people deceive others by giving a false impression of themselves – they pretend with a false show of godliness so that people might perceive them differently. Following his mother's lead Jacob's action was a practical illustration of the hypocrite. Who he claimed to be was different from who he really was. In verses 19 and 20 Jacob told his father four lies: "I am Esau": "I have done…" (his mother did it all): "He told his father goat meat was actually venison": "He claimed God helped him while it was his mother who did everything." Jesus in Matthew 23:25–27 illustrated deceivers as people who clean the outside of a cup yet hide the dirt inside, like whitewashed tombs that are full of all sorts of impurities. *"Woe to you, scribes and Pharisees, hypocrites. For you clean the outside of the cup and of the plate, but within they are full of extortion and self-indulgence. [26]You blind Pharisee, first clean the inside of the cup, that its outside may become clean also. [27]"Woe to you, scribes and Pharisees, hypocrites. For you are like whitened tombs, which outwardly appear beautiful, but inwardly are full of dead men's bones, and of all uncleanness.""* (NHEB.)

Often, those who engage in deception are motivated by their desire for personal gain. We are to be truthful and sincere in our dealings with others and not take advantage of anyone. All liars will have their dwelling in the eternal lake of fire with the deceiver – Satan – and his angels if they fail to repent. To speak or act in such a way, with the intent to deceive or mislead others, is an ungodly trait. When we let the word of God transform our lives by living according to it rather than exhibiting deceptive behaviours, our actions will inevitably be Christlike. The way of Christ is the way of truth but the way of deceit is the way of the evil one, for he has been a deceiver from the beginning of creation. He is a liar – the father of all liars: *"He was a murderer from the beginning, and does not stand in the truth, because there is no truth in him. When he speaks a lie, he speaks on his own; for he is a liar, and its father."* (John 8:44 NHEB.) Anyone who lies speaks Satan's native language and identifies with Satan as his father.

Children of God should be careful not to be identified with the vice of deception. Deception is sinful and destructive, but a heart renewed by Christ can be delivered from the grip of deceit and liberated by the truth. Apostle Paul, in his letter to the Colossians, admonished all Christians, saying: *"Do not lie to one another, seeing that you have put off the old self with its practices, ¹⁰and have put on the new self, who is being renewed in knowledge after the image of his Creator"* (Colossians 3:9–10 NHEB).

We must endeavour to be mindful of the kind of influences we subject ourselves to. Unlike Jacob, who succumbed to the advice from Rebekah, we must never allow people to persuade us to carry out deceptive acts.

TOPIC 3: DAY OF RECKONING

GENESIS 27:30–34

Facing the repercussions of every unrepented misdeed, either openly or secretly, is inescapable for anyone, especially on the day of reckoning. Man was created with freewill. Nevertheless, we are both free and bound. We possess the liberty to act in whatever way we desire, but are not entirely free of the consequences of our actions. This truth was illustrated in the life of Esau as depicted in Hebrews 12:16–17: *"that there be no sexually immoral or profane person like Esau, who sold his own birthright for one meal. ¹⁷For you know that even when he afterward desired to inherit the blessing, he was rejected, for he found no place for a change of mind though he sought it diligently with tears."* (NHEB.)

Esau arrived home one day famished. He requested some food from his brother Jacob who was cooking at the time. Jacob asked that Esau give him his birthright in exchange for some food. Esau replied, *"What good is the birthright to me?"* (Genesis 25:32 NHEB.) Esau was the firstborn and so had certain rights and privileges accorded to him. In his father's absence he was to be in charge of the household, have a greater portion of Isaac's inheritance and have the blessing Isaac intended to give him. All these did not bother him during a momentary hunger. Esau was a careless man who sold his birthright for one morsel of meat.

After Jacob had taken the blessing Esau cried with a great and exceedingly bitter cry – not because he had sold his birthright but because he had lost the blessing. No amount of tears could undo what had been done.

We should not be quick to criticise Esau but instead learn from him and not make the same mistake concerning our spiritual inheritance – our soul's salvation. This day for Esau could be likened to the day of reckoning for everyone; a day, each person will reap the consequences of their actions. Given the numerous teachings and warnings from countless evangelists over time about the day of reckoning, the fact that it is over 2,000 years since the death and resurrection of Christ, and the fact that the final day of reckoning for humanity has not yet come, there is a tendency to become used to these warnings and live as though that day will not exist. However, it does not change the fact that the day is coming when every person will reap what they have sown. *"For we must all appear before the judgment seat of Christ; that each one may receive the things in the body, according to what he has done, whether good or bad."* (2 Corinthians 5:10 NHEB.)

God has set out a day when He will judge mankind for their sins through the One He has appointed – the Lord Jesus Christ. In light of this, it will be wise to ponder on this day, every day of our lives, and live in anticipation of it. If we find ourselves not anticipating this day, we should be concerned. It is an indication that our stand with God is faulty and hence, we must make amends immediately while we can, for, by the justness of God, no amount of tears will save us on that day. Those who treasured their spiritual inheritance, who lived their lives in absolute submission to the will of God, will dwell with God for eternity, while those who lived in rebellion against His word will have their place in the eternal lake of fire.

Many Christians like Esau are careless with their spiritual inheritance and place more value on this world's ephemeral things than on their spiritual lives. They compromise their stand with God at the slightest opportunity: they are slaves to their lustful passions and desires and have no restraint over their flesh. They have rejected the way of sacrificial living and settled for a lifestyle of carnality. Christianity, to them, is merely a profession, for they bear no evidence of a changed life. Professing to be Christians, they live instead like sinners and love what God detests. They are myopic, living for momentary gratification, and are not bothered about eternity. They see a life of holiness as too demanding, forgetting that no man will see the Lord without it.

We should be more concerned about our soul's salvation, for life is but a moment compared to eternity. We can, within a moment, lose something invaluable, just as Esau did. *"For if we sin willfully after we have received the knowledge of the truth, there remains no more a sacrifice for sins, [27] but a certain fearful expectation of judgment, and a fierceness of fire which will devour the adversaries."* (Hebrews 10:26–27 NHEB.) Nothing, no matter how enticing, is worth our eternity with God.

It is not too late for those who are not yet partakers of the spiritual inheritance. They are to renounce their sinful lifestyle, accept Christ as Lord and decide to obey Him at all costs: *"Today if you will hear his voice, do not harden your hearts…"* (Hebrews 3:15 NHEB.)

Furthermore, worthy of note is the fact that time and seasons bring moments of reckoning, even outside the final day of judgement. Apart from the eternal consequence, sin also comes with an immediate or physical effect. The day of reckoning is also when someone comes face to face with the unpleasant consequences of their past actions in life. For instance, the day of reckoning for a randy lecturer is when he is caught and exposed and proper disciplinary actions are meted out against him. Likewise, the day of reckoning for an armed robber is when he is apprehended by the authorities and judgement is passed on him for his crimes.

That said, we ought to be careful about how we live our lives, knowing full well that the choices we make have the propensity to dictate the course of our lives and determine our eternal destination. *"Therefore watch carefully how you walk, not as unwise, but as wise"* (Ephesians 5:15 NHEB).

TOPIC 4: ESAU'S RESENTMENT

GENESIS 27:41

Resentment is an intense feeling of anger or indignation towards another. It is persistent anger within our hearts to the extent that we may fantasise about hurting the other party. It is often characterised by an unforgiving spirit, critical attitude and bitterness. If resentment is allowed to fester in the heart it contaminates the heart and may lead to hatred and/or murder. However, if the spirit of forgiveness is allowed to rule over the heart resentment can be dispelled.

Isaac was old and death was approaching. He intended to bless Esau but asked Esau to prepare some wild game for him first. Rebekah eavesdropped on their conversation and before Esau returned from hunting, plotted with Jacob for Jacob to deceive Isaac and take the blessing. When Esau arrived and learnt that Jacob had taken his blessing he held a grudge against his brother and determined to hold this grudge until the death of their father; then, he would take revenge by killing Jacob. This is the implication: as long as Isaac was alive Esau's soul would be troubled with the feeling of resentment towards his brother. Assuming he had succeeded in killing Jacob, would that have brought his blessing back? Would another wrong from him make right the first wrong from Jacob? Are resentment and murder the most appropriate approaches to this situation? It is noteworthy to consider that Esau had earlier traded his birthright, so he was angry about what was not his.

Looking at his conduct at the time, Esau showed no trace of remorse in his attitude. He refused to see where he had gone wrong. There was no confession of his former careless act nor acknowledgement that the blessing had been justly lost. His sorrow was for the loss of the blessing, which he felt was still his. For this reason, he felt, since he could not have the blessing, that his brother also should not have it.

A similar case of resentment is recorded in Genesis 4, where Cain allowed his anger and jealousy to reach the point of harbouring resentment against his brother – Abel – because his brother's sacrifice was accepted and his sacrifice rejected. He neglected God's warning against the anger he held in his heart against his brother, which eventually led him to murder Abel.

Matthew 5:22 tells us that it is not only the one who kills another but also the one who harbours anger against another that is subject to judgement. *"But I tell you, that everyone who is angry with his brother without a cause will be liable to judgment; and whoever will say to his brother, 'Raqa,' will be in danger of the council; and whoever will say, 'You fool,' will be in danger of the fire of hell."* (NHEB.) Anger harboured towards another can lead to vengeance, and in being vengeant we are attempting to act in place of God as both judge and executioner. A judge, because we decide which punishment is appropriate for the wrong done, and an executioner, because we execute the punishment. Therefore, vengeance is rebellion against the authority of God.

Every day, people hurt us intentionally or unintentionally. How we handle it determines what the outcome will be. We will either have a positive or negative result at the end that can make or mar our relationship with others and determine our degree of happiness. Often, resentment manifests when people offended by others allow the hurt to germinate and flourish in their hearts. Anger at the wrongs done to us, when not adequately managed and harboured for a long time, becomes resentment.

Resentment influences our actions towards the offender negatively. It displays itself in ways that can be self-destructive and harmful to others. It can simmer and then gradually reach boiling point, causing physical and mental exhaustion. Not only is resentment detrimental to our souls, it can also be detrimental to our physical wellbeing.

For us to be free of resentment, we must come to the understanding that God requires us to forgive those who have wronged us, irrespective of the type or degree of offence. Our Lord and Master, Jesus Christ, demonstrated this attitude when He was ridiculed, tortured and crucified, yet He forgave and prayed for His persecutors. Similarly, in Acts 7:60, Stephen exhibited love and forgiveness to his persecutors. *"He kneeled down, and shouted out, "Lord, do not hold this sin against them." When he had said this, he fell asleep."* (NHEB.) We must also extend a hand of forgiveness to those who hurt us and let the word of God serve as our comforting resource to help us deal with the effects of any hurt or experience that may endanger the salvation of our soul. Ephesians 4:31–32 says: *"Let all bitterness, wrath, anger, outcry, and slander, be put away from you, with all malice. ³²And be kind to one another, tenderhearted, forgiving each other, just as God also in Christ forgave you."* (NHEB.) We must endeavour not to repay evil with evil but repay evil with good.

God has commanded us to forgive our offenders, not once but as many times as possible. No offence is beyond our forgiveness. The Bible does not provide any exception as regards offences that should be forgiven: *"For if you forgive people their trespasses, your heavenly Father will also forgive you. ¹⁵But if you do not forgive people, neither will your Father forgive your trespasses."* (Matthew 6:14–15 NHEB.) Many times in life, just like Esau, we have reasons based on our understanding that justify our resentment of others. People might mistreat, disrespect or even take advantage of us by robbing us of what we truly deserve. But by the wisdom of God, resentment is not the appropriate approach to handling such circumstances. Ecclesiastes 7:9 says: *"Do not be hasty in your spirit to be angry, for anger rests in the bosom of fools."* (NHEB.)

Satan is constantly seeking an occasion to tempt us to sin. Harbouring anger in our hearts means opening a door for Satan to come into our hearts, and you know what will follow when Satan comes in – resentment, malice, hostility, hatred and even murder. Anger must not be allowed to rule over us and should be avoided. Colossians 3:8 says, *"but now you also put them all away: anger, wrath, malice, slander, and shameful speaking out of your mouth."* (NHEB.)

Resentment does not reflect strength, but our weakness in controlling our anger. It does not hear the language of love and forgiveness but seeks to hurt others. A Christian's improper response to offences is an expression of spiritual immaturity.

Forgiveness is the antidote to resentment. The Bible says, *"Esau hated Jacob…"* (Genesis 27:41 NHEB.) Hatred is a choice and so is forgiveness. The call to Christianity is a call to a selfless life. It is a call to obey Christ above our thoughts, desires and all we perceive to be right by our understanding. Forgiveness is not possible if we are proud and full of ourselves – it takes humility to forgive. It is a selfless act that is easier for those whose interests are not their priority but their obedience to God. The more we focus on the severity of the offence or what we have lost, the more difficult it will be to forgive, but when we take our focus off the offence, concentrating instead on God and making a firm decision to obey His word, by His grace we will find the strength to forgive. Forgiveness might not be easy, but we are to forgive, nonetheless.

The Christian's mark is the love of God within our hearts, and this love is not conditional; it is not based on how we are treated by others, for we are to love both our loved ones and our enemies. Forgiveness is a reflection of this love. When we harbour resentment or bitterness in our hearts towards others and refuse to forgive them, God will not forgive us our sins, nor will He attend to our prayers. Psalm 66:18 says: *"If I cherished sin in my heart, the Lord wouldn't have listened."* (NHEB.)

CHAPTER 3

TOPIC 1: INDIVIDUALITY OF OUR WALK WITH GOD

GENESIS 28:10–15

All humans are masterpieces created by God and no two persons are entirely alike. As much as God relates with people in groups, nations or tribes, He also relates with people individually. According to His unique plans for our lives, God deals with us concerning what He wants us to do in His kingdom. In a world as vast and populated as ours, none of God's children is unnoticed, lost in the crowd or purposeless.

The individuality of God's relationship with us could be seen in the revelation of Himself to Jacob. Having successfully, with his mother's aid, executed the plan to claim the blessing meant for Esau, Jacob found himself needing to escape his brother's murderous vengeance. It was while he was en route to the territory of his mother's family that, in his low moments, alone in a strange land in the night and with a stone as a pillow, he had an encounter with God. God saw fit to relate with him as an individual. Jacob had the vision of heaven in a dream, of angels ascending and descending and of the God of his grandfather, Abraham and of his father Isaac, standing above and introducing Himself personally to him. He made a commitment to his relationship with God from that time on.

God recognises us uniquely, loves us personally and calls us individually. We are not faceless numbers out of the masses; we are not photocopies but original individuals in our relationship with

God. Our walk with God is not primarily a family or group endeavour but a personal one. While Abraham had a good relationship with God, Jacob was required to develop his relationship with God. His relationship with God could not be inherited but had to be cultivated individually.

A person might be born into a Christian home or attend Christian gatherings regularly, but this does not make them a Christian. Everyone must realise the need for Christ, admit their sins and accept Christ personally as their Lord to begin their personal walk with God. Similarly, we cannot entirely run the Christian race on other people's experiences or knowledge of God. They can be sources of guidance or encouragement in our Christian walk but not the sole foundation for our conviction. Our conviction must be founded on a personal relationship and on experiences of our dealings with God. Our personal conviction in God will keep us steadfast in faith amid the trials and temptations we will face in the world. Our Christian walk must be based on the word of God – the Bible – and Christ should be our role model. We can also have human role models as long as their lifestyles correspond to the life of Christ. We are not called to follow the crowd or what is generally accepted, but to follow Christ. Hence, we must know Him personally.

Just as we are uniquely different in appearance, character and other factors, we differ in purpose. Jeremiah 1:4–5 says: *"Now the word of the LORD came to me, saying, ⁵ "Before I formed you in the belly, I knew you. Before you came forth out of the womb, I sanctified you. I have appointed you a prophet to the nations.""* (NHEB.) How overwhelming that the Lord God Almighty chooses us individually for His purpose. God is very much interested in and committed to dealing with us based on our individual purposes. For instance, someone purposed for a pastoral ministry might be used by God differently to another who is called by Him to be a gospel artist. We can see how God manifested and used men for different purposes in the Bible. Noah's purpose differed from Moses', just as Paul's purpose differed from John the Baptist's.

Also, the assignments of God's servants are unique to them and are in line with their generations' needs at the time. For instance, Moses' assignment was different from Joshua's, Joshua's was different from Samson's and Samson's was different from Elijah's. Their walk with God was peculiar to them; they had unique assignments exclusive to God's requirements for their generations.

In line with the individuality of our purpose and walk with God, we may encounter different situations and circumstances concerning our purposes. When God allows us to pass through certain circumstances we must not compare ourselves to others who are not passing through similar experiences. Regardless of how challenging our experiences might be compared to others, such experiences may just be necessary to actualise our purpose. It might be the will of God for one of His servants to die in persecution and for the other to live longer, preaching the gospel. This is well illustrated in John 21:21–22 when Jesus spoke to Peter concerning how Peter would die. John was with Jesus when Jesus talked to Peter, so Peter asked Jesus, *""Lord, what about this man?" [22] Jesus said to him, "If I desire that he stay until I come, what is that to you? You follow me.""* (NHEB.)

Furthermore, since God deals with us as individuals, He assigns responsibilities to each of us according to our purpose. Where responsibility is given, accountability is inevitable. Hence, we shall all individually account for how we responded to His offer of salvation. Romans 14:12 says: *"So then each one of us will give account of himself to God."* (NHEB.)

Interestingly, it is God's earnest desire that everybody, in all the tribes and nations of the earth, come to have a walk with Him. The summary of the Bible is the story of an Almighty and self-sufficient God, having His abode in heaven, sincerely longing and desiring to have a relationship with men. He is actively looking for men whom He will call His own, who would be vessels through whom He will make His glory manifest, who will be living expressions of the supernatural life. He is willing to walk with anyone regardless of their past, no matter how grievous their sin. He has made provision through His Son Jesus Christ to cleanse us from every stain of sin, make us as white as snow and give us eternal life if we put our trust in Him. John 3:16 says: ***"For God so loved the world that he gave his only Son, so that whoever believes in him will not perish, but have everlasting life."*** (NHEB.) Answering the call of God to repentance qualifies a person to begin a walk with Him.

While God desires a personal and intimate relationship with us, we have a role in ensuring the relationship is well cultivated. We must detach ourselves from sin, focus on our relationship with God and please Him through our obedience to His word with emphasis on salvation.

TOPIC 2: GIVING GOD CONDITIONS

GENESIS 28:20–22

Two men met a beggar while walking through a street on a frigid and windy day. Afflicted by the pangs of hunger, the beggar pleaded that the men offer him some money so he could feed for that day. The first man dipped his hand into his pocket, gave the beggar some money and walked away. The second man also dipped his hand into his pocket and was about to stretch his arm towards the beggar when he made a statement to himself: "God! I hope you are watching! As I am giving this man this money, I expect you to give me back and even more." (Johnny, 2022.)

The second man's gesture sadly mirrors the state of some people's relationship with God. Rather than a wholehearted and absolute devotion to God, their service and commitment to Him is anchored on conditions. They demand a reaction for every action they deem worthy of a reward or a blessing.

One man who exhibited this trait in the scripture was Jacob. Fleeing from his brother Esau to his mother's relatives in Haran, Jacob made a vow to God in a manner that had strings attached. He predicated his decision to serve God with conditions, as many people do. He elected to put the cart before the horse by telling God to fulfil His promises first and have his personal needs met before he would accept the lordship of God. This gesture can be said to be flawed in approach. By implication, it can be reasoned that if God did not meet those conditions Jacob might have had difficulties making God his Lord.

Jacob's conditional approach to serving God portrays a similar scenario evident in some people's acceptance of God and a relationship with Him today. It is not an entirely strange sight to see people base their choice of accepting Christ on conditions that relate to their needs and an expectation that life from that moment on will become a bed of roses as a result. When prompted towards salvation, some people have the mindset that, unless Jesus gives them clothes to wear, food to eat, a lucrative job or a child of their own, their allegiance to Jesus will not be absolute. This sort of attitude is not only one that is peculiar to prospective converts but also to those who already have a relationship with God. Whether within or outside religious gatherings, we make our commitment and service to God conditional when we decide to give in the church or show care to the needy solely because we want God to reward us. In truth, it is far from a pleasant view seeing people choose to become Christians for the material benefits they hope to get from God and not because of the salvation of their souls. If ever there is a device available that can reveal minds and motives, one wonders how many people will be counted as Christians for the right reasons and not for selfish motives. When our motives for serving God are characterised by conditions, we become easy targets for the devil to manipulate. When our relationship with God is based on conditions other than our soul's salvation it becomes easy for our faith to be destabilised when the storms of life rage at us, and we discover that the Christian journey is not always a bed of roses.

It is imperative to place firmly in our minds the fact that God desires our relationship with Him to be devoid of conditions or strings. He requires our walk with Him to be borne out of love and our service to Him to be rendered with wholehearted commitment. For what it is worth, the decision to follow Christ or obey His commands should be motivated by our love for God and the salvation of our souls. As such, these should be the driving force of our relationship with God and not any fleeting gain. All the material possessions we hope to get from God cannot be compared in worth to our soul's salvation. Matthew 6:33 says: *"But seek first the kingdom of God and his righteousness, and all these things will be given to you as well."* (NHEB.)

As God is the very reason for our existence, He knows what we need before we ask. Any condition attached to following God only shows a lack of trust in Him to sustain us. Our trust is supposed to be absolute, not optional, paramount, not conditional in our relationship with God. Regardless of the multitude of unpleasant occurrences that could come his way, Prophet Habakkuk made a resolution to keep the Lord as his God: *"For though the fig tree doesn't flourish, nor fruit be in the vines; the labor of the olive fails, the fields yield no food; the flocks are cut off from the fold, and there is no herd in the stalls: ¹⁸yet I will rejoice in the LORD. I will be joyful in the God of my salvation. ¹⁹The LORD, the Lord, is my strength. He makes my feet like deer's feet, and enables me to go in high places."* (Habakkuk 3:17–19 NHEB.) Whether in good times or bad, our trust in God and our devotion to Him must remain absolute and resolute.

CHAPTER 4

TOPIC 1: PARENTS' TRADES

GENESIS 29:4–9

One notion the world often advocates these days is, "Parents should teach and encourage each of their children to choose and focus on a career path that will lead them to success in life." This is good and commendable, but some people usually fail to underscore the significance of multifarious skills in a diversified global economy, forgetting that no knowledge is wasted knowledge. In addition to pursuing their careers, it is wise that children also pay attention to and learn their parents' trades.

Laban, for example, actively involved his children in his livestock business during their upbringing. Though it was a prevalent practice for children to ply the business line of their parents in Laban's era, it is commendable for Rachel to have dedicated herself as a shepherdess to her father's business. This is quite interesting – a lady herding her father's sheep. This may be an uncommon occupation one would expect a lady to venture into. But Rachel was different: she became actively involved in her father's profession and diligently learnt the art of shepherding. After she had acquired the requisite skills for shepherding, Laban reposed confidence in her to the extent of allowing her to personally take the sheep out for open grazing and watering. Beyond all doubt, her parent's encouragement, together with her personal interest, commitment and diligence, must have contributed significantly to her accomplishment as a trained shepherdess. While carrying out her daily activity she met Jacob, who later became her husband.

There is wisdom in how Laban trained Rachel to become a shepherdess. No parent can precisely predict what the future holds for their children. No parent has the privilege of knowing if any of their children will end up choosing the same career as theirs, as Rachel followed the course of her father's occupation. Hence, parents are encouraged to get their children involved in the day-to-day running of whatever business they do from the children's tender ages. This will acquaint them with what the business entails and how it is being run. Proverbs 22:6 says: *"Train a child in the way he should go, and when he is old he will not depart from it."* (NHEB.) This does not impede them from following their chosen career path in life. And children's chosen career paths do not negate the importance of knowing whatever profession or business their parents are involved in. When knowledge in any field of endeavour is acquired it does not vaporise into thin air; instead, it provides the children with an extra edge in life. After all, no acquired knowledge is useless. If they do not utilise it now, it may be helpful in the future.

Imagine a child being at home and his father has to pay or delegate someone to care for his business in absentia. It does not sound pleasing to hear. In actuality, it will be an honour for the father to see his child be in charge whenever he is not around. Even in the event of his demise, such a child can easily take control, having acquainted themself with the know-how of their father's business. This will ensure smooth continuity and the child will know that their parents' occupations are essential, even if they decide to follow a different career path. Against this backdrop, if a father's occupation is manufacturing, it is wise for a child to familiarise themself with producing the products the father specialises in, even if the child's dream profession is to be a doctor. Likewise, for a child of a tailor who dreams of becoming a lawyer, having the know-how to sew clothes will not affect this dream. For a child whose mother owns a supermarket, having adequate knowledge of how to manage such a business will help the mother and may also be of immense benefit to the child in the future. Therefore, while parents need to send their children to schools and encourage them to follow their dream professions, this should be done without undermining the need to acquaint them with their vocations. No knowledge is wasted; it might come in handy in the future. Who knows?

It is worth noting that, in a bid to acquainting the children with the family business, especially if it was not done from their childhoods, a prudent approach should be employed. It is incumbent on parents to devise wise methods to make their children see why they should develop an interest in and know their businesses, even if they have already chosen different career paths.

What if a child refuses to listen to their parents? Should the parents apply force? No! No Christian parent should do such a thing. Though some parents try to coerce a child into following their profession, nothing justifies this approach. There should be no reason for parents to impose their professions or preferred careers on their children. Rather, they are to encourage them, arouse their interest, and, if they still refuse, the parents are to guide and support them in their preferred area of interest.

Sometimes, however, in sending their children to higher institutions, some parents may try to compel them to follow their career path. Forcing children to study courses they never show interest in can be challenging for the children. Some children may yield easily, but it may be quite hard for others. This may lead to a strain on the parent–child relationship. Unyielding children may not accept their parents' career choice and the parents may also oppose the personal career choice of such children, leaving parent and child at loggerheads. This is a serious issue, as some parents have ruined their children's futures because they refused to accept their career choices. A loving parent should understand that what is at stake is their child's future and not their own ego, reputation or continuity. Instead of being adamant, a loving parent should observe the child's passion, understand their strengths and weaknesses, and encourage, advise and support them in their dream career.

By and large, children should endeavour to learn and devote themselves to their parents' trades as long as it does not go against God's word.

TOPIC 2: INTEGRITY

GENESIS 29:15–30

Diamonds are rare and not easily possessed by everyone, and so is integrity. Integrity is a rare quality that is not easily found in many. Integrity is required in all spheres of life but is notably absent in many lives. Every aspect of human endeavour greatly suffers because of the want of integrity. It is very conspicuous how many people break truces at will, how they easily say one thing and do another. Many people's words hold no value anymore; sadly, we are in a world in which many people's words are no longer their bonds.

Laban exemplified one of the many problems the world is struggling with – a lack of integrity. He was the one who called Jacob to the negotiation table on the premise that he should work and be rewarded. "Tell me what your wages would be," Laban said to Jacob. All the while, Jacob had found himself submerged in the tides of love. He desired only one thing – not livestock, land or money, but Rachel, Laban's daughter. Jacob laid out his terms of service – seven years of service for Rachel's hand in marriage and Laban agreed. The seven years of service passed swiftly. Jacob's wedding day arrived and his wedding night could not have come any sooner. The euphoria, merriment and anticipation filled the heart of Jacob, but something was to cut short his joy. In the morning, Jacob discovered that his father-in-law, Laban, had not given him the daughter he had longed for. He had been given Leah, the older daughter, rather than Rachel. Jacob confronted Laban, who hung everything on the premise of their culture – the first must marry before the second. It was quite a twist in the tale and a display of dishonesty on Laban's part. When Jacob laid out his contract terms, Laban should have explained their custom of not marrying the younger daughter before the older daughter. Instead, for seven years Laban concealed that fact from Jacob. And for seven years, he knew Jacob was in love with Rachel and not Leah. Jacob was angry and Laban decided to make an alternative suggestion on how he could marry the one he truly loved, thereby taking advantage of Jacob's love as a medium for further service.

If there is one thing that can earn us people's trust or distrust it is integrity. Judging from day-to-day interactions, it does seem like second nature for people to say one thing and do another. Unfortunately, our society is replete with many "Labans" regarding integrity. For the purpose of deception, many are those who utter words they never intend to keep. Many are those whose integrity suffers due to their tendency to make promises or accept tasks that could be overwhelming because of the fear of disappointing people. Consequently, they lose people's trust as they become less credible and reliable.

Integrity is the quality of being honest or truthful and consistent in adherence to moral principles. It is choosing to do the right thing in every circumstance, whether convenient or not. A person of integrity understands that they are bound by their word. Integrity is not to have different shades of ourselves but to be consistent in character – to be the same at work, church, school, among friends and family members. God's expectation for all Christians is that they maintain their integrity and moral uprightness no matter what circumstance they find themselves in, whether convenient or not. Showing moral rectitude in words and actions with people we meet daily builds the trust they have for us and, as a result, doors can subsequently open for our benefit. The world itself lacks people with integrity, so when such a person is found they are like diamonds – many people desire to have them.

Characters in the Bible are examples for us to learn from. In Laban, we find a man who displayed a lack of integrity but in Samuel, we see a man who called a whole nation to examine his integrity, and no speck was found. Samuel stood before the nation of Israel after he had judged them for several years and said: *"Here I am. Testify against me before the LORD, and before his anointed. Whose ox have I taken? Whose donkey have I taken? Whom have I defrauded? Whom have I oppressed, or from whose hand have I taken a bribe so that I would overlook something? Testify against me, and I will restore it to you. ⁴They said, "You have not defrauded us, nor oppressed us, neither have you taken anything of any man's hand.""* (1 Samuel 12:3–4 NHEB.) How many of us can say this and get a similar response?

In imbibing the nature of integrity, we build trust in others. They take what we say as binding and need no further proof to certify that we will keep our words. It is this level of trustworthiness that Christ requires us to reach. In Matthew 5:37, He instructed that our yes should be yes and our no, no. *"But let your 'Yes' be 'Yes' and your 'No' be 'No.' Whatever is more than these is of the evil one."* (NHEB.) People can trust our yes and no as binding, based on our previous display of trustworthiness and integrity. Let us never forget that the reputation of a thousand years can be destroyed by an action. God demands integrity from every Christian. It is the will of God that we deal honestly with every man and live in a way that is worthy of the trust of others. Integrity is consistency in doing what is right in any circumstance. It goes beyond a single act of honesty: it is a habit, a lifestyle of morality regardless of the situation. We should grow to the point that our words and works will always say the same thing.

One might ask, What if there is a justifiable reason why we cannot keep our promises? There are times in our lives when we make promises with the full intention of fulfilling them, but then we find it hard to keep our promises because of unexpected challenges. In handling such situations, firstly, the reason must be justifiable. If the reason is justifiable, we must not keep the other person in the dark but tell them why we may not fulfil the promise or why we may fulfil it at a later date. In so doing, we still keep our trustworthiness and maintain the quality of our integrity. We must also be careful not to make promises or accept tasks we will be unable to fulfil. It is better to tell a person, "I cannot" than to say "I can" and then fail to do it.

Furthermore, one cannot truly walk with God and lack integrity. How do we intend to win souls for Christ when people do not even trust what we say? Lack of integrity is counterproductive to our soul-winning mission because the world's gaze is ever on us, and when we are known for inconsistency of character, our ability to attract people to Christ diminishes. To trust the message of salvation from us, people should trust us to keep our simple commitments.

The habit of acting on what God expects makes us true children of God. Integrity always has its roots in our hearts. When the heart is right with God and the pleasing of the Master is our everyday muse, integrity will be a non-detachable quality of our being.

TOPIC 3: LOVE: A REQUISITE FOR CHRISTIAN MARRIAGE

GENESIS 29:16–30

A young couple, both of whom were previously divorced, visited an older couple celebrating their 50th wedding anniversary. "Fifty years!" the young husband thought. "That is quite a long time to be married to one person" Out of curiosity, he approached the old couple and said, "It is strange that two individuals can live happily for so long. How did it happen?" The old gentleman smiled, looked at his wife with love in his eyes, held her hand and said, "It would have been a lot longer without her; our love for each other made 50 years seem like five years." (Johnny, 2022.)

How beautiful! It was quite a spectacle for the old man and the old woman to continue their journey on the path of marriage. Their hands were gnarled but still clasped; their faces were seamed but still radiant; their bodies were frail, but their love was still strong.

Marriage is a sacred and unique human relationship. Love is an essential factor in marital decisions. But often, people enter into the lifelong commitment of marriage with the wrong motive. Love, as an essential factor, has been substituted for many other things. Many people are motivated to marry because of wealth, connection, circumstance, physical appearance and sometimes custom.

As a young man running for his life, Jacob's top priorities were his safety, provision and hope of returning in peace. Although his mother had used marriage as a cover for his flight from home, his request to God at Bethel revealed his major desires – safety, provision and a peaceful journey; marriage was not yet a priority. But after just a few moments with Rachel at the well the scope of Jacob's focus was extended. From then on, it was obvious: Jacob was in love with Rachel and he did not hide it. From helping the young shepherdess with her flocks to choosing to marry her instead of being paid for his services, Jacob showed that he had fallen head over heels for Rachel. Little wonder Solomon acknowledged that one of the things beyond him was understanding the relationship between a man and a young woman. *"There are three things which are too amazing for me, four which I do not understand: ¹⁹The way of an eagle in the air; the way of a serpent on a rock; the way of a ship in the midst of the sea; and the way of a man with a maiden."* (Proverbs 30:18–19 NHEB.)

The Bible said that the seven years Jacob served for Rachel *"seemed to him but a few days, for the love he had for her."* (Genesis 29:20 NHEB.) Love made seven years of service look like a jolly ride. Love is requisite for a successful marriage; getting married to someone you love is like a refreshing drink of water to a weary wilderness traveller. Although love does not solve challenges – every couple goes through their share of ups and downs – it will undoubtedly give them reason to hold on to their shared value and affection during challenging seasons *"for love is strong as death..."* (Song of Solomon 8:6 NHEB.)

Interestingly, Laban pulled a fast one when the Jacob–Rachel love was about to culminate in marriage. Laban gave Jacob Leah, a woman who was not the subject of his hopes and aspirations. In years to follow, Leah would become the victim of a loveless marriage – having to compete for her husband's affection with her sister as a co-wife who had captivated her husband from the first day he met her. Getting married to someone without the foundation of love is like building a house on an unstable foundation: it may collapse sooner or later. This kind of couple would be struggling to cope with what others enjoy. Laban had claimed their custom as the reason for him giving Leah before Rachel. Though today, it might not be on the grounds of custom. For whatever reason, no parent should impose their child on another in marriage or impose another on their child in marriage. No one should go into a marriage in which there exists no love or, worse still, in which the other is obviously in love with someone else. Since marriage is a lifelong commitment, imposing a spouse on one's child where there is no love may not bode well for that child's marriage's security and longevity. The love between couples is like a lubricant between bolts and nuts: once it is absent, friction is inevitable. Therefore, marrying someone without genuine love may lead to persistent conflict and ultimately divorce, which God detests and discourages. A parent's interest should be about the love shared and the godly background of their child's spousal choice.

Marrying for the wrong reasons is not only initiated by parents. Many people choose to marry for the wrong reasons. Today, wealth has become the invaluable spice in spousal choice. Physical appearance has become an inducement for marriage. Naturalisation by marriage has motivated many people to go into marriage. People are hardly marrying for love these days. And what are the effects of these wrong motives? Increasing divorce rates, unhappy families, child neglect, domestic abuse and more. If the main spice of marriage, love, is not there, people do not enjoy the union; they merely endure it.

Though wealth, physical appearance and other factors may attract you to a person, love is what will keep you glued to that person if those factors are not there. Love will keep you in your marriage when your spouse is experiencing financial struggle; love will keep you in your marriage when your spouse is advancing in age and is no longer as charming as they used to be. Love will make you fight every single day for the interests and welfare of your family. Love is that special feeling you get when at old age, you look into your partner's eyes and know that the feeling you share is just as wonderful, beautiful and captivating as when you knew each other many years ago. Money cannot buy that; beauty cannot give you that; connections cannot do it. Only one thing can make marriage endure so long yet feel so sweet – its name is love! *"Many waters can't quench love, neither can floods drown it…"* (Song of Solomon 8:7 NHEB.)

One of the wrong notions people have is that love before marriage does not really matter. They opine that love develops within the marriage. This may be true in some cases. There are instances in which couples have learnt to love themselves while in marriage. But the truth is that, as much as there is a possibility that love develops in marriage, it is risky and not an advisable option for intending couples. There is always a great possibility that hostility can develop in a marriage where love never existed. There should be proof of affection between the couple before a marriage commitment.

Intending couples should be careful about how they handle their affection for each other before marriage. Sex before marriage is no godly proof or demonstration of love; allowing that affection to lead to sin could hinder the Holy Spirit's guidance in that relationship.

Though love is of utmost importance in marriage, a believer must not marry an unbeliever simply because of love. It will be hard to achieve the 'oneness' that God desires for an ideal marriage if couples have different beliefs. Marriage is an intimate relationship that unites two individuals as 'one flesh'. This does not mean couples must think or feel alike in everything because marriage does not extinguish individuality. But a relationship so intimate that one literally and figuratively becomes part of the other requires two people who share the same belief.

Although love is essential and plays a vital role in a marriage's success, the kind of love that can stand and weather the test of time is the love that can only come from commitment first to God and then to each other. God's love helps us become better people – we appreciate others' strengths, help with their weaknesses and see that we do not hurt them. It helps us forgive one another freely, notwithstanding the offence committed. The kind of love exhibited by Christ for the church is God's expectation from a husband to his wife. Ephesians 5:25 says: *"Husbands, love your wives, even as Christ also loved the church, and gave himself up for it"* (NHEB). Thus, we cannot talk about love in marriage outside God because God is love and He is the Originator and the Sustainer of marriage.

In reality, there is no perfect couple and no perfect marriage. Since we are imperfect, we are bound to make mistakes. Love in marriage does not eliminate our partner's flaws but enables us to correct them in love where necessary. When marriage results from genuine commitment, it becomes a testimony to others on how true love should be. A blissful marriage thus requires the love of God as revealed in 1 Corinthians 13:4–7: *"Love is patient and is kind; love does not envy. Love does not brag, is not proud, ⁵does not behave itself inappropriately, does not seek its own way, is not irritable, does not keep a record of wrongs; ⁶does not rejoice in unrighteousness, but rejoices with the truth; ⁷bears all things, believes all things, hopes all things, endures all things."* (NHEB.)

TOPIC 4: GOD'S COMPASSION

GENESIS 29:31–35

God may conceal the purpose of His ways, but His ways are not without purpose. They are laced with love and compassion. The accurate measure of God's compassion is that it is without measure.

Jacob, Rachel and Leah's story is a story of a broken promise, adorable love, marital rivalry and a compassionate God. It was not Leah's fault, neither Rachel's nor Jacob's; it was Leah's father's action in marrying her to Jacob that put her in a tight corner. She was going to live with a man who would not show her love from his heart; she would live seeing her younger sister and now co-wife being loved and given more marital attention. Leah's children's names were a reflection of her plight. She had hoped that her husband would love her due to the children she bore for him. Note her remark in Genesis 29:34: *"Now this time will my husband be joined to me, because I have borne him three sons..."* (NHEB.)

Genesis 29:32 says, *"Leah conceived, and bore a son, and she named him Reuben. For she said, "Because the LORD has looked at my affliction.""* (NHEB.) God, in His compassion, understood what Leah was going through and opened her womb. This was compensation and a comfort in her plight. One cannot help but wonder how Leah went through life wallowing in the canal of misery she had been made to endure. Fortunately, she was not alone, even though she might not have realised it initially. God was with her and was interested in her situation. God's intervention proved to be a comfort that she greatly needed when everything seemed gloomy for her. Leah gave birth to six sons and a daughter for Jacob before Rachel's first son was born. God was moved by the sorrows within Leah's heart due to all she was going through.

God's compassion in this particular story did not end with Leah. Rachel also enjoyed His compassion when God opened her womb when she feared she could not give birth and only her sister could. As Leah kept giving birth, the tables kind of turned, making Rachel the disadvantaged one in the marriage. In her words to Jacob, "Give me children or else I die" we see how sad she had become in the marriage. God showed His concern for Rachel and blessed her with children. Genesis 30:22–23 says, *"God remembered Rachel, and God listened to her, and opened her womb. ^{23} She conceived, bore a son, and said, "God has taken away my reproach.""* (NHEB.)

Compassion is a fundamental and distinctive quality of God. In God's compassion, He acts on behalf of the disadvantaged. The Bible is saturated with instances of God's compassion; it flows through the pages of the Old and New Testaments. Psalm 72:12–14 says: *"For he will deliver the needy when he cries; the poor, who has no helper. ¹³He will have pity on the poor and needy. He will save the souls of the needy. ¹⁴He will redeem their soul from oppression and violence. Their blood will be precious in his sight."* (NHEB.) God is concerned about what concerns His children. The fact that we might not have an immediate response when we share our burdens with Him should not make us disheartened and feel it is unnecessary to trust Him. God is moved by our grief. No one on earth cares for us as much as God does. What would have been the fate of barren Hannah if God had not had compassion for her (1 Samuel 1:1–28) or the fate of the Jews when Haman plotted against them as recorded in the book of Esther? The list is endless.

At several instances in His ministry, Christ showed compassion to the oppressed, hungry, diseased, demon-possessed and those who needed salvation. He displayed compassion and admonished His followers to do the same. Christ demands that we live and act compassionately, not only towards those who are kind to us but also to the unkind. Matthew 5:47 says: *"And if you only greet your brothers, what more do you do than others? Do not even the Gentiles do the same?"* (NHEB.)

Finding people who need compassion is by no means a difficult task; we only need to look around us. Note that compassion goes beyond having feelings for others' plight; it entails acting upon these feelings to ease them of their pains however we can. One measure of our likeness to Christ is our sensitivity to the needs and sufferings of others. 1 John 3:17–18 says: *"But whoever has the world's goods, and sees his brother in need, and closes his heart of compassion against him, how does the love of God remain in him? ¹⁸Little children, let us not love in word only, neither with the tongue only, but in deed and truth."* (NHEB.) Therefore, all who are called by His name ought to cultivate compassion within them.

Leah's experience is illustrative for us as believers, especially in trying times. Often, we allow ourselves to be overwhelmed by our circumstances to the point at which we think God is detached from our lives. What we may not know, however, is that He is very much involved and compassionate about the storms that betide us. Whatever experiences, challenges, injustices and oppositions we face, God is working through them in His own way; we only need to trust Him.

Just as only a living Saviour could rescue a dying world, only a compassionate God can rescue people who are victims in a non-compassionate world. So, we should run to Him and trust in Him, for His compassion is new every morning.

What would have been the world's fate if God did not have compassion and had not offered His only Son? While God's ultimate compassion for the world has already been displayed by the gift of salvation through His only Son's death, we have the responsibility to accept His gracious gift by living according to His word with emphasis on salvation.

CHAPTER 5

TOPIC 1: RACHEL'S ENVY

GENESIS 30:1

One husband. Two sisters. Different fates. The story of Rachel and Leah is unfortunately riddled with episodes of envy. While Rachel's marriage to Jacob was borne out of love, Leah's marriage to him came about due to Laban's mischievous act. Despite all the love Rachel enjoyed, she lacked something her sister enjoyed – a child. This contrast in fortune sparked envy in Rachel, making her confront her husband about her childlessness. Rachel's envy and competition with her sister led her to name the second child born to her, through her servant, Bilhah, as Naphtali, meaning, ***"With mighty wrestlings have I wrestled with my sister, and have prevailed..."*** (Genesis 30:8 NHEB.) Whereas Leah's fruitfulness should have been a thing of joy for Rachel, envy made her perceive it as a competition. It is not difficult to see the ill effects envy can have on relationships, even on those with blood relations.

Regardless of how some might attempt to justify Rachel's envy, envy is never a feeling we must accommodate as God's children. God has made all of His creations differently and with a unique purpose in life. By comparing ourselves with others we allow envy to blind our eyes from seeing and appreciating the uniqueness of who we are or what we possess. When envious feelings are allowed to fester, we become discontented with ourselves and what God has done for us and instead shift focus towards other people's successes, happiness and gifts. When we allow envy to possess our hearts we can develop resentment and hostility towards other people due to their possessions or positions. As a feeling that God frowns upon, envy often rides along in the company of other sins when left unchecked. At the point where we allow envy to lead us into bearing ill will towards others who possess what we desire, we become susceptible to more behaviours that run contrary to God's word. The truth is that envy is a feeling many would not want to confess to but one that many are guilty of. When ruled by envy, our actions tend to be tailored to hurting others, even to our detriment. When propelled by envy, we assume an attitude that makes us selfish rather than selfless.

The envy of seeing his offering rejected and his brother's offering accepted drove Cain to murder his brother, Abel, in anger. It was also envy that made Joseph's brothers contrive to sell him into slavery – having initially plotted to murder him – due to his dreams and the greater affection shown by their father towards him. Indeed, envy is a fire that has destroyed families, friends, relationships and organisations. It is also like a cancer that can gradually destroy one from within if left unchecked. Proverbs 14:30 says: *"The life of the body is a heart at peace, but envy rots the bones."* (NHEB.)

It is worth noting that when we permit envious feelings to submerge us in sin, we risk estranging ourselves from God and endangering the salvation of our souls. Galatians 5:19–21 says, *"Now the works of the flesh are obvious, which are: sexual immorality, uncleanness, lustfulness, [20]idolatry, sorcery, hatred, strife, jealousies, outbursts of anger, rivalries, divisions, heresies, [21]envyings, murders, drunkenness, orgies, and things like these; of which I forewarn you, even as I also forewarned you, that those who practice such things will not inherit the kingdom of God."* (NHEB.) In tackling the cancerous feeling and behaviour that is envy, it is imperative to address the root. When Jesus talked about what defiles a man, He highlighted the heart as the source. Since envious thoughts and actions spring from the heart, it is essential to let Christ penetrate our hearts and purge us of every impurity, including envy. After we receive the newness of life in Christ we can only avoid exhibiting deeds of the flesh such as envy by walking in the Spirit. Galatians 5:24–26 says: *"Those who belong to Christ have crucified the flesh with its passions and lusts.* *25If we live by the Spirit, let us also walk by the Spirit. 26Let us not become conceited, provoking one another, and envying one another."* (NHEB.) By walking in the Spirit, we are choosing to walk in love.

When we yield to the voice of the Holy Spirit and let His abiding presence saturate our hearts with love, we will always be happy for others' progress rather than being envious of them. 1 Corinthians 13:4 tells us: *"Love is patient and is kind; love does not envy..."* (NHEB.) When the love of Christ domiciles our hearts we will feel contentment for what we have rather than resentment for what others have. When love rests in the abode of our hearts we will not have any ill will to hurt others or act against the word of God to have what they have.

If indeed we desire God to meet a need of ours, we can choose the option of seeking His face in prayer rather than displaying envy towards others, as exemplified in the contrasting attitudes of Rachel and Hannah. Loved by their husbands but shared with another, Rachel and Hannah experienced barrenness while their co-wives witnessed fruitfulness. Though both suffered from the same problem, their approaches differed. While Rachel envied her sister's fertility, Hannah chose to direct the burden of her barrenness to the Lord – the Giver of children. *"She was in bitterness of soul, and prayed to the LORD, and wept bitterly."* (1 Samuel 1:10 NHEB.)

By seeking God's face when in lack and demonstrating love rather than envy, we will be showing the kind of attitude that God desires us to have and the kind of attitude that would endear people to Christ rather than away from Him.

TOPIC 2: MISDIRECTED REQUEST

GENESIS 30:1–2

"No one can receive anything, unless it has been given to him from heaven." (John 3:27 NHEB.) This statement is sublime; it reveals the sovereignty of God in the affairs of man. No matter how prestigious

your position or level you have attained, nothing is worthwhile in this life outside the will of God. God is the source of every good and perfect gift. One of these good and perfect gifts is the fruit of the womb: *"Look, children are a heritage of the LORD. The fruit of the womb is his reward."* (Psalm 127:3 NHEB.)

After a wedding, most people expect the newly wedded couple to bear children in the early years of their marriage. In Rachel's case it was appropriate and understandable for her to be expectant of this. As a matter of fact, it was long overdue for her to conceive and have her children. Nevertheless, her request was misdirected. How? Rachel's barrenness took a toll on her, and seeing her sister, Leah, giving birth to children made it worse. She envied Leah and became so frustrated that she angrily demanded a child from Jacob, her husband, with a threat to die if her request was not granted. This made Jacob upset and he asked, *"Am I in God's place, who has withheld from you the fruit of the womb?"* (Genesis 30:2 NHEB.) Jacob acknowledged the divine hand of God in her challenge. He understood that children were gifts from God. As such, it was God's prerogative to give them to whomever He willed. While addressing his wife's misdirected request, he acknowledged his inability and made her understand the fact that he was not in the position to give her what God in His wisdom had withheld.

The lesson to learn here is crucial, and great attention must be accorded to it. No one can help someone whom God, in His wisdom and sovereignty, has withheld help from. Any attempt to direct a request that only God can grant to anyone or anything apart from God is a misdirected request. It is dishonouring and unwise to place the confidence and expectation meant for the Creator on His creatures. Hence, no matter the intensity of the challenges confronting us, and regardless of the longevity of the delay in having our need(s) met, our requests, as Christians, should by no means be misdirected to any human, as Rachel did, nor to any idol, but to God alone. By this, God is honoured and acknowledged as the sole source of every good gift and godly help.

Just as Jacob responded to Rachel's misdirected request, the King of Israel's response to a woman's request in 2 Kings 6:24–27 also acknowledges the supremacy of God in the affairs of humans. The King of Syria had besieged Samaria and there was a severe famine. One day, when the King of Israel passed by on the wall, a woman cried to him for help. By the King's response to her, he acknowledged God as the source of help. *"It happened after this, that Benhadad king of Syria gathered all his army, and went up and besieged Samaria. ²⁵There was a great famine in Samaria. Look, they besieged it, until a donkey's head was sold for eighty pieces of silver, and the fourth part of a kab of dove's dung for five pieces of silver. ²⁶As the king of Israel was passing by on the wall, a woman cried to him, saying, "Help, my lord, O king." ²⁷He said, "If the LORD doesn't help you, from where could I help you? From of the threshing floor, or from the winepress?""* (NHEB.)

One biblical character that rightly directed her request was Hannah. She was barren, just like Rachel. Because of her barrenness she was mocked and despised by her rival – Peninnah. Despite the delay in her conception, her anguished soul and the reproach, Hannah remained committed to serving God and properly directed her request to the right source – the Almighty God. No doubt, the frustrations caused by her co-wife would have been overwhelming. Yet that was not enough to propel her to misdirect her request to her husband or any other human. Her prayer to God is worth noting: *"LORD of hosts, if you will indeed look on the affliction of your handmaid, and remember me, and not forget your handmaid, but will give to your handmaid a son, then I will set him before you as a Nazirite until the day of his death. And he will not drink wine or strong drink, and no razor will come on his head."* (1 Samuel 1:11 NHEB.) By this prayer, Hannah recognised children as a heritage and reward from God. When in need of them, we should always go to Him alone.

Does this now mean it is wrong to make requests to any human? Obviously not! There are certain things God has placed within humans' power to enable them to help one another. There is nothing wrong with children making certain requests of their parents. It is appropriate for siblings to ask fellow siblings what they lack. It is not against God's will for the needy to make a request from someone whom God has blessed to meet their needs. In reality, it is God's will for us to help one another with whatever He has entrusted us with. It is, however, wrong to repose our confidence in humans as if they are the source of such help. Psalm 118:8 says: *"It is better to take refuge in the LORD, than to put confidence in man."* (NHEB.) Even when we receive assistance from humans we must acknowledge God as the One who used them to render such help. Thus, it is inappropriate to place humans in the position of God by recognising them as the source of help or by requesting from them something God alone can provide. The psalmist's stance in Psalm 121:1–2 when he was in need is worth emulating by all and sundry. He declared: *"I will lift up my eyes to the hills. Where does my help come from? ²My help comes from the LORD, who made heaven and earth."* (NHEB.) While we all need help for one thing or another, true and lasting help can only emanate from God, not humans or idols.

This leads us to another form of misdirected request: making requests or seeking help from any form of idol. This certainly is an act of dishonouring God, as it violates God's commandment and has attendant grievous consequences. Whoever does this has pitched his tent with the devil. As for the devil, he has nothing good to give. Though disguised as good, his gifts are given with an evil intent to lure the receivers. Such gifts are detrimental, as the devil will seek to claim in return something of greater value – your soul's salvation. That is always the devil's trick: he usually gives with one hand and collects double with the other hand. In light of this, absolutely nothing should move any child of the living God to make a request or seek help from the devil, no matter how complex the challenge may be.

As Christians it must be registered in our hearts that experiencing the storms of life at some point in our walk with God is inescapable.

Whatever the challenge may be, be it prolonged sickness, acute lack, joblessness, stagnation or persecution, we should not allow it to keep us wallowing in the mud of misery, whiffling by the boisterous wind of worry or being weighed down by the overwhelming cloud of uncertainty to the extent that we consider misdirecting our requests. No, we must not succumb to such pressure. Instead, with the overflowing joy of salvation in our hearts, take it to the Lord Jesus in prayer. Philippians 4:6 says: ***"Do not be anxious about anything, but in everything, by prayer and petition with thanksgiving, let your requests be made known to God."*** (NHEB.) We can make our requests known to God through prayers, not by getting worried or misdirecting our requests, as this will not bring the needed solutions to our challenges but instead only worsen them and cause us undue pain.

A hymn writer Joseph Medlicott Scriven (1820–1886) penned this lovely hymn during a challenging moment:

What a friend we have in Jesus, all our sins and grief to bear.
What a privilege to carry everything to God in prayer.
O what peace we often forfeit,
O what needless pain we bear,
All because we do not carry everything to God in prayer.

This hymn teaches us to cast all our cares on God because He knows our needs at every point in time and is always committed to meeting them as we take everything to Him in prayer. If God can meet the greatest need of mankind – salvation – then we can rest assured that our needs, rightly directed to Him, will receive His response. Even if such a response seems to take a long time, it is worth waiting for. God always responds to our requests according to His timing within the confine of His will. While we are waiting, whether our requests are eventually granted or not, let us keep trusting God, especially for our soul's salvation, and avoid doing anything that is against the word of God.

TOPIC 3: GOD'S APPOINTED TIME

GENESIS 30:20–24

Man naturally desires that everything be done at his pace and in the shortest time. This has given rise to the fast-paced world we now live in – a world greatly inclined towards speed and convenience. Just as one sends a mail and expects to receive a reply within a short time, we generally imagine that our prayers should be answered similarly, making it even more difficult for us to walk with God's timing. There is no doubt that one of the hardest things for many Christians to do is wait on God's appointed time to answer a request. We are used to getting what we want, which makes it hard to adjust to God's clock. To truly walk with God, one must learn to adapt to God's time and wait patiently for the fulfilment of His promises. Ecclesiastes 3:11 says: *"He has made everything beautiful in its time. He has also set eternity in their hearts, yet so that man can't find out the work that God has done from the beginning even to the end."* (NHEB.)

With the flames of envy burning in her heart, Rachel's frustration at her barrenness knew no bounds. At some point she had furiously demanded that her husband give her children – as if Jacob had the power to give children. At God's appropriate time, He remembered Rachel and blessed her with two sons. God's delay was not denial; He was working according to His will and timing.

The Bible records that "God remembered Rachel" (Genesis 30:22), and a question that could come to mind is, Does God forget? In a natural sense, we understand remembrance as a recollection of something forgotten, and if God is indeed omniscient, how come He forgets like mortal man? The Bible uses the concept of anthropomorphism to assist us in understanding the workings of God. We may come across phrases such as *"I will even set my face against that person…"* (Leviticus 20:6 NHEB) or *"Who is like the LORD our God, who has his seat on high, ⁶Who stoops down to see in heaven and in the earth?"* (Psalm 113:5–6 NHEB.) Anthropomorphism is essentially presenting the divine as having a human form or traits (The Free Dictionary, 2003–2022). By using human terminologies and representation we may get a better understanding. So, "God remembers" does not mean He had forgotten; instead, it simply means God responded at the appointed time.

People naturally have various dreams or desires they want to achieve. Many people could have the same need as Rachel; for others, it could be something else: job, money or health, for example. But the problem comes when these wants seem not to be answered. We feel God has forgotten us; we become weary and begin to worry. God has a set time for everything under the sun. Usually we do not get instant answers to our prayers and at times it looks as if it will not come to pass. But as Christians we are to put our trust in God, knowing that He is in control of every situation and that at the appointed time He will bring to pass that which He has promised. Since God knows when it is best for our request to be answered and what is good for us, we have to wait patiently for the appointed time of God. While waiting, we are to keep trusting and obeying Him in everything. When we decide to walk according to God's clock and not insist that He works according to ours, we will find peace and can rest our minds because we have chosen to rest our heads peacefully on the pillow of God's sovereignty. Times of trials are not meant to kill us or ruin us; they are not the time for us to wear long faces, go about complaining and murmuring, behave as if the whole world is falling apart. Rather, such times are times to pray and exercise faith in God, times of absolute trust, submission and obedience, because *"all things work together for good for those who love God, to those who are called according to his purpose."* (Romans 8:28 NHEB.)

God's love for us is like an endless stream of refreshing water. To truly walk with Him we must imbibe the nature of trust, for God could be using our case for a more far-reaching effect than we could ever imagine or ask for. Lazarus' death and his resurrection further illustrate this. Mary and Martha – sisters of Lazarus – had requested Jesus' presence because their brother was sick. They expected Christ to come immediately so that Lazarus would not die. But on hearing the news, Christ delayed by two days and Lazarus was dead by the time He decided to go. Jesus was late – or so was the thinking of Mary and Martha. But Jesus had a greater purpose for His seeming delay: He intended to reveal in a greater way the glory of God. God's apparent delay is always for a reason. Many believers' faith has been built on occasions in which everything seems logically and humanly impossible. However, God intervened in those situations. The stories of women giving birth after many years of barrenness, stories about seemingly incurable cancer cured, stories of people on the brink of death coming back to life are but a few illustrations of God's seeming delay building the faith of believers and displaying His glory to the world.

In our personal walk with God, the path of patience and trust is of the essence. Their lack means looking for alternative means to solve our problems. This may offer respite, but it is always the counterfeit of what God intends for us, and in the process, we put our salvation in jeopardy. We must learn to be totally submissive to God, trusting Him, even if it seems that the answers to our prayers are delayed. Our attitude should be that if God does not meet our heart's desires for reasons best known to Him, we will not go against God's word. Rather than going against His word we should keep trusting and obeying Him, having these words of Jeremiah 29:11 engraved on the tablets of our hearts: ***"For I know the plans that I have for you,' says the LORD, 'plans for your welfare, and not for calamity, to give you hope and a future.'"*** (NHEB.)

As Christians we must not be tempted to take God's seeming unresponsiveness to our requests as forgetfulness. Though life challenges us, prolonged afflictions and waiting time may illustrate that God has forgotten us, while in reality He has not. No doubt, He may allow us to go through trials of faith and other life challenges, but still, He has promised never to forget us. ***"Can a woman*** *forget her nursing child, that she should not have compassion on the son of her womb? Yes, these may forget, yet I will not forget you."* (Isaiah 49:15 NHEB.)

As Christians, we are to take our burdens to the Lord and leave them there, which means no more fretting or worry, just trusting that the will of God is best for us. Therefore, having made our requests known to God at any time concerning anything, while waiting for the answers we must not develop any impression that God is insensitive to our prayers, needs and wants and instead trust Him to answer us at His time.

God's seeming delay is always for a reason. There are times when we might look back and be grateful that God did not answer some of our prayers when we made them or answer them in the way we expected. We must never forget that God is not deaf and neither is He sluggish or insensitive. He works according to His time and His will, and He is always on time; He is never late.

We sometimes have wrong perspectives of answers to prayers and teach others the same. We tell them to take all their troubles to the Lord and that He will certainly deliver them from all of it, without teaching them about the will and sovereignty of God and that sometimes challenges are God's will. Take Psalm 55:22, for example: *"Cast your burden on the LORD, and he will sustain you..."* (NHEB.) Some might quote this and interpret it to mean, "Cast your burden upon the Lord and He will certainly remove it." But the promise here is that He will sustain you. It is not assurance that the challenge will go away immediately, especially if God intends it to work out His purpose in your life. The assurance here is that God will give you grace amid the trial. God's grace is what gives us the ability to bear the burden; it provides us with the forbearance and the peace of mind to go through the situation. Even if our request is not fulfilled, our love for the Father should be ever-glowing and ever-growing.

TOPIC 4: THE EFFECT OF A CHRISTIAN'S PRESENCE

GENESIS 30:25–30

Within us are abundant treasures. One of these is the divine wisdom promoting creativity and making all our endeavours successful. Also, in our voices is the hope of peace for turbulent homes around us, and flooding our hearts is the love to lift the downtrodden and heal the hopeless. These, among many others, are the blessings showered by God upon His children to impact lives and create change.

To leave a positive impact on people and our environment is an attribute of God's children. It is the evidence of God's presence with a person and manifests visibly in every aspect of his life. Jesus says in Matthew 5:13–14 that His followers are the light and salt of the earth. *"You are the salt of the earth, but if the salt has lost its flavor, with what will it be salted? It is then good for nothing, but to be cast out and trampled under people's feet. ¹⁴You are the light of the world. A city located on a hill cannot be hidden."* (NHEB.) Naturally both salt and light have the inherent capability to affect things around them. Salt enhances flavour and serves as a preservative. Light dispels darkness and illuminates everything around it.

Jacob was a source of blessing in his uncle's house in Paddan Aram. He had found himself running from the wages of his deception – his brother's rage. On his way to Haran, Jacob encountered God and began his personal walk with God. As a result of the presence of God everything he laid his hands on prospered. Jacob was a vessel of divine favour and blessings in his uncle's house; his presence in Laban's house transformed the face of Laban's livestock business. He added value to everything in Laban's life. Laban recognised that he had come to be blessed by God because of Jacob so when Jacob requested to leave, Laban pleaded with him to stay, saying: *"If now I have found favor in your eyes, stay here, for I have divined that the LORD has blessed me for your sake."* (Genesis 30:27 NHEB.)

As Jacob was an embodiment of God's blessings, so are all God's children. These blessings manifest wherever we find ourselves and are felt by whomever we come across. Indeed, *"Blessed is the one who doesn't follow the advice of the wicked, or take the path of sinners, or join in with scoffers. ²But his delight is in the law of the LORD, and on his law he meditates day and night. ³And he is like a tree planted by flowing streams, that brings forth its fruit in its season, and its leaf does not wither, and whatever he does shall prosper."* (Psalm 1:1–3 NHEB.) The last part of that Psalm says, *"whatever he does shall prosper"*. Note that there has to be a doing for the blessing to manifest; it is not automatic.

Looking at the people blessed by God in the Bible shows that blessings were on work done, trade exercised or skills acquired. Abimelech felt God's presence in Isaac's life; Pharaoh and Potiphar saw it in Joseph; Saul saw it in David. In this way God's presence manifested through their diligence. The laziness of a child of God inhibits the outward expression of the blessing he carries, which is against God's purpose for him. Jacob did not wait for the blessings to come: he was diligent in his work and God blessed and increased the work of his hands. He took Laban's business as his business and worked assiduously for God to reward his hard work. An analysis of Genesis chapters 29 and 30 reveals that Jacob was diligent in herding his uncle's flock.

As Christians we move with the presence of God. God's blessings surround us but these blessings will not translate to anything if we decide to do nothing. A Christian should be ready to engage in any honourable venture wherever he finds himself. We ought to pursue excellence, growth and expansion in our work to effectively harness the blessings we are given, for God's blessing is not an encouragement for laziness. When we are ready to roll up our sleeves and do honourable work God will prosper it. *"And whatever you do, work heartily, as for the Lord, and not for people, ²⁴knowing that from the Lord you will receive the reward of the inheritance; for you serve the Lord Christ."* (Colossians 3:23–24 NHEB.) Working diligently begins with our service to God and extends to our businesses and jobs. A Christian employee should be known for keeping to the rules that govern the organisation they work in; a Christian businessperson should be known for their honesty in dealing with clients. A Christian's lifestyle should earn positive commendations to God's glory and not bring reproach to the name of God. We should mirror Christ and shine with righteousness and love, in a world full of evil, for everyone to see. *"Even so, let your light shine before people; that they may see your good works, and glorify your Father who is in heaven."* (Matthew 5:16 NHEB.)

The most significant impact we can have on others is influencing them to surrender their lives to Jesus. The godly effect is the best influence we can have on anyone. The call to salvation is a call to be separated from the world. While being separate, we are to have a maximum impact on the lives of people around us by how we live. When people see the light of God in us they will be attracted to turn over to the Giver of the light.

CHAPTER 6

TOPIC 1: REACTION TOWARDS OTHERS' PROGRESS

GENESIS 31:1–2

Life is an exciting phenomenon and human nature makes for quite a fascinating study. You work really hard at something and finally your work pays dividends. You are elated at your accomplishment, except that certain people around you begin to treat you as if you offended them in some way. Interestingly, many people are scared of seeing others rise above them.

Jacob found himself in such a scenario in his uncle's house. The summary of the first 14 years of Jacob's service from Laban's point of view was: *"I have divined that the LORD has blessed me for your sake."* (Genesis 30:27 NHEB.) That sounds like a happy man who had profited from Jacob's services and God's favour on those services. Jacob was the supposed jewel in Laban's household, the diamond that reflected God's glory. He had requested to leave but Laban pleaded with him to stay. Apparently Laban was only interested in Jacob's staying to increase his wealth. But after a while Jacob was accruing more wealth than his uncle. As is natural with the intrigue of human nature, Laban's attitude towards Jacob began to change.

Laban's smile turned to a frown and the reason can be deduced from the murmurings of Laban's children: *"Jacob has taken away all that was our father's. From that which was our father's, has he gotten all this wealth."* (Genesis 31:1 NHEB.) This reflects many people's attitudes. As long as Jacob was creating wealth for Laban the smiles kept flowing; now that Jacob was making that same wealth for his own family – which Laban should have been happy with as his uncle and in-law – murmuring set in and tension built up. It was just a matter of time before a full-blown confrontation would ensue between Laban's and Jacob's families.

Greed and selfishness were the propelling force behind Laban's ill-treatment of Jacob. The case is no different from conflicts affecting people today. Many people are not happy when others outgrow them. How do we react when people rise above us on the ladder of success? How do we respond when we notice others' attitudinal changes when we rise above them?

In our reaction to others' growth, we must learn to be contented with what we have, be happy with those who are happy and not let jealousy find a place in our hearts. Jesus taught us to love our neighbours. This love of Christ entails putting the interests of others before our own. When we do this we will not find ourselves jealous of their happiness but rejoice with them when they are happy. For instance, if we desire certain spiritual gifts but do not receive them we should not envy a fellow Christian who does receive them. If our colleagues are promoted – a promotion that we deserve or are due for – and we are not we should not be embittered. Masters in any field of endeavour should be happy with their servants' progress; they must be fair to them and rejoice with them when they become independent and seem more blessed and favoured.

There could be times when a brother sees another testifying about things he wishes he had, and he might experience the urge to ask God: "Father, what of me?" This may be a manifestation of the person's level of trust in God or his understanding of the word of God.

Our trust in God eliminates negative attitudes towards others' progress. We learn to trust God when we have the proper knowledge of the word of God. The Bible teaches us that our days on earth are numbered, and, like a flower that blossoms beautifully and fades before long, our days will pass away. Our achievements and possessions will mean nothing to us when we are gone but we do not just fade away: we awake to another life – a permanent life. Why should we desire anything in life so much that we sin against God by envying, hating or disdaining others because of their possessions? Our focus should be on where we will spend our eternity, whether in eternal bliss – if we are obedient to God – or in eternal condemnation – if we are disobedient to God in this life. We must know that whatever we have in this life is given to us by God, and that if He withholds anything from us in His sovereign will we are not to fret. We are to trust His will as being best for our lives, knowing full well that He cares for us and has our best interests at heart.

On the other hand, how do we react when we notice others' attitudinal change following our elevation? We know for sure that our success may not sit well with everyone, but we must always live by the standards that distinguish us as Christians. Our standpoint must always be love, notwithstanding the changes in attitude from others. The world's reaction to our success should not deter us from expressing the love of Christ towards them, *"For if you love those who love you, what reward do you have?..."* (Matthew 5:46 NHEB.)

Jesus gave us one solution to interpersonal problems of life that will ensure our eternal salvation is not at risk, and that is love. Love is not envious; it is love that would make a master rejoice when their servant performed better than they did. It is also love that would make a servant who had been cheated pray for the good of the master nonetheless. We are to emulate the selfless love of Christ by showing love to everyone and esteeming others better than ourselves: *"make my joy full, by being like-minded, having the same love, being of one accord, of one mind; ³doing nothing through rivalry or through conceit, but in humility, each counting others better than himself; ⁴each of you not just looking to his own things, but each of you also to the things of others."* (Philippians 2:2–4 NHEB.)

TOPIC 2: GOD'S INTERVENTION

GENESIS 31:1–13, 22–29, 41–42

If any has seen the hen in a fierce rage at a hawk, an eagle's rush to a falling eaglet or a mother's leap to the cry of her child, they will understand a little of God's intervention in the safety of His children, for God's commitment to the protection of His children is far greater than them all.

God's involvement in the affairs of man started at the creation. As our Creator, God is attentive and very much involved in our affairs. He usually steps into the affairs of man to prevent some events from occurring. Sometimes He causes events to happen for the good of His children, and at other times He changes the event's outcome altogether. God's intervention conveys genuine concern, love and compassion for His obedient children.

There is a tendency for a person to be less conscious of God's involvement in man's affairs because God is invisible. Some might perceive God to be confined to a faraway heaven with limited dealings with humans. Against this notion came a voice from heaven to King Nebuchadnezzar in Daniel 4:17: *"so that the living may know that the Most High rules in the kingdom of men, and gives it to anyone he wants, and sets up over it the lowliest of men."* (NHEB.)

God is not confined to heaven. Though He dwells in heaven, His eyes are over the earth. God shows interest in our affairs and intervenes as He deems fit. He intervened in Jacob's plight in his uncle's house and for his safety when he ran away from him. Since Jacob started working for Laban he had been on the receiving end of unfair treatment. Laban deceptively made Jacob marry his eldest daughter – Leah – leaving him with no option but to work another seven years for Rachel. Laban made a habit of taking advantage of Jacob in their terms and conditions of engagement. He continuously modified

Jacob's wages in ways that were aimed at ensuring Jacob's growth was suppressed. While Jacob might have grappled with maltreatment from Laban during this period, God never forsook him. The Lord appeared to him, asking him to return to the land of his fathers. Jacob gathered his wives, children and all he had acquired under Laban and fled. When Laban learnt about Jacob's act he got together all his brethren and pursued Jacob for seven days with the intention to carry out some form of retribution against him. God observed all Laban had done to Jacob and was unwilling to let Laban have his way this time, so He intervened in Jacob's situation by ensuring his safety. When Laban reached Jacob he said, *"It is in the power of my hand to hurt you, but the God of your father spoke to me last night, saying, 'Take heed to yourself that you do not speak to Jacob either good or bad.'"* (Genesis 31:29 NHEB.)

God intervenes for His children in diverse ways and circumstances, but His intervention always aligns with His will and purpose. For instance, He intervened to deliver Shadrach, Meshach and Abednego from the fiery furnace after they disregarded Nebuchadnezzar's order to bow to an idol as a result of their fear of God. *"Nebuchadnezzar spoke and said, "Blessed be the God of Shadrach, Meshach, and Abednego, who has sent his angel, and delivered his servants who trusted in him, and have changed the king's word, and have yielded their bodies, that they might not serve nor worship any god, except their own God.""* (Daniel 3:28 NHEB.) God also intervened for the Israelites by commanding Balaam to bless them instead of cursing them as Balaam intended (Numbers chapters 22, 23 and 24).

God watches to protect us from harm and evil and to prevent us from sin. When we go astray, He demonstrates His intervention by attempting to redirect us from the road of destruction to the path of salvation. When we are cheated or victimised He does not abandon us to our peril. Hence, we should always hope and rely on God's dependable arm, for we are safe there. When we are weak, and it seems that the whole world is crashing down upon us, we can still trust His intervention in the lowliness of our hearts. He always intervenes at the right time. Indeed, He is concerned about every detail of our lives here on earth. *"Are not two sparrows sold for an assarion coin? Not one of them falls on the ground apart from your Father's will, 30but the very hairs of your head are all numbered. 31Therefore do not be afraid. You are of more value than many sparrows."* (Matthew 10:29–31 NHEB.)

We may sometimes find ourselves in circumstances in which we expect God's intervention, but we do not see it. We should not be disappointed but trust His will as being best for our lives in such cases. Remember, the disciples were greatly loved, but God allowed most of them to pass through torture and martyrdom. Sometimes, our preconceived expectation of His intervention may not always play out exactly. Remember that God's ways are different from our ways, and that His thoughts are higher than our thoughts. Our soul's salvation is paramount to Him. Hence, He intervenes with our salvation as the ultimate aim. If He does not intervene as we expect we should trust that it is for our good. We should, therefore, be willing to accept God's will and manner of intervention, for we believe that all things work together for the good of those who love God and are called according to His purpose. Also, God's strength is perfectly revealed in our weakness or helplessness. Let us remember that God always has us in mind, whatever the case may be. *"'For I know the plans that I have for you,' says the LORD, 'plans for your welfare, and not for calamity, to give you hope and a future.'"* (Jeremiah 29:11 NHEB.)

Before we can hope for God's intervention on our behalf we must make sure we are in Christ and live by His word daily. When we go against His word we move outside His coverage. Outside Christ, no anchors can calm the boat when the storms of life rage. We can only find true peace and protection in Christ Jesus when we trust and obey His word.

TOPIC 3: PARTING AMICABLY

GENESIS 31:1–31

Relationships exist for various reasons and purposes. Some relationships do not last for a lifetime; they may need to come to an end at certain times. While some end smoothly, for others, their end could come with some misunderstanding. The end might be initiated by one or more parties in the relationship or by circumstances. Whichever case it may be, parting amicably could be challenging and complex, depending on the situation and the reason for separation. Recognising the time and knowing the 'need and how' of ending the relationship matters. Ending relationships should, as much as possible, be done peacefully so that all parties involved can part ways without holding a grudge or any form of bitterness. Having misunderstandings with others does not always mean it is time to part ways. When we choose to call it quits, we should do so after ensuring that God's guidance is sought and followed; then, the parting is done amicably.

From his records in the Bible, Laban is the kind of employer no one would readily want to serve. He deceived Jacob, making him work for 14 years instead of the initial seven years agreed for his daughter Rachel. After several more years of service Jacob approached Laban to inform him of his desire to leave with his family. Laban persuaded Jacob to stay and agreed to Jacob's wages terms. Even with the agreement, Laban still cheated Jacob; as Jacob put it, Laban changed the terms ten times. Agreed, Laban's attitude towards Jacob had worsened, and his change of disposition and his sons' attitudes towards Jacob were of great concern to Jacob. The tension built between the two families to the extent that Leah and Rachel were united in acknowledging their father's love of money over family. God eventually gave Jacob the go-ahead to return to Canaan, promising to be with him. However, none of this was a good enough reason for Jacob to sneak away without informing Laban.

About two decades before this incident Jacob had had reason to run away from his twin brother Esau, after conniving with his mother to deceive his father and receive the blessing Isaac intended for Esau. Now a rich family man, Jacob was again faced with the fear of harm, this time from his father-in-law, who was also his employer. He did what he had done two decades earlier: he ran away. Genesis 31:20 described it thus: *"Jacob deceived Laban the Syrian, in that he did not tell him that he was running away."* (NHEB.) He parted ways with a man he had worked and lived with for several years – his uncle and the father of his wives – by sneaking away at night.

It was not surprising that Jacob sneaked away. Jacob's stay with Laban, especially during the years in which he worked to raise his own capital, was full of tension and suspicion, with each trying to outsmart the other. A tense and acrimonious relationship is unlikely to end amicably. When the Bible teaches us to live in love and peace it is for our good: *"If it is possible, as much as it is up to you, be at peace with all people."* (Romans 12:18 NHEB.)

Onesimus, a slave of Philemon, ran away from his master in Colossae. Somehow, Paul's and Onesimus' paths crossed in another city and through Paul's ministration Onesimus gave his life to Christ. When Paul realised that Onesimus' parting with Philemon (who was Paul's friend and spiritual son) was not amicable, Paul had to send him back to Colossae with a letter to Philemon, reconciling the master and servant. We know that letter now as 'Paul's Epistle to Philemon'. Philemon and Onesimus could part ways later but it would most likely not be under the circumstance with which they initially parted.

To have an amicable separation from people we must learn to forgive any mistreatment or wrong done to us. Colossians 3:13 says: *"bearing with one another, and forgiving each other, if anyone has a complaint against another; even as the Lord forgave you, so you also do."* (NHEB.) Whether leaving a church, a workplace, a parents' house or vacating a rented apartment, parting in unamicable ways is contrary to Christ-likeness. Hence, to ensure our soul's salvation is not endangered, we must endeavour to let go of any bitterness that may prevent us from relating and parting amicably with people.

To think that we would never meet a former employer or friend we left unceremoniously would be to have a very myopic grasp of the future. It does not matter whether the other party was at fault; for all we know, the employer or friend that you part ways with rudely today may be in a position to determine your success tomorrow, for example through giving recommendations; it would almost be impossible to get a positive recommendation from someone you left unceremoniously. Parting ways from one's superior spitefully could also prevent whatever blessing or knowledge that would have been passed down. Elisha remained utterly devoted to his master till the very end and, by this, received the blessing necessary for his ministry after the departure of Elijah. The prophet and his servant eventually parted ways, but not before the master said: *"Ask what I shall do for you, before I am taken from you..."* (2 Kings 2:9 NHEB.) That is what he would have missed if he had parted with his master in an unamicable way. While the prophet got carried by chariots of fire into heaven, his servant replaced him and performed more miracles than his master.

That said, while our separation from people should be amicable, it does not necessarily mean it has to be with a fanfare. However, it should be in such a way that the next meeting will not be tense. Imagine how Jacob felt when he was about to meet Esau after several years. If they had parted ways harmoniously the tension Jacob felt would not have been necessary (Genesis 32:3–12). People who have been together and parted in love need not fear when next they meet.

In relationships with underlying misunderstandings, in which parties feel strongly about leaving, care should be taken that bodily harm is avoided, property rights are respected, personalities are not insulted, and anything that could result in former friends or partners not being able to look each other in the face when next they meet is avoided.

Ensuring amicable departure should, however, be done with caution. To part amicably we should not go against God's word in our attempt to appease any aggrieved party. After one has exhausted every biblical reconciliation procedure for situations like these, it is better to obey God than to lose one's salvation trying to please people; however, we should not allow the adverse or antagonistic action of the other party to create resentment in our hearts.

TOPIC 4: RASH CONCLUSIONS

GENESIS 31:32

There are moments during which our utterances can cause the rise or fall of others; words can be either an extinguisher or a wildfire. Therefore, we must be careful with the conclusions we make in critical moments.

God initiated Jacob's return to the land of his father. However, unknown to Jacob, while he was absconding with his wives, children and all his possessions, Rachel had stolen her father's household idols. When the news of his secret departure came to Laban's notice on the third day Laban pursued him furiously, and on the seventh day, caught up with Jacob on the mountain of Gilead. Though Laban did not hurt him, having been forewarned by God, he demanded from him, saying: *"why have you stolen my gods?"* (Genesis 31:30 NHEB.)

Without giving it a second thought, Jacob asserted: *"Anyone you find your gods with shall not live…"* (Genesis 31:32 NHEB.) This rash conclusion shows that Jacob was sure he had not taken the idols. The question is, was he also certain about the innocence of every member of his household? He spoke with confidence, as if he knew that they were all clean. Unknown to him, the idol was with his beloved wife, Rachel. In that sudden swirl of emotion Jacob had unconsciously put the life of Rachel at risk with his rash proclamation that whosoever had Laban's idols should be killed. Jacob would not be made to rue his statement, for as Laban searched, Rachel devised a means to hide her father's idols from him.

Trust is an essential commodity in a relationship; being able to strike your chest and vouch for the integrity of another person is a beautiful feeling, but we must not fail to remember the weakness of human nature. Someone may have an excellent virtue but may falter on a day of temporary lapse. That is why it is advisable to always be cautious in matters that call others' integrity to bear.

Many have been victims of their words by making statements without proper deliberation. Such was the case with Herod. Herod's impulsive promise to Herodias' daughter in Matthew 14:7–9 led to the death of John the Baptist. He would never have considered the possibility of a young girl demanding, of all things, the head of John the Baptist. If he had considered the possibility of such an outcome he probably would have limited her options.

It is shocking and sad how a small number of words can cause damage that will bewilder many. Words spoken in haste are the words we speak without considering all the possible consequences. Drawing rash conclusions has a tendency to bring about unpleasant eventualities which can occur under different circumstances. Therefore, it is essential to obtain the facts about any situation, problem or person before jumping to any conclusion.

We are warned to be mindful of what we say because once words leave our mouth they can never be retrieved. Proverbs 18:21 says: ***"Death and life are in the power of the tongue; those who love it will eat its fruit."*** (NHEB.) Drawing rash conclusions is not wisdom. Sometimes we place people on the chopping block without knowing. Learning from Jacob's case, it is wise to consider the one per cent chance of a matter not being the way we presume and investigate every issue before arriving at a conclusion. Even when we arrive at a conclusion that supports our earlier conviction, it is best to be modest in our actions and utterances. James 1:19 admonishes us: ***"But let every*** *person be swift to hear, slow to speak, and slow to anger"* (NHEB). We should learn to tame our tongues and control our emotions so that we do not fall into the trap of drawing rash conclusions we may later regret. No one can know the heart of another and no one is infallible, so we should give everyone the benefit of the doubt without seeing it as questioning their integrity.

CHAPTER 7

TOPIC 1: GUILTY CONSCIENCE

GENESIS 32:3–21

Great fear descended upon him as he pondered the danger his family would be exposed to. The news of 400 men and his brother coming to meet him and his family haunted his heart. How would he do it? How could he possibly protect them from the seeming impending carnage that was about to be inflicted on him by his twin brother, the brother he had taken advantage of, the brother he did not mind starving if his brother did not sell him his birthright and the brother he and his mother connived against to steal his father's blessing. The guilt of the past and dread of the future overwhelmed him, leaving him trembling.

Jacob's guilt about his past deed against his brother Esau came back to haunt him as he prepared himself for what he thought would be retribution from his brother. His exhibition of fear was evidenced in his prayer for help and his attempt to appease his brother. Jacob addressed Esau as "my lord" and labelled himself as "your servant" to express his vulnerability when at the mercy of Esau. It can be said that if Jacob had not wronged Esau he would not have had reason to be apprehensive of his brother because his conscience would have been clear, but since it was not, the venom of guilt bit deep into his conscience. Apostle Paul wrote in Acts 24:16: *"This being so, I also do my best to always have a clear conscience toward God and people."* (NHEB.)

We all possess an inherent sense of what is right and wrong. This is called the conscience: it evaluates our thoughts, words and deeds.

It provides us with satisfaction when we sense that we are right and haunts us when we perceive that we have done wrong. Typically, the conscience is relative to an individual's societal values and beliefs. It is not the same for everyone: what may seem inappropriate to someone in a particular locality may be accepted elsewhere. But as Christians, we are one family in Christ; thus, our beliefs and values are guided by God's word. Our consciences are influenced by our knowledge of the instructions of God. Hence, a satisfactory feeling erupts in us when we conform to God's standard, but we are plagued by a guilty conscience whenever we violate it.

Jacob's guilty conscience shows how the conscience works when we have committed an offence, especially when we face the person we offended. The conscience becomes a mirror reflecting the wrongs we did. It can work for or against a person. For some, the conscience can make them realise their wrongs so that they make amends where necessary, while for others, it works against them by making them prisoners of their guilt and can sometimes lead them to taking the wrong approach to silence the guilt.

When the guilt of our wrong actions overwhelms us, the first line of action should be to seek forgiveness from God. King David's reaction to his guilt is worthy of emulation: *"David's heart struck him after that he had numbered the people. David said to the LORD, "I have sinned greatly in that which I have done. But now, LORD, put away, I beg you, the iniquity of your servant; for I have done very foolishly.""* (2 Samuel 24:10 NHEB.) Only God can clear our consciences from guilt because He alone has the authority to forgive our sins. The appropriate action to take towards removing our guilt is, first, to ask for forgiveness from God. When God forgives us the guilt is removed together with the fear of punishment. Though sometimes we still face the consequences, we can be bold enough to relate with God unhindered and also face the victim of our offence to either seek forgiveness or carry out restitution if necessary, *"let us draw near with a true heart in fullness of faith, having our hearts sprinkled from an evil conscience, and having our body washed with pure water"* (Hebrews 10:22 NHEB).

It is important to note that a guilty conscience does not necessarily mean a change of heart or repentance, though it can lead to repentance. For instance, a man caught in the act of fornication may feel guilty to the extent of resolving to part with all sexual sin. However, if he finds an easy way to bypass the trouble he is in, he could forget all about the initial guilt he felt and continue with the sin at the next available opportunity. On the other hand, guilt for sin makes a Christian better because it pricks the conscience. The effect of a guilty conscience as a result of sin helps lead the Christian back to the right path, since his conscience is influenced by God's word. 2 Corinthians 7:10 says, *"For godly sorrow works repentance to salvation, which brings no regret. But the sorrow of the world works death."* (NHEB.) But there could be a point at which the conscience loses its sensitivity. This happens when a Christian continuously and deliberately goes against its promptings. Ignoring the conscience over time weakens or kills it. In such an instance, a believer feels comfortable doing wrong. Without an active conscience, a believer sins without restraint. This is a dangerous position for a person to be in, for they could end up eternally damned. One can only regain spiritual sensitivity through the grace of God.

In some situations, in doing the right thing, such as reporting a neighbour's misbehaviour to the authorities or standing up for the truth, believers can feel the weight of a guilty conscience if their action leads to the severe punishment of others. This could be normal, but we must not let it stop us from always acting in accordance with the word of God *"because if our heart condemns us, God is greater than our heart, and knows all things."* (1 John 3:20 NHEB.)

By and large we are to continuously renew our minds with God's word so that the societal norms and values we had imbibed before our encounter with Christ no more influence our consciences. As children of God, the word of God should be the sole determinant of our actions. Hence, to keep our consciences free of guilt, we must refrain from whatever contradicts God's word.

TOPIC 2: PRAY AND ACT

GENESIS 32:9–16

A child who barely communes with his father would not be as bold in approaching him as the one who communes regularly. Communion here is not just stepping into his father's presence to make requests or reports about certain discomfort; it is an interaction. For a son to have a good interaction with his father he must be on good terms with the father, not just for what he stands to benefit, but for being there as his father. He must make every attempt to obey his father in all things. The child who communes more with their father has a special place in his heart.

Prayer and meditation time for a Christian represents that time of communion with the Father. Prayer has been described as the 'fuel' a Christian needs to keep his relationship with his heavenly Father going. This underscores the inevitability of prayers. However, as important as prayer is, it should not be assumed that every other action necessary to actualise our desire is not needed once we pray.

The fear of the unknown and a guilty conscience was what propelled Jacob's calculated action and desperate prayer in his attempt to obtain Esau's mercy and favour. He feared the unknown because he did not know how Esau would react when they eventually met – having been notified that Esau was coming to meet him with 400 men. Although we can notice traces of fear and desperation in his prayer, there are lessons to learn from Jacob's prayer and what he did after the prayer.

In his prayer, Jacob acknowledged God as the source of his prosperity and expressed his need for God's intervention. He knew that only God could grant him favour and mercy in the sight of Esau. He went ahead to remind God of His covenanted promises towards him and that his return to the land of Canaan was in obedience to His instructions. Jacob also recognised his unworthiness of God's mercy and faithfulness, from which he had thus far benefited. No doubt, at this point, he displayed an attribute of someone with a broken spirit and contrite heart in his supplication. Elements of Jacob's prayer could be summarised with three words – adoration, consecration and request. As children of God, our lives, not just our prayers, should not lack these elements. We need to constantly worship God as our source of life and salvation. Our lives should be continuously consecrated by living holy for God and righteously among those around us. Our request should be such that we ask in faith – trusting that He will respond and that He knows what is best for us.

Jacob did not only pray, but he also played his part as a human. He sent out gifts to Esau. Although this act was done out of fear, he put everything in place to pacify his brother's anger. Prayer does not take away man's responsibility in certain situations. At times, we treat our prayer life like rubbing a magical lamp and asking a magician to grant us our wishes. The truth is that sometimes prayer requires action on our part. Two believers could be praying for business opportunities and growth. One gets up from his place of prayer and proceeds to his bed. There he stays all day till the next prayer time. The other brother gets up from his place of prayer, calls his customers and makes new contacts. Of the two, the one who acted after praying will most likely have his prayers answered, while the other might never see any answer to his prayers. The brother who worked after praying showed he had faith in God and that he believed his prayers would be answered.

Nehemiah is one of the great examples of men who prayed and acted. His prayer had the earlier elements we discussed in Jacob's prayers. He acknowledged God, consecrated his life and his nation and then made his request to God. After his prayers he rolled up his sleeves and got to work – requested and obtained the King's permission, mobilised his people and personally supervised and partook in rebuilding the ruined walls of Jerusalem. Even as he worked he was praying; he returned to work after praying. No wonder the work prospered in his hands; distractions could not stop him.

As Christians, we should ensure that our prayers for others are backed up by the required actions. For instance, in interceding for the sick or the needy, our duty does not end with prayers and with saying nice and motivational words to them but by doing something practical about their needs, such as providing for them after praying. The Bible emphasises that we put our faith into action by doing good deeds: *"What good is it, my brothers, if someone says he has faith, but has no works? Can faith save him? ¹⁵And if a brother or sister is naked and in lack of daily food, ¹⁶and one of you tells them, "Go in peace, be warmed and filled;" and yet you did not give them the things the body needs, what good is it? ¹⁷Even so faith, if it has no works, is dead in itself."* (James 2:14–17 NHEB.)

We must always couple our prayers with good works. When we pray for the salvation of others' souls we should act by telling them about Jesus and His righteousness. When we pray to God to provide for the poor, we must go the extra mile by practically providing for their basic needs. When seeking God's mercy and forgiveness for the wrong we have done to others, we must also seek forgiveness from the offended.

Note that accompanying our prayers with actions does not imply that we act contrary to God's word. A student who prays to pass his examinations must get up and work but that does not include seeking ways of cheating in the examinations. It is worth noting that living in disobedience hinders answers to prayers, while obedience to God's word enhances our communication with God. We have nothing to fear when we obey God, for the Lord will accomplish His purpose in our lives.

Acting in line with the word of God is an indication of our faith, but it does not guarantee answers to our prayers if God in His sovereignty wishes to withhold the answers. It is essential to note that God's answer might be yes, no or wait. If God says no, we should accept His will as best for us because, as a loving Father, He knows what is best for us. Instead we should pray for the grace to endure the circumstance without compromise, to achieve God's purpose for our life. If the answer is wait, He knows what we need, what is good for us at every point in time. Hence, we should always factor in the will of God in our prayers and be willing to submit to Him.

CHAPTER 8

TOPIC 1: RECONCILIATION

GENESIS 33:1–17

"I thought we were brothers!" The pain behind those words can overshadow years of peaceful coexistence, love and blissful memories if forgiveness is not considered at all. It is not easy to recover from pain inflicted by a person one is close to.

We have all been on both sides of hurt. Either we have wronged others or have been wronged by others. Usually, these wrongs cause an estrangement in our relationship. This is where reconciliation comes into play. Reconciliation happens when two or more people who were formally aggrieved at each other decide to make peace. Sometimes, all it takes to mend ways with people is three words: "I am sorry" or "I was wrong" or "You were right." Reconciliation occurs when friendly relations are restored between two previously clashing parties. As an indication of the complexity in human dealings, conflict is bound to originate when there are differences in personalities, orientation or ideology. As if that is not enough, there is the inherent human tendency to resort to ungodly behaviours such as selfishness, covetousness, deception or greed, which often lead to conflict. As believers, God's expectation of us when we offend people or have been wronged is to seek reconciliation.

The last time the twin brothers had had the opportunity to stay in the same environment was about 20 years previous, when their father blessed Jacob instead of Esau following Jacob's deceit. As a result, Esau was angry and resolved to kill Jacob after their father's death. Jacob was sent away from home to Laban in Haran. After many years they met again, though not as they had left each other. Jacob now had wives and children, and Esau was also a great man, having abundant possessions. Despite what had transpired between them, one thing is striking about their reunion: Esau had forgotten the past and was happy to meet Jacob. *"Esau ran to meet him, embraced him, fell on his neck, kissed him, and they wept."* (Genesis 33:4 NHEB.)

Considering their estranged relationship, it would undoubtedly have posed a challenge for Jacob to actualise his desire for reconciliation with the brother he had greatly wronged. Yet he was not alone: He had God with him. He had prayed for God's intervention before meeting Esau. *"Jacob said, "God of my father Abraham, and God of my father Isaac, the LORD, who said to me, 'Return to your country, and to your relatives, and I will do you good,'* [10] *I am not worthy of the least of all the loving kindnesses, and of all the truth, which you have shown to your servant; for with just my staff I passed over this Jordan; and now I have become two companies.* [11] *Please deliver me from the hand of my brother, from the hand of Esau: for I fear him, lest he come and strike me, and the mothers with the children.""* (Genesis 32:9–11 NHEB.) Jacob's role in ensuring reconciliation is quite commendable. His prayer to God and insistent presentation of gifts to Esau revealed his desire to make peace.

Esau, on his part, demonstrated a commendable attitude. He was receptive to reconciliation and forgave Jacob for what Jacob had done. Considering the degree of wrong done to him, Esau could have continued to begrudge his brother; instead, he decided to let go of the wrongs. His enthusiastic reception and physical affection demonstrated his joy at reuniting with his brother. By accepting the gift presented by Jacob and offering to leave some of his men behind to escort Jacob and his family to their destination, Esau proved beyond doubt that there was no fragment of bitterness or shards of resentment in the deepest recesses of his heart.

What could have caused this smooth reconciliation between the brothers? Attributing it to time might fall below proper placement because time without God does not heal wounds. Attributing it to their riches is not appropriate because rich people without God can retain their malice for years. That the brothers met in benevolence and kindness was the effect of God's favour. He worked on Esau and showed His faithfulness to Jacob who He had promised to be with. God works in various ways, and while humans rage He restrains them from doing harm by His power: *"The king's heart is in the LORD's hand like the watercourses. He turns it wherever he desires."* (Proverbs 21:1 NHEB.)

Like Esau and Jacob we should learn to put grievances or disputes behind us and work towards reconciliation if it depends on us. Romans 12:18 says: *"If it is possible, as much as it is up to you, be at peace with all people."* (NHEB.)

In our relationship with God, reconciliation puts us in the right standing with Him. And in our relationship with others, reconciliation crosses distances, overcomes hostilities, resolves differences and cultivates peace. To understand the need to reconcile with those who have hurt us and vice versa, we need to look to God, who reconciled us to Himself through Christ. The fact that humanity needed reconciliation is an indication that our relationship with God was broken due to man's disobedience in the Garden of Eden. Since sin alienated us from Him, the death of Jesus gave us an opportunity to be reconciled to Him, as contained in Romans 5:10: *"For if, while we were enemies, we were reconciled to God through the death of his Son, much more, being reconciled, we will be saved by his life."* (NHEB.) We were once God's enemies, but now we are products of forgiveness and reconciliation. We did not earn or deserve our reconciliation, and we did not reach out to God first; instead, He reached out to us. God was the one who accomplished our reconciliation at the cross; this reconciliation is available to mankind by faith in the gospel. All we are asked to do is receive Him in faith and walk in that love and reconciliation. We should show this love to those who may have wronged or hurt us. Having an attitude of forgiveness and reconciliation is being like Christ.

Reconciliation may make us uncomfortable and push us out of our comfort zone as we pursue peace with people we naturally find most problematic. But always remember: *"For if you forgive people their trespasses, your heavenly Father will also forgive you. ¹⁵But if you do not forgive people, neither will your Father forgive your trespasses."* (Matthew 6:14–15 NHEB.)

Beyond a shadow of a doubt, forgiveness constitutes an indispensable part of reconciliation. When we refuse to reconcile with those who hurt us, we endanger the salvation of our souls. There is no limit to how often we are to forgive others. Jesus instructed us to forgive our offenders as many times as possible: *"Watch yourselves. If your brother sins, rebuke him. If he repents, forgive him. ⁴And if he sins against you seven times in the day, and seven times returns to you, saying, 'I repent,' you must forgive him."* (Luke 17:3–4 NHEB.) As Christians, we should always be ready to forgive our offenders no matter the offence.

A relationship is easier to mend when the offender apologises to the offended. But what if the offender does not apologise? To many, therein lies the problem! We ought to swallow our pride and bitterness and take the initiative. Taking the first step is imperative in reconciliation. Jesus taught us to take the initiative, saying, *"If your brother sins against you, go, show him his fault between you and him alone. If he listens to you, you have gained back your brother."* (Matthew 18:15 NHEB.) Sometimes, instead of confronting a person, we go to everyone else to plead our side of the story, validate our feelings and justify our anger; we do not go to the person we have an issue with. If there is a ruptured relationship we should first go to the other party before involving another person.

In the same vein, we must be humble enough to admit our wrongs and initiate reconciliation with those we have offended. Our humility must be such that we do not feel too pompous to make peace with those we have wronged, regardless of our position or status. Additionally, we can endeavour to restitute where there is a need, if it is possible. In situations in which those we offended seem resistant and unwilling to reconcile with us, we should commit the matter to God's hands. In truth, reconciliation may not always be smooth or go as expected, especially if the other party is an unbeliever or a young believer in the faith. However, with prayers, God can heal the wounds and soften the hearts of those we offended to the point at which reconciliation becomes a reality.

We should note that reconciliation with one another is requisite for our relationship with each other in the body of Christ. To show the importance of reconciliation, Jesus said: *"If therefore you are offering your gift at the altar, and there remember that your brother has anything against you, [24] leave your gift there before the altar, and go your way. First be reconciled to your brother, and then come and offer your gift."* (Matthew 5:23–24 NHEB.)

Finally, in reconciling our broken relationships, we must never forget to ask God for assistance. He does so much in the background we do not know of, and we should always be grateful for that. The reconciliation process may sometimes be challenging; that is why we need God's help. As Jacob did, whenever we want to go about reconciliation it is in our best interests to go to God first to settle the matter in prayer before confronting the person with whom we have a misunderstanding, for without God we can do nothing.

CHAPTER 9

TOPIC 1: RAPE

GENESIS 34:1–2

Go through newspapers and social media platforms, watch the news on the television; one thing that is often on the media is repeated incidents of rape. It seems as though each passing day emboldens more and more people to indulge in this depravity. The list of people coming out to narrate their ordeals keeps growing with each passing second. The plague of rape in our society is hanging like a chandelier, visible for all to see.

The issue of rape does not start today; it dates back many centuries. This chapter records an incident of non-consensual sexual relations. As Dinah went out to visit the women of the land, Shechem – son of Hamor, the Hivite and ruler of that area – saw her, took her and raped her.

Many people will relate to Dinah's plight because many have also been victims of this uncultured act. The rape count is on the rise, lives are being destroyed and emotional traumas haunt many. You hear sad stories of people going into depression; you hear of heart-wrenching ordeals and of people having psychological trauma. You even hear of cases in which people who cannot come to terms with the torment commit suicide in a bid to escape their emotional anguish. This is the extent to which rape has decimated lives and is still playing havoc in our society.

Rape is a crime with health, social and emotional implications, but most importantly it is a sinful act against God. God commanded the

Israelites in Deuteronomy 22:25–29, saying, *"But if the man find the lady who is pledged to be married in the field, and the man force her, and lie with her; then the man only who lay with her shall die: [26] but to the lady you shall do nothing; there is in the lady no sin worthy of death: for as when a man rises against his neighbor, and kills him, even so is this matter; [27] for he found her in the field, the pledged to be married lady cried, and there was none to save her. [28] If a man find a lady who is a virgin, who is not pledged to be married, and lay hold on her, and lie with her, and they be found; [29] then the man who lay with her shall give to the lady's father fifty shekels of silver, and she shall be his wife, because he has humbled her; he may not put her away all his days."* (NHEB.) Although the consequences of rape stated in this law do not apply to us today, God still frowns on rape just as He did in times past.

Rape is a hydra-headed menace that produces multi-dimensional effects, not only on the victims but, by extension, the family and society. The attack and the killing of the unsuspecting men of the city by Dinah's brothers resulted from the act of rape. The horrible experience of Tamar, David's daughter, who was raped by her half-brother, and the murderous revenge of Amnon by Absalom, are a few of the adverse effects of rape (2 Samuel 13).

Rape is an abominable sexual act that can be traced back to lust, which in turn can be linked to a sinful heart. A heart that is sinful, without the life of God, can exhibit actions that are not only an offence against God but inhumane. A corrupt heart is hardened against the feeling of shame or guilt.

It is typical for rapists to aim the arrow of blame at the devil when they are caught committing the depraved act. The truth is that rape perpetrators often let the flame of their desire ignite them into performing the action. The devil's influence on a person is effective to the level that that person allows. Every man who sins in this way is enticed by his evil desires. *"But each one is tempted, when he is drawn away by his own lust, and enticed."* (James 1:14 NHEB.) Therefore, we need to turn to the only One that can deliver us from a life ridden with sin, Christ. We should run to Him for the gift of salvation to enable us to walk in the Spirit.

To anyone who has been a victim of rape, your story does not end there. Do not make the unrecoverable mistake of committing suicide in a bid to escape the trauma. If it so happens that you are raped, Jesus does not condemn you. His arms are wide open to receive you. Do not even hold bitterness against the culprit but rather, in love, pray for the forgiveness and redemption of that person's soul. And if you report the attack to relevant authorities it must be done with pure motives. If your motivation is to help the culprit see the wrongs of his ways and prevent other people from falling into that dilemma, there is nothing wrong with that. If rape results in pregnancy, you should not travel the lane of abortion, which is murder and a sin against God. It is better to accept such responsibility, though painful, than go against the command of God.

People, especially Christians, have an essential role to play concerning rape victims. Many are the lives lost to suicide, and many are the hearts dying in silence because of stigmatisation and scrutiny. When we come across rape victims, rather than stigmatise them we should, in love, try to show them that all is not lost, that in Christ there is rest and hope for the future.

Unaffected people are also advised to take precautionary measures not to fall prey to this abominable act. Rape is terrible and very condemnable, but people need to stop putting themselves in situations that may create room for this evil to occur. A wise African saying captures this mindset: "While blaming the hawk, advice should be given to the chicken." That is to say that while blaming the rapist, advice should be given to people to avoid a situation in which they could be exposed to being raped. Liberty of movement, dressing and association comes with the responsibility of ensuring that we do not expose ourselves or tempt others through our liberties. For instance, indecent dressing through the exposure of various erogenous zones of a female body can arouse sexual desires in some men, putting the woman in danger of rape. Also, to avoid the risk of being drugged, caution should be taken when having a drink with someone.

To all those guilty of the sin of rape, it is not too late to retrace your steps. The Lord invites all with this burden to come into His rest. His rest provides you with the purification of your soul, His rest provides you with mortification of the flesh, and His rest provides you with the ability to live above sin.

TOPIC 2: REVENGE

GENESIS 34:1–31

The complexities of human relationships due to diversities of personalities often make it practically impossible for people not to step on each other's toes at some point. When this happens, God's expectation of His children regarding our reactions is unambiguously stated in the scriptures: ***"Do not be overcome by evil, but overcome evil with good."*** (Romans 12:21 NHEB.)

Often, whenever someone is assaulted, the impulse is to retaliate, not minding the aftermath of such an action. However, wrong actions cannot be used to rectify another wrong action. That itself is wrong, for two wrongs do not make a right. Instead, it becomes a lose–lose situation, as nobody wins when an act of revenge is carried out. Several times, revenge comes at a price; it often leaves a person without the desired satisfaction to move on freely with life. It can also leave a person with the fear of a counter-attack. Such was the case of Simeon and Levi.

When the sons of Jacob learnt that Shechem had raped Dinah they were furious. Dinah had been sexually assaulted against her will. It was a despicable act that could have led to painful emotions and post-traumatic episodes for her. This did not go well with her brothers, especially Simeon and Levi. Even when Shechem came with his father to demand Dinah's hand in marriage and a willingness to pay whatever they named as the bride price, they replied deceitfully, giving conditions while having a different intention. After they had deceitfully convinced Shechem and his father to circumcise themselves and the entire men of that city, Simeon and Levi avenged their sister's sexual assault by murdering all the men in the town. At this point, one may wonder whether such a vengeful reaction was necessary. Certainly not! Did their action undo what had been done? Obviously not! Instead, by their obnoxious action, they provoked their father and gave him a bad reputation among the neighbouring cities, and, but for the fear God instilled in those cities, they could have been attacked. Some years later, they incurred curses upon themselves because of their vengeful act. *"Simeon and Levi are brothers. Their swords are weapons of violence. ⁶My soul, do not come into their council. My glory, do not be united to their assembly; for in their anger they killed men. In their self-will they hamstrung cattle. ⁷Cursed be their anger, for it was fierce; and their wrath, for it was cruel. I will divide them in Jacob, and scatter them in Israel."* (Genesis 49:5–7 NHEB.) If they had repressed their fury and trod the path of peace by forgiving Shechem, the murderous act could have been averted.

The effect of vengeance is often devastating. Even the thought of it must not be entertained in our hearts as children of God much less acting on it. We must painstakingly safeguard the threshold of our hearts against any vindictive reflection. Vengeance usually begins with vengeful thoughts, and these thoughts tend to replay or magnify the injury, hurt or loss suffered due to the other party's action. Immediately we sense such thoughts we are not to entertain them within our hearts, for they could spur us to action. We are not to allow ourselves to get to the point at which we begin to fantasise about various means by which we can exact our vengeance. For the very reason that an act of revenge cannot undo the evil done to us it is wrong and unnecessary. It will only gratify the heinous desire in us to inflict pain on the one who has wronged us. Certainly it will never reverse the deed nor will it contribute anything positive to the first injury inflicted on us. Revenge might seem emotionally rewarding at first, but in the long run, rather than bringing healing to the injury inflicted on us, it will open up a cycle of retaliation, creating a chain of bitterness, malice and all other evil actions associated with it. In the end, it will make the situation far more worse than it would have been had the decision to forgive been taken.

Hence, no matter the degree of the hurt or wrong meted out to us, our reaction must always be the kind that brings glory to God's name. We must not succumb to the overwhelming craving of the flesh or the voices of those around us who want us to retaliate. We must not be pressurised to the point where we throw away all godly virtues and react in a manner inconsistent with God's word, thereby exhibiting the same trait we condemn in others. Instead, we are to subdue evil acts with good deeds. In the natural sense, doing good to those who act wickedly against someone may be pretty difficult and look like a strange thing, but it is practical with godly love through the help of the Holy Spirit. This is God's expectation of His children, from the dispensation of law, and it has not changed. In Leviticus 19:18, God instructed the Israelites, saying: *"You shall not take vengeance, nor bear any grudge against the children of your people; but you are to love your neighbor as yourself. I am the LORD."* (NHEB.)

Likewise, today as Christians we are the light of the world, and by this, we can only illuminate the heart of an evil person whose life is permeated with darkness by relating with him in love just as Jesus teaches us in Matthew 5:44: *"love your enemies, and pray for those who persecute you"* (NHEB). By this, we will demonstrate a better way to live – the way of love – to such a person. Revenge is a hurtful action, and no one will want to hurt someone they love. But if we only express love to those who love us, God's love is not domiciled in our hearts – for the unbelievers also love those who love them in return. The love of God is pure, and it must be expressed indiscriminately irrespective of the other party's qualities. *"Above all things be earnest in your love among yourselves, for love covers a multitude of sins.* " (1 Peter 4:8 NHEB.) With love, there is no limit to the offences which a Christian should forgive. We must forgive at all times regardless of the gravity of atrocity perpetrated against us. Let this statement of our Lord Jesus Christ in Matthew 6:14–15 be registered in our hearts: *"For if you forgive people their trespasses, your heavenly Father will also forgive you. ¹⁵ But if you do not forgive people, neither will your Father forgive your trespasses."* (NHEB.) These scriptural verses should always serve as a reminder to us each time we are confronted with the choice of vengeance or forgiveness. The Lord will not forgive us our sins if we refuse to forgive those who wronged us, nor will we be beneficiaries of His mercy if we refuse to be merciful to our offenders.

Revenge, under any circumstance, is not an act that should be exhibited by any child of God; never is it a solution to the already perpetrated act. So as Christians, regardless of how grievous the offences committed against us, recompensing evil with evil should not be our subsequent course of action. Instead, we should develop and exhibit the godly way of overcoming evil acts with good deeds out of pure love. *"not rendering evil for evil, or reviling for reviling; but instead blessing; because to this were you called, that you may inherit a blessing."* (1 Peter 3:9 NHEB.)

TOPIC 3: THE ACT OF IGNOMINY

GENESIS 34:30

An African adage says, "The children disrupted the soldier ants, but the ants are now attacking the elders." The origin of this adage is quite an interesting one. It was common for children in some rural African settings to go running ahead of their parents on farm roads. Sometimes they come across troops of soldier ants marching and well organised. The children scatter the ranks of ants and the angry ants disperse all over the bush, sometimes not very far from their previous formation. Soon, the parents appear on the scene, oblivious to what had transpired. As they unknowingly walk into the angry mob of ants the ants find their way up their dresses and into those parts of the body not easily accessed without undressing, then the biting begins – and so this adage was created.

Simeon and Levi were no children – at least not of the age to play with ants on farm roads. However, their action was such that it did not only affect them but their entire family. Like those children who scattered the ants, they did not stop to ponder what their actions would mean for their parents and the rest of their family. Jacob's sons murdering and plundering a whole community could have been perceived as a declaration of war on the surrounding communities. Those communities' natural reactions would be to rally for a counter-attack, and but for the fear God instilled in them (Genesis 35:5), Jacob's family would have faced extinction. Jacob puts it: *"You have troubled me, to make me odious to the inhabitants of the land, among the Canaanites and the Perizzites. I am few in number. They will gather themselves together against me and strike me, and I will be destroyed, I and my house."* (Genesis 34:30 NHEB.)

It is common to hear such words spoken by parents to their children: "Do not bring shame to the family" or "Make the family proud." This establishes the fact that actions always have far-reaching effects; they do not centre only on an individual but create a ripple effect that can positively or negatively affect one's family. An individual's actions may not affect the individual only but can bring glory or shame to the family as well. To children who bring shame to their family, Proverbs 17:25 addresses them in this light: *"A foolish son brings grief to his father, and bitterness to her who bore him."* (NHEB.)

Simeon and Levi acted rashly, thus exposing the whole family to danger. Their action was going to spark repercussions. Those given to anger are always prone to folly. It is as said in Proverbs: *"He who is slow to anger has great understanding, but he who has a quick temper displays folly."* (Proverbs 14:29 NHEB.) Simeon and Levi are not alone in bringing disrepute to one's family; the world is replete with their kind. We are all born to different families and many of us are guilty of bringing disgrace and heartache to our families. We scatter the ants and our families feel the bite. There have been times when a child gets pregnant out of wedlock, bringing disgrace and dishonour on her family, and cases in which a short-tempered child kills someone in a fight, the police are involved and the whole family loses sleep and peace for days. It is an unending tragedy in the world we find ourselves in.

But there is a bigger picture here, which transcends our earthly families and which many Christians are guilty of – bringing disrepute to our spiritual family. As Christians, we are part of God's family and our actions rub off on the whole family. The way the world perceives Christians is dependent on the deeds of those who bear the name. The eyes of the world are ever gazing on the lives of believers, waiting, looking for reasons to strengthen their opinions and arguments against God and the religion we profess, and we, through our actions, give them reasons on a platter. It was to this effect that Paul wrote: ***"For "because of you the name of God is blasphemed among the nations," just as it is written."*** (Romans 2:24 NHEB.)

Simple actions – those we might think of as trivial – can cause people to speak evil against the body of Christ. Our reaction to temptation, our disposition to commit offences, and our involvement in sin have a telling effect on our soul and the image of the whole Christian family.

Christians have a lot to learn from the action of Simeon and Levi. Every believer belongs to one family, which is the church, and just as the heinous act of Jacob's sons brought reproach to their father, Christians can also live in such a way that gives occasion for the blasphemy of God's name among the heathen. We can, by our actions, make Christianity stink among unbelievers. When we profess to be Christians but our lifestyles contradict this, we instigate unbelievers to make a mockery of our faith. If we claim to be saved from sin and live as though we have never known Christ before, we also leave the world with an impression that the gospel of Christ has no power to save. Rather than winning over those in the world by our conduct, we make ourselves a poor representation of what a Christian should be and further strengthen their alienation from God. The world hears the story of a loving, merciful and compassionate Saviour but sometimes sees hate, wickedness and sin worn by those expected to be His followers. There are few things that could make an unbeliever further alienated from God than a religion filled with hypocrites; a hypocritical Christian does more harm to the kingdom of God than an unbeliever. There is an expectation of how Christians should live; when we live in direct contradiction to this expectation we bring reproach and dishonour to the body of Christ. It will be better for us not to identify with Christ if we are unwilling to submit our necks to His yoke of discipleship and live our lives worthy of His gospel. We cannot be ambassadors of a God whose earnest desire is to save the entire world from sin if our lives do not reflect this salvation. People should be able to emulate us because they are sure that we are heading to heaven, but it is difficult to lead people to where we are not going.

The carriage of the identity – Christian – demands a demonstration of character that conforms with God's expectations rather than the cravings of the flesh. True repentance requires us to be first transformed from the inside and then to manifest the inward transformation for all to see. Christians are lights and should shine as one. When we live as lights, men will receive our testimonies, and the family of God on earth and in heaven will rejoice.

As Christians, our actions are supposed to bring other people to Christ, not discourage them from the path. When our lifestyle speaks of the love of God, we will be able to draw others to Christ, and by so doing, their souls will be saved. But on the flip side, if our actions bring reproach to the family of God, not only does this portray a bad image of Christianity, but it could also discourage new converts.

It must be firmly rooted in our hearts that as those who choose to align their identity with Christ we inevitably fall under the scrutinising microscope of the world. And since we are ambassadors of Christ, we must represent Him well everywhere we go and abstain from all appearance of evil that will bring dishonour to His name. This is only achievable when we are rooted in the word of God, giving God our hearts and affections, having salvation as our focus and doing everything not to risk it. Christians, being in God's family, being the ambassadors of Christ, are the image and representatives of Christ here on earth. Our lifestyle should resemble the Lord's so much that we will not need to introduce ourselves as Christians. If we are to convert the world we must first be converted. We are to be living epistles of Christ, and those around us should see our lives and easily reckon that, indeed, we are followers of Christ.

CHAPTER 10

TOPIC 1: CONSECRATION

GENESIS 35:1–4

When we dedicate ourselves to God, we may think we are doing a lot for Him, but we only do ourselves a favour. The reality of what we do at that point is to release the unholy things in our lives and when we are empty, He fills us with His holy treasures, making us vessels to be used by Him. The sacred call to forsake a life of sin for a righteous way of life is a call that requires the consecration of our lives from all manner of distracting and unholy influences. Consecration entails our separation from anything impure or unholy capable of contaminating our spiritual lives. For God's presence to be made manifest in our lives, we must enter the place of consecration. Consecration involves embracing all that is pleasing to God, and it is a voluntary, personal and sacrificial decision.

While he was at Shechem, God instructed Jacob to go to Bethel, dwell there and make an altar to Him. Before Jacob set out on his journey he assembled his household and prepared them for the trip. He demanded that they discard from among them every idol, change their garments and purify themselves. He understood that the Lord is a Holy God and that those who would appear before God ought to rid themselves of every form of blemish and be consecrated. A crucial lesson that we should learn from the Bible is that consecration is the fundamental requirement for God to enable Him to commune with man effectively.

After the children of Israel had encamped in the desert of Sinai God intended to meet with them. He gave them specific instructions through Moses before the meeting. They were to wash their clothes, consecrate themselves and be ready on the third day. Subsequently, when the children of Israel were about to come out of the wilderness to cross over the River Jordan, Joshua said to the people: *"Sanctify yourselves; for tomorrow the LORD will do wonders among you."* (Joshua 3:5 NHEB.)

Christianity is a journey of consecration: our new birth in Christ is not the end but the beginning of a journey of consecration. For the very reason that God is holy, His children must embrace holiness and purity. We must come out from the world and be separate. Consecration does not automatically happen to every believer after the new birth. Instead, it is a decision that we must make every moment of our lives; it is not a one-off action. It is not what we do before a church service; it is a way of life.

To be used by God, consecration is imperative. *"Now in a large house there are not only vessels of gold and of silver, but also of wood and of clay. Some are for honor, and some for dishonor. ²¹ If anyone therefore purges himself from these, he will be a vessel for honor, sanctified, and suitable for the master's use, prepared for every good work."* (2 Timothy 2:20–21 NHEB.) "If anyone therefore purges himself from these" is very much key in these verses. We ought to consciously take necessary steps to rid ourselves of every impurity and blemish, to be sanctified and useful for the Lord, fully prepared and ready to do His bidding. Trust and obedience to the word of God are the requirements we must have to remain in the state of consecration. This is the responsibility of every Christian.

Consecration is not only the basis of our communion with God; it is the basis of our spiritual growth and our usefulness in the hands of God. We cannot grow spiritually if we refuse to consecrate ourselves; neither can we be useful to God. We must surrender ourselves wholly to God, submitting our will to Him. Romans 12:1–2 says: *"Therefore I urge you, brothers, by the mercies of God, to present your bodies a living sacrifice, holy, acceptable to God, which is your spiritual service.* ^{2}*And do not be conformed to this world, but be transformed by the renewing of your mind, so that you may prove what is the good, well-pleasing, and perfect will of God."* (NHEB.)

In the Old Testament, consecration included physical observations such as rites of the outward cleansing of the body and garments. Today, consecration is of the heart and a life of holiness. Jacob's family were to hand over molten and carved images; for us, besides carved images, idols include things we set up for adoration that occupy and engage our minds and take the place of God in our lives. For a deeper walk with God, we need to hand over those things that separate us from God or something we esteem above God.

Consecration for believers is a lifestyle and not a build-up to a particular occasion. When God was about to descend on Mount Sinai the Israelites were asked to consecrate themselves for three days. They consecrated themselves for three days before they crossed the Jordan with the Ark of the Covenant. Here lies a difference between the Old Testament consecration and that of believers today. Now, we are royal priests, a temple of the living God, we are to put ourselves daily on the altar as a living sacrifice. We are not to set aside days, places and occasions to consecrate ourselves. A situation in which we are conscious of living a holy life because we have a role in a Christian gathering is outright mockery and hypocrisy. There are cases where a person sets apart days to be holy or situations in which someone declines fornication on a particular day because they will be leading choir ministration the next day. These are outright compartmentalisations of holy living and hypocrisy. As Christians, we have one kind of life, and that is the life of Christ. Once we are saved, this life will be shown in all spheres of our existence.

Many Christians in generations past and present have neglected the issue of consecration. But the reality is that to be anything in the hands of a Holy God or to be a vessel that God uses, consecration experience is necessary. Therefore, giving the Holy Spirit control over our lives and living a life characterised by victory over sin, self,

Satan and the world is not optional. *"Therefore do not let sin reign in your mortal body, that you should obey it in its lusts. [13]Neither present your members to sin as instruments of unrighteousness, but present yourselves to God, as alive from the dead, and your members as instruments of righteousness to God."* (Romans 6:12–13 NHEB.)

TOPIC 2: GOD'S PROTECTION

GENESIS 35:5

Protection is one of the essential needs of humanity. One chief desire of governments is to devise a way of ensuring the security of lives and properties in their nations. Business owners hire security personnel, intending to safeguard the properties and resources of their organisations. The influential are not left out; they also engage the security guards' services to protect their lives and properties. Understandably, these are steps in the right direction. However, the reality of the matter is that unless the Lord protects an individual, a family, a city, an organisation or a nation, any means deployed to ensure adequate and flawless protection will be an exercise in futility. No protection outside God is sufficient, reliable and impeccable. *"Unless the LORD builds the house, they labor in vain who build it. Unless the LORD watches over the city, the watchman guards it in vain."* (Psalm 127:1 NHEB.)

Only in God can anyone find adequate, dependable and flawless protection. The actuality of God's protection over those who have pledged their allegiance to Him is one phenomenon that is impossible to dispute. This fact is evidenced across the Bible pages, even in our contemporary Christian community. On God's protection, Apostle Paul, in his letter to the Romans, wrote: *"If God is for us, who can be against us?"* (Romans 8:31 NHEB.) This is a rhetorical question, but the response is not far-fetched. One with God is "majority", for He is the greatest ally anyone can ever have. He is by far greater than all our adversaries. If God is on a man's side, all the armies of the earth and all the powers of darkness combined can do him no harm. This is what the psalmist understood when he wrote: *"The LORD is my helper; I will not fear. What can man do to me?"* (Psalm 118:6 NHEB.)

Jacob, in reality, should have had no cause to fear any potential adversary. His entire journey from Mesopotamia was completed without any attack. When Laban pursued Jacob to cause him harm after Jacob had absconded, God intervened and prevented Laban from doing so. Even when Jacob feared the worst before meeting Esau, God intervened. God had always been with him and had assured him of His protection. Why the sudden fear, then? The incident was still fresh in Jacob's memory – the killing of the men of Shechem in cold blood by Simeon and Levi in avenging the sexual assault against Dinah, their sister. Jacob knew the cruel massacre was evil and could elicit a possible counter-attack from neighbouring cities, which he was not prepared and equipped for; this was the reason for his fear. As they journeyed towards Bethel in obedience to God's instruction, God protected them by stopping their potential assailants attacking them, having already overclouded the surrounding cities with terror. God's protection was a mark of His faithfulness to preserve the entire family of Jacob as He had promised to keep him wherever he went. *"Look, I am with you, and will keep you, wherever you go, and will bring you again into this land. For I will not leave you, until I have done that which I have spoken of to you."* (Genesis 28:15 NHEB.)

God, in His sovereignty, uses several approaches in protecting His own. In Jacob's case, He withheld Jacob's potential adversaries from harming him and his household. For Hezekiah and the people of Judah, when King Sennacherib laid a siege against Judah, God fought on their behalf. In one night, the angel of the Lord went to the camp of the Assyrians and 185,000 soldiers were slaughtered. Consequently, the impending danger was averted. *"It happened that night, that the angel of the LORD went out, and struck one hundred eighty-five thousand in the camp of the Assyrians. When men arose early in the morning, look, these were all dead bodies. [36]So Sennacherib king of Assyria departed, and went and returned, and lived at Nineveh."*(2 Kings 19:35–36 NHEB.) At times, God could indirectly use circumstances to prevent us from engaging in certain things that are appealing to us but detrimental to our lives, families or the salvation of our souls. In another instance, God could cause His children's enemies to fight against each other in the way that He instigated the adversaries of Judah to fight against one another during the reign of King Jehoshaphat. *"When they began to sing and to praise, the LORD set ambushers against the children of Ammon, Moab, and Mount Seir, who had come against Judah; and they were struck. ²³For the children of Ammon and Moab stood up against the inhabitants of Mount Seir, utterly to kill and destroy them: and when they had made an end of the inhabitants of Seir, everyone helped to destroy another. ²⁴When Judah came to the place overlooking the wilderness, they looked at the multitude; and look, they were dead bodies fallen to the earth, and there were none who escaped."* (2 Chronicles 20:22–24 NHEB.) The list is endless. One fundamental thing is that irrespective of the method used by God, He always protects His own.

God is not only willing but more than capable of delivering those who are His from their adversaries: *"God is our refuge and strength, a very present help in trouble."* (Psalm 46:1 NHEB.) Just as a mother hen watches over her chicks, rising to defend them from harm, the Lord watches over His people and protects them. God never fails to protect His children.

For us to enjoy God's protection in all its ways, deciding to become God's child is a primary step we must take. Not only that, we must then live the rest of our years in obedience to God. More so, we must repose our trust in God's ability to protect us at all times. It is total trust in God and obedience to His word that will guarantee the protection of His children. A human father would be more inclined to meet the needs of children who obey and trust him than children who disobey or disregard him, and so it is with God. For us to enjoy His protection, we must trust and obey Him.

It should be noted that, despite our trust in God and obedience to His word, there might be moments in our Christian journey when it seems that God is not with us, especially when we are confronted with different obstacles and His protection is not in view. In such situations we ought to keep trusting God, obey His word and accept whatever happens as His perfect will for us. We are not to go against God's word in an attempt to ensure our safety. Though some of the episodes may not play out the way we anticipate, ours is to joyfully accept God's will for our lives in all circumstances. There may also be occasions when we find ourselves being persecuted for our faith and we beckon to the Lord, and it seems that help is not coming; we are not to lose hope but to trust His will as best for our lives. God will not allow anything to befall His children if it is not for their good at the end. As with Stephen we are to remain faithful to God even to the point of death in the face of severe persecution. Stephen was a man who loved God and was filled with the Holy Spirit and wisdom. When he was being persecuted one might have expected God to protect him from being killed, yet he was stoned to death by the antagonists of the faith he stood for. At that moment, it was God's will for him to suffer and to die for the sake of the gospel. It was not that He was incapable of preventing Stephen from being killed. Stephen was eventually received into the glorious abode (Acts Chapters 6 and 7). God is sovereign, and His ways are higher than our ways. Though sometimes, we may not fully comprehend His ways or His dealings with us, let us rest assured that He will definitely lead us to a glorious end.

Jesus has promised to abide with us till the very end of the world, and if Jesus is with us always, we have nothing to fear. The only thing that can plunge us into the shadow of fear is sin. Sin is a separator – it separates a man from his Creator. Isaiah 59:1–2 says: ***"Look, the LORD's hand is not shortened, that it can't save; neither his ear heavy, that it can't hear: ²but your iniquities have separated between you and your God, and your sins have hidden his face from you, so that he will not hear."*** (NHEB.) Sin can prevent us from enjoying God's protection. Though sin may not make God abandon the erring child completely, that child will be vulnerable to the enemy's attack. Being condemned to eternal punishment is inevitable if the child does not repent before breathing their last. To avoid this, consistent obedience to God's word with an emphasis on salvation is vital.

Peradventure, you are no longer enjoying God's shield due to sin; His arm of salvation is still wide open, you can return to Him now. After that, you can use the Lord's name, the strong tower, for safety in times of danger. Proverbs 18:10 says: ***"The name of the LORD is a strong tower; the righteous run into it and are safe."*** (NHEB.) One must personally seek protection under the shadow of God's wings, but this involves more than just using God's name. As highlighted in the scriptures, we need to trust the bearer of that name and live in harmony with His righteous standards. We must actuate God's protective presence in faith while we place a value on constant fellowship with Him through prayer and the study of His word. When these are done, no matter how precarious the world might be or severe the circumstances confronting us may seem, even if our bodies suffer, one thing is sure, our souls as God's children are secure in His hands.

TOPIC 3: NAMING

GENESIS 35:10, 16–18

Imagine a world in which humans, objects or animals have no names. Truly, identifying one person or one thing from another would be an arduous task. From the beginning of life on earth, naming has been ingrained in our cultures. The first man had a name – Adam – and God instructed him to name all the animals He brought to him. Names are crucial to human beings: they are our primary identity. A name is a medium by which one person is distinguished from another.

Names given to children become their identity; they mark them out from others. Also, the sort of name a parent gives a child is very important. Many choose names they think sounds "cool". Little or no attention is placed on the meaning of a name. Names are important, not because they sound nice, but sometimes for the meaning they symbolise. God changed Abram's name to Abraham to reflect God's purpose for him. Sarah called her son Isaac, implying that God had brought her laughter and that everyone who heard about it would laugh with her. Many other characters in the Bible were named or renamed for various reasons, but one thing is sure, the naming of a person was significant in ancient times.

In Genesis 32:28, God gave Jacob another name – Israel. *"He said, "Your name will no longer be called Jacob, but Israel; for you have fought with God and with men, and have prevailed.""* (NHEB.) This chapter records an emphasis on that name. "Jacob" was given to him because he held his brother's heel during birth, and God gave him the name Israel to reflect God's purpose for his life. Like Jacob, his son's name, Ben-Oni, was given due to the scenario that transpired during his birth. Rachel experienced some complications during her labour, which led to her demise. But as her life trickled down like sand in an hourglass she named her baby Ben-Oni which means "son of my sorrow" (Campbell, 1996). From Rachel's eyes, we can understand why she called her son that. Yet Jacob did something remarkable. Not wanting to tie his son to a name with a negative meaning, he named him Benjamin instead, meaning "son of my right hand".

Similarly, in 1 Samuel 4:19–22, a child was born during unpleasant events and his mother named him Ichabod because the glory had departed from Israel. *"His daughter-in-law, Phinehas' wife, was with child, near to be delivered. When she heard the news that the ark of God was taken, and that her father-in-law and her husband were dead, she bowed herself and gave birth; for her pains came on her. [20]About the time of her death the women who stood by her said to her, "Do not be afraid; for you have given birth to a son." But she did not answer, neither did she regard it. [21]She named the child Ichabod, saying, "The glory has departed from Israel"; because the ark of God was taken, and because of her father-in-law and her husband.* ^{22}*She said, "The glory has departed from Israel; for the ark of God is taken.""* (NHEB.) Indeed, it was a gloomy day in Israel but that did not justify giving an inglorious name to an innocent baby. Both Ben-Oni and Ichabod portray negative meanings.

We are fully encouraged to take a leaf from Jacob's book. What he did should be emulated by parents in terms of the necessity of giving names to their children with positive connotations. No matter the circumstances surrounding a child's birth, no child should be made to bear a name with a negative cloud hovering over it. Every parent has the responsibility of giving their children names with positive meanings. Parents must not be careless when it comes to naming their children. Sometimes a bad name given to a child could affect their status among their peers or in their social circles in general.

It should be noted that names do not necessarily translate to a child's destiny. There have been cases of people named "Christian" whose lives have not depicted Christ-likeness. There are cases of people called "Mercy" whose attitudes have been far from merciful. A 'good name' boils down to all the choices a person makes through life's pilgrimage. Your name may have positivity and a godly reference tied to it, but if you make all the wrong choices in life it does not matter if you are named David, which means beloved, John, meaning gracious God or even Jesus; you will be identified with all the wrong choices you have made. Good names are advisable and encouraged, but the most important thing is the character and attitude of the one bearing the name. We must not be like Judas Iscariot, who had a name with a positive meaning – praise – but ended up doing something that was not praiseworthy. We must not act like Samson – the sun – who was divinely born as a Nazirite to God but, due to his sexual indiscipline, fell off the path of his calling. Our characters are like a mirror: they reflect our authentic identities and describe us more accurately than our names.

Unless divinely inspired, the names we give to our children do not reflect their destinies. That is the difference between God naming or renaming a person and a parent naming a child. God, being omniscient, gives names with the knowledge of the future; He does not give names in hope but in certainty. God changed Abram's name to Abraham to show that He had made him the father of many nations.

As established earlier, the names we give to our children can impact their emotional wellbeing. Against this backdrop, every parent must pay close attention to the names they give to their children and never let the birth circumstances sway their minds into giving a child a name that has negativity surrounding it. Because children are gifts from God, they must be treasured, and so should their names be.

Some people have already been given unpleasant names. To all those with ungodly names, or names with negative meanings, do not despair! You can choose to change your name; it is totally up to you. Know one thing for a fact: your name does not define you, whether you decide to keep the name or change it. So, set your mind at peace, and continue to live the life that God would be most pleased with.

TOPIC 4: REUBEN'S ABOMINABLE ACT

GENESIS 35:22

Considering the magnitude of Reuben's offence in sleeping with Bilhah – his father's concubine – which was deviant and despicable, pertinent lessons can be drawn from it.

Reuben's disgraceful act was not accidental; actions like these are usually premeditated and fantasised about before execution. Having conceived the idea, he went out of his volition and defiled his father's bed covertly. The information about how, where and when he did it is apparently out of reach. However, what he thought was a secret was not hidden from his father, Jacob. Jacob's immediate reaction when he heard of such ignoble news is not written in the Bible.

Nevertheless, long after Reuben might have forgotten his drop of stone in the pond, the ripples went on in his father's heart till his deathbed pronouncement. Reuben's sin found him out; instead of receiving the firstborn's blessing from his father he was given a negative pronouncement. Jacob said: *"Reuben, you are my firstborn, my might, and the beginning of my strength; excelling in dignity, and excelling in power. ⁴Boiling over as water, you shall not excel; because you went up to your father's bed, then defiled it. He went up to my couch."* (Genesis 49:3–4 NHEB.)

God's disapproval of Rueben's action was later revealed when the law was given. God, in expressing His disapprobation of this kind of action to the Israelites, said: *"You shall not uncover the nakedness of your father's wife: it is your father's nakedness."* (Leviticus 18:8 NHEB.) Reuben sleeping with his father's concubine was not just an act of sexual immorality; it was an act of dishonour to his father.

The root of Reuben's abominable intercourse with his father's concubine can be seen in Jesus' teaching in Matthew 15:19; without a doubt, the lustful action originated from Reuben's heart. *"For out of the heart come forth evil thoughts, murders, adulteries, sexual sins, thefts, false testimony, and blasphemies."* (NHEB.) Sexual sin often begins in a heart with a lustful desire. It drives a man uncontrollably and passionately into sexual immorality when it is entertained and nurtured. The passion of lust generates an inward heat like fire, and if not brought under control is highly destructive. Have you ever seen a wildfire? You would notice the terrifying speed and impact with which the fire consumes the entire bush. Lust works similarly, and it would not be far-fetched to call it a fiery desire. When allowed to burn inside, it speedily consumes the mind and emotions of its victim. When lust casts its shadow on a man he does not care about the consequences of his actions; he does not care about what he will sacrifice to gratify his inordinate sexual desire. Such was Reuben's act; his lust drove him to perpetuate the abominable act.

Reuben later paid for his actions by losing the blessing of the first son. Likewise, we have something of inestimable value to lose when we let the passion of lust drive us into sexual immorality. Be it incest, rape, fornication, adultery or any other related act of sin, whenever we indulge in such actions, we stand to forfeit the salvation of our souls. The question we must ask ourselves is: is the fleeting gratification of our flesh worth the loss of our souls? If our soul's salvation and the satisfaction of a sexual urge outside marriage are placed side by side, and we are to choose, which of the two will hold the most value to us? If the answer is the salvation of our soul we have made the right choice, but we need to make every effort to ensure our lives correspond with our choice.

While God disapproves of any act of sexual immorality, He desires those involved in such acts to forsake their sinful ways and, with penitent hearts, seek forgiveness from Him. 1 John 1:9 says: *"If we confess our sins, he is faithful and righteous to forgive us the sins, and to cleanse us from all unrighteousness."* (NHEB.) The blood of Jesus is more than enough to cleanse you from all your sins. God is always ready to wipe your slate clean and allow you to start all over again in a way that aligns with His word.

Considering that abominable actions like Reuben's and other related sexual immorality and perversion are manifestations of the flesh, we will not fulfil its desires when we walk in the Spirit. *"walk by the Spirit, and you will not carry out the desires of the flesh."* (Galatians 5:16 NHEB.) This can only be achieved when we are filled with the Holy Spirit. The Holy Spirit will provide us with the power to live above all sin. Also, we must acquaint ourselves with the word of God and allow it to guide our thoughts, words and actions. By this, we will be able to make decisions consistent with God's will and live in love and fear of the Almighty.

CHAPTER 11

TOPIC 1: ESAU'S COMPROMISE
GENESIS 36:6–8

One mentality that often pervades the nooks and crannies of the world we live in is the "It's my right" philosophy. Like a cloud of smoke, it blinds our mind to what is more critical – peace. For many people, letting go of their rights makes them fear looking weak or gullible. What they fail to realise, however, is that sometimes compromise is not an act of weakness but one of strength. It takes strength of character to forgo what is rightfully yours, for peace to reign. Esau demonstrated this strength of character when the harmony between him and his brother faced a potential threat due to their booming prosperity.

The canoe of thoughts finally rowed to the shore of the decision in his mind. It was time. There was no need to hold back, nor was there much wisdom staying back. He had to go, his household and all his possessions as well. Along with his brother, Jacob, Esau had become a bountiful beneficiary of God's prosperity. The peaceful coexistence with his brother in Canaan seemed likely to be hit by a wave of discord if not swiftly averted. As it stood, it was separation from Jacob that could maintain their peaceful relations. Without reluctance, Esau decided to leave the land of Canaan for his brother and choose the land of Seir for himself. Without allowing the cloak of ego to impair his reasoning, Esau was able to forgo his settlement for the sake of peace. He also showed selflessness as his grandfather had shown towards Lot. When a dispute had arisen between Abraham and Lot's herdsmen Abraham towed the path of compromise with his nephew,

Lot. Due to his additional possessions making coexistence no longer possible, Abraham made the wise choice of calling for a separation to prevent conflict emerging between himself and Lot (Genesis 13).

While it cannot be overlooked that the hand of God played a role in ensuring Jacob's descendants dwelt in Canaan, Esau's gesture is instructive for us as believers in our relationship with people. Without a fragment of doubt, compromise forms an integral part of any successful relationship, whether with family members, coworkers or friends. While it is understandable and legitimate at times to insist on having our way or standing our ground, it is sometimes necessary to cede our right, give up privileges or forfeit our claim for the greater good. Romans 12:18 says: ***If it is possible, as much as it is up to you, be at peace with all people.*** (NHEB.) For the wise, the cost of peace is much less than the cost of discord. However, it is a price that requires many compromises, tough decisions and a selfless attitude.

One approach that is a *sine qua non* in making compromises for the greater good is humility. Unlike Esau, many of us tend to surf on the sea of pride when it comes to letting go our right so that peace can thrive. Our egoistic nature often pushes us to obstinately cling to our rights, regardless of the consequences involved. When we allow our egos to dictate our actions and refuse to give up our rights, we risk severing relationships with our loved ones. When we allow our egos to thrive in situations that require us to compromise our rights, we put material possessions above our soul's salvation. The antidote to pride is the word of God. By adherence to the principles of God we can dispel the vice of pride from our lives. The summary of the teachings of Christ in regard to relating to one another is "selfless humility". When our hearts are filled with humility, our attitude of contending for things will be redefined. Humility will enable us to make sacrifices to enable peace to reign.

Selflessness is one factor that can ensure peace when we choose to make compromises. Philippians 2:4 admonishes us: ***each of you not just looking to his own things, but each of you also to the things of*** *others."* (NHEB.) When we are selfless it is easier to compromise our interests for the benefit of the interests of others. This can mean forgoing our rights by letting people have their way in matters that could have ended in conflict. As difficult as it may be, making a compromise with people portrays a good image of us as Christ's ambassadors. This was highlighted when Paul admonished the Christians disputing among themselves in 1 Corinthians 6:7 regarding the making of compromises for the sake of their faith: *"Therefore it is already altogether a defect in you, that you have lawsuits one with another. Why not rather be wronged? Why not rather be defrauded?"* (NHEB.)

In as much as making compromises portrays a good image of us as Christians, we must remember that it should not translate to us going against God's word. If our compromise prompts us to tell a lie, help someone engage in diabolical acts or offer a bribe to obtain a favour we must resolutely avoid it by all means. God does not condone sin, nor does He give a middle ground for it. As such, if our compromise, even if it is humanly justifiable, warrants us to act against God's word we would do well to sidestep it. However, if our compromise aligns with His word we must not hesitate to seize it as an opportunity to demonstrate our Christlike nature.

While we may forfeit properties, opportunities or positions that we are deserving of or that are rightfully ours, in the process, we will ultimately be gaining far more precious and imperishable rewards in the life to come.

CHAPTER 12

TOPIC 1: PARENTAL LOVE AND FAVOURITISM

GENESIS 37:1–4

Parental love is essential for a child's wellbeing. Every child needs their parents' love; thus, parents ought to show love to all without preference for one over others. Yet, the tidal waves of parental favouritism have rocked the boat of many families. Some parents have chosen to esteem one child over the rest, thereby setting in motion a shipwreck waiting to happen.

History repeated itself. The game of favouritism that had ravaged Isaac's family was playing out again in Jacob's family. Jacob, who had experienced the subtle rivalry in his father's house, should have learnt the danger of preferential love for a child at other family members' expense. We see him replicating his parents' exact attitude concerning him and his brother Esau. Genesis 25:28 tells us that, *"Isaac loved Esau, because he ate his venison. Rebekah loved Jacob."* (NHEB.)

Jacob's love swayed to Joseph. His actions, especially giving Joseph a coat of many colours, coupled with Joseph's dream about his future of superiority over his brothers, stirred up hatred in his brothers' hearts, which eventually led to them selling Joseph into slavery and separating him from the family. To Jacob, his reason for loving Joseph more was because he was the child of his old age. It could also be because Joseph was honest in reporting his older brothers' evil deeds (Genesis 37:1–3). Some parents love one child more than their other children because of the child's character. Others love a child they presume to have more potential. Other reasons could be a child's achievement or resemblance to the parent.

Parental favouritism is such a menace that it has engendered a lot of family problems. The expression of preferential love for a child is not without consequences. These consequences can be profound for all the children throughout their lives. It can affect their relationship with their siblings and their parents. Many parents' conscious or unconscious acts of favouritism open the door for the devil to come into their homes. When a cloud of bias hovers over a home, it casts a huge shadow and relegates love to the background. Siblings who were supposed to love each other and work together develop bitterness, envy, jealousy and hatred for one another; these behaviours should not be found in a home. For instance, in Jacob's family, Joseph's brothers conspired to kill him but later sold him off to slavery, telling their father that his beloved son had been devoured by a wild animal. This left him sorrowful and heartbroken. When hatred among siblings leads to the conception of murder, it can be devastating.

Also, children who are less loved feel cheated and neglected. Children feeling this way may act up to win their parent's attention, making matters worse. They may also indulge in inappropriate behaviours, becoming the black sheep they believe their parents already see. They may lack self-acceptance, which can affect different aspects of their lives and their emotional wellbeing in adulthood. They may not believe in themselves or be able to withstand criticism from the outside world. In the same vein, children who are loved less are susceptible to falling into the wrong hands that seem to show them the kind of affection their parents never gave them.

Imagine what could have happened if Jacob had shown as much love to his other children as he did to Joseph or given them all coats of many colours. It can safely be said that if Jacob had treated his children fairly, the friction that caused a rift within his family and led to Joseph's brothers hating everything about him would have been averted. While some parents struggle to conceal their preference for a child they have more affection for, parents should completely discard favouritism from their homes. No matter what, parents should display impartiality in love by treating their children equally and punishing them equally when they misbehave. Reports of misconduct by a child must be appropriately handled to not create acrimony in the family.

Parental love is the first love children experience and the first love they understand. When children receive love, they learn to give love. When parents show love to their children, they will not yearn for love outside the family. Parents' love helps children develop an identity and builds self-confidence, and gives them the capacity to share that love with others. Parents should ask the Holy Spirit to direct their actions so that no family rift develops.

Favoured children also have a responsibility. Often they tend to add fuel to the fire because they do not know how to handle a parent's favouritism. To prevent strife in the home, they must endeavour not to become boastful towards their less favoured siblings. Even if parents fail to mask their favouritism, a favoured child can still try to make their siblings not feel less loved.

On the other hand, if you find yourself at the disadvantaged end of parental favouritism, do not let the situation embitter you and make you develop a negative attitude towards your siblings or parents. Sometimes, you may need to wisely talk with your parents to let them know your observations. This could go a long way towards addressing the situation, since some may not have known the effect of their indeliberate actions. You ought to always live in obedience to God's word and be on your best behaviour at all times. Although the experience may be heartrending, you should endeavour to always respond with love. A response in love can correct the wrong attitude of others.

The stories in the Bible are meant for our learning. Sometimes it is better to learn from the experiences of others rather than experiencing them ourselves. Jacob's favouritism had a damaging effect on his family and we must learn from his experience. God has entrusted us with His wonderful gifts – children – and He has created every child uniquely. He expects us to be impartial in our display of love for them; it is expected that all our children be treated with equal love.

TOPIC 2:   CONTINUUM OF SIN

GENESIS 37:1–36

It is a generally accepted truth that one sin often begets another. An unrepented evil opens the door to further temptation, leading to other sins more grievous in their effects on others. Continuum of sin occurs when a sin, not adequately addressed, grows into another sin or sets a cycle of other sins in motion. It also occurs when one commits several other sins in a bid to cover up the initial sin. Both scenarios played out perfectly in the account of Joseph and his brothers.

In this chapter, the genesis of the continuum of sins between Joseph and his brothers was the ill feelings of envy and hatred they nursed in their hearts towards him, due to Jacob's apparent preferential love for Joseph. Their hatred for him was difficult to conceal because they could not speak kindly to him. This hatred was aggravated by Joseph's dreams; they hated him the more when he told his dreams to them. Their hatred further degenerated into a conspiracy to murder their brother. The timely intervention of Reuben prevented this plan developing. They later decided to sell Joseph off to the Ishmaelites for 20 pieces of silver and conspired to tell their father that a wild animal had devoured his beloved son. Joseph was lost in a foreign land as a slave and their actions made their father mourn deeply for a child who was not dead.

Harbouring envy and hatred within the heart is one of the best ways to get entangled in a series of sins. These vices instigate people to perceive those they hate as enemies and, in so doing, carry out a series of actions against them in a bid to cause harm one way or another.

Little wonder James 3:16 says, *"For where jealousy and selfish ambition are, there is confusion and every evil deed."* (NHEB.)

Let us look at Cain and his dastardly act of murder against his brother; it began with the sin of resentment. God noticed this and warned him about the anger he harboured in his heart against Abel. But Cain refused to heed God's warning and, in time, the vice within his heart culminated in the act of murder against his sibling, Abel. Genesis 4:6–8 says, *"The LORD said to Cain, "Why are you angry? Why has the expression of your face fallen? [7] If you do well, will it not be lifted up? If you do not do well, sin crouches at the door. Its desire is for you, but you are to rule over it." [8] Cain said to Abel, his brother, "Let's go into the field." It happened when they were in the field, that Cain rose up against Abel, his brother, and killed him."* (NHEB.)

Another story that illustrates the continuum of sins in the Bible is the account of David and Bathsheba – the wife of Uriah. Rather than repent and turn to his God, David tried to save himself from the dilemma his adultery had plunged him into with other sinful actions. After Bathsheba took in, he began thinking up ways to conceal their affair. He sent for Uriah from the battlefield to make him sleep with Bathsheba so that he would think he was the father of the child, but this plan did not work. David further arranged for Uriah to be killed. David's continuum of sins began with unbridled lust in his heart, then adultery and finally murder. Note that no matter how hard David tried to conceal his sin, his evil deed was eventually exposed. The same was true of Joseph's brothers.

To avoid a continuum of sins, sin must immediately be acknowledged, confessed, repented of and forsaken: *"He who conceals his sins doesn't prosper, but whoever confesses and renounces them finds mercy."* (Proverbs 28:13 NHEB.) Unrepented and wilful sins are fatal to the soul: they harden the heart and the conscience against God. One whose heart is hardened by sin feels no remorse or contrition for his sins; such a person is on the path to damnation. We are not to carry out further evil actions to conceal our sins, and neither are we to entertain sin in our hearts lest it spurs us into ungodly acts.

Evil actions are usually preceded by evil desires within the heart. James 1:14–15 says, *"But each one is tempted, when he is drawn away by his own lust, and enticed.* ¹⁵*Then the lust, when it has conceived, bears sin; and the sin, when it is full grown, brings forth death."* (NHEB.) Evil desires give birth to sinful actions, which lead to death – separation from God. It is impossible not to have external enticements to sin, but these enticements will have no hold on us when there are no corresponding desires within our hearts. This is why we ought to saturate our hearts with the word of God: *"In my heart I have hidden your word, that I might not sin against you."* (Psalm 119:11 NHEB.) With the help of the Holy Spirit, we are to subject our hearts to the pleasing fragrance of God's word. We are to allow it to dispel all forms of vice such as hatred, resentment, inordinate affection and covetousness. It is difficult for sin to thrive in a regenerated heart saturated in God's word. When our hearts and desires are pure, our actions will, in turn, be pure.

Sin has an entangling nature. It seeks to rule or dominate its victims. Little wonder that Christ said, *"Truly I tell you, everyone who commits sin is the slave of sin."* (John 8:34 NHEB.) Nevertheless, just as God instructed Cain before he murdered his brother, God desires that we live above sin. When we yield ourselves to sin we become servants to it. But if we decide to exercise our dominion over it by faith in the finished work of Christ on the cross for our soul's salvation, and have a willingness to resist it at all costs, we will be victorious over it. Let us always remember that God is faithful and that He will not suffer us to be tempted beyond what we can handle.

The concept of the continuum of sins could be likened to a spark of fire amid dry bushes: if it is not immediately put out it will consume the entire bush. Sin, not properly handled, has the propensity to dictate the course of our lives and, ultimately, our eternal destination.

Some who have found themselves severely entangled in sinful habits might never have imagined their lives could turn out in such a manner. They only started with an evil action and repeated this action until it became a habit and a way of life. This would never have happened if they had handled the sin appropriately at the initial stage. Sin should be treated like a plague and should be given no place in our hearts or lives.

TOPIC 3: THE PATH TO AN EXPECTED END

GENESIS 37:1–36

The journey through life is one that some often desire or expect to be as smooth sailing as that on a cruise ship. But while there will be moments of bliss, periods of happiness and times of triumph, there will also be phases when we encounter obstacles and trials on the path towards God's expected end for us.

This was a scenario that remarkably played out in the life of Joseph. Joseph's dreams had contained a future filled with promises, greatness and honour. As with many people, Joseph would have expected to accomplish those dreams. Indeed, he might have expected a ride to a future of bliss without encountering any hurdle on his way. But Joseph's life and his path to a promising future suffered an agonising twist during a sudden turn of events. The next series of events that followed Joseph's dreams was as traumatising as it was excruciating. From his brothers' jealousy to their conspiracy to murder him, Joseph's path to a glorious future began with a stride on a thorny road. In the process of being sold into slavery and thrown into prison, Joseph experienced a reality check that would have made his dream seem like nothing more than a figment of his imagination. By this time, it would not have been a surprise if the memory of Joseph's dreams had faded away in the recesses of his mind.

Indeed, just as Joseph's journey to his glorious future was littered with difficulties and temptations, the path to our soul's salvation and the fulfilment of our purpose is also replete with challenges. The fact that God has destined us for greatness and promised us eternal life does not translate to us having a smooth ride towards its fulfilment, nor does it make us immune from trials. This understanding seems to be lacking in some believers, unfortunately. They operate with a mentality that things will always work out in their career, business or other endeavours because of God's promise of a great future for them. This misconception is further exacerbated by some servants of God who mislead people into thinking that the Christian journey will be a bed of roses once they surrender to Christ. This is why many people get frustrated, bitter, lose their passion for serving God and ask all the "whys" in life: "If God is good, why the loss?", "Why the broken relationship?", "Why the sickness and challenges?", and many more. Though we may never understand His reasons, and though the bits and pieces of our lives may not make sense during times of trial, we must know that everything God allows to happen in our lives – good or seemingly bad – is designed to work out for our good in the end. Romans 8:28 says, *"We know that all things work together for good for those who love God, to those who are called according to his purpose."* (NHEB.)

While God desires us to experience comfort and happiness in this world, we must realise that trials are part of His divine plan to lead us to an expected end. Those who have come across scriptures such as Jeremiah 29:11 tend to misconstrue it as a promise of a blissful life and a stressless Christian journey: *"'For I know the plans that I have for you,' says the LORD, 'plans for your welfare, and not for calamity, to give you hope and a future.'"* (NHEB.) Granted, this scripture is an encouragement and must be balanced holistically with other passages that speak of challenges, such as John 16:33: *"In the world you have oppression…"* (NHEB.) The believer's journey to an expected end is correspondent to the wilderness experience faced by the Israelites. They experienced bouts of hunger and thirst, moments of danger and episodes of wars and only a handful survived the journey from Egypt to Canaan, because of unbelief. Similarly, the road to our soul's salvation is filled with a series of trials, temptations and difficulties, which must be navigated in faith and obedience to God before we can be victorious.

There are cases in which a person's severe turbulence in life is a result of identifying themself with God. While those who once loved them may be cautious, this does not mean that God is not with them or that they are not on the right path. We must never let the obstacles on the way to the expected end make us abandon the course.

God desires that we remain steadfast in the faith and that we cling to His promises when we do not get that promotion at work, the healing we desperately want, or fail at that business endeavour we thought would flourish. We have to trust that God is in control of our lives even in the face of challenges; we are to trust Him when it seems that though He has promised us success we are instead experiencing the opposite. We must never lose hope or go against the word of God. David should be an example for us. Despite being anointed king he still had to endure moments of despair and years of evading his adversaries before becoming king. Even when he had the opportunity to kill Saul and become king, he refused because he was careful not to go against the word of God; he chose instead to wait on the Lord. When we understand that God is weaving every circumstance for our good we will not be discouraged in going through life because of disappointment, bitterness, loss, frustration or because we feel God's plan has not come to pass.

Further, when trying periods surface during the journey towards our purpose or in our Christian walk, we must never succumb to the temptation to go against God's word. While disobedience to God's word will undoubtedly derail us from the path of righteousness and God's plan for us, obedience will keep us on the path to fulfilling our purpose and ensuring the salvation of our souls. Despite the challenges he encountered, Joseph never let them propel him to act in disobedience to the word of God. Even when his master's wife seduced him to commit adultery with her, Joseph never compromised his godly standards but remained loyal to God's word.

Though the path to God's expected end for us is anything but easy, the thorns of difficulty do not equate to the crown of victory and the expected future that awaits us at the end of our journey. Let us always reassure ourselves with this hope in the word of God in 2 Corinthians 4:17–18: *"For this momentary light affliction is working for us a far more exceeding and everlasting weight of glory; [18]while we do not look at the things which are seen, but at the things which are not seen. For the things which are seen are temporal, but the things which are not seen are everlasting."* (NHEB.)

TOPIC 4: INTEGRITY

GENESIS 37:2

Often, evil thrives, not because the evildoers are stronger, but because the good people compromise by looking the other way, out of fear for the consequences of standing up for what is right. The sad reality remains that evil in our society will continue unabated if the beacons of integrity do not rise up to nip it in the bud because of fear. When we allow evil to thrive in our offices, homes, churches, societies or anywhere we find ourselves, we are, by implication, dimming the light of uprightness and aiding the darkness of moral decadence.

Joseph always brought reports of the evil deeds of his brothers to their father, Jacob. Compared to Joseph, his brothers seemed to have lacked integrity, for they carried out actions which they could not do in their father's presence. Joseph did not allow himself to be influenced by their lack of integrity. This act of Joseph was possibly part of the reason he was despised by his brothers. People generally do not want their evil deeds to be exposed. Those who want to expose them stand to face stiff persecution, but Joseph preferred to suffer his brothers' hatred than allow evil to thrive.

Note that integrity was a way of life for Joseph. The account of his life contains several other episodes of acts of integrity that are worthy of mention. While he was in Potiphar's house there was no report of untruthfulness or malpractice, despite him being in charge of everything. Even when his master's wife pressurised him to commit immorality with her, Joseph held on tenaciously to his integrity because he feared God. Even so, he was wrongly accused and thrown into prison as a result.

While Joseph was in prison, the prison keeper committed the prisoners to his care and Joseph managed the affairs of the prison with integrity. That is not all: Joseph's integrity was evident when he was a ruler in Egypt. Despite being exalted to such a high position in a strange land, there was no report of misdeeds during his time as Pharaoh's second-in-command. Integrity preserved him all the way: *"The integrity of the upright shall guide them, but the perverseness of the treacherous shall destroy them."* (Proverbs 11:3 NHEB.)

Joseph maintained his integrity in the afore-cited instances because he resolved to trust and obey God always, irrespective of the consequences. Though his integrity exposed him to tribulations, God was always with him and caused everything to work out for his good in the end. This is evidence that integrity can be costly and that we may suffer for standing up for what is right. Nonetheless, we must trust God for our wellbeing without compromising our integrity, regardless of the consequences. Joseph was a man of integrity both at home and everywhere else he found himself. He remains a worthy model of integrity to Christians.

Integrity is being sincere and transparent in everything we do. It goes beyond a single act; it is a habit, or a lifestyle of honesty and moral uprightness, regardless of the circumstance. Integrity also means "wholeness". It is a wholeness of character – not to say something or act in a particular way and mean something else. Not only is integrity doing what is right, it is also the quality of being morally incorruptible.

As Christians we must be willing to stand up against evil wherever we find it, and not mind the consequences. When we see evil and do nothing about it, we indirectly allow evil to thrive. For instance, a Christian who works in an organisation and is aware that a colleague is stealing funds belonging to the organisation yet turns a blind eye, acting as though no wrong is happening, is indirectly helping the evil to thrive. Such an act is not one of integrity. It is best to first approach such an erring colleague and warn them. If every effort to dissuade the person from misbehaving fails, they should be reported to the proper authorities.

Let us carefully consider James 4:17 in light of this: *"To him therefore who knows to do good, and does not do it, to him it is sin."* (NHEB.) We not only err when we act in disobedience to the word of God but also when we refuse to do what is right. The awareness of a good and the ability to carry it out makes it our responsibility. We must not encourage evil by our refusal to act. A Christian's integrity should be such that people fear discussing evil plans or carrying out evil acts around them, for they know that they will not be a partaker and that their plans could be exposed. If one does not stand up against something, that silence could be mistaken for approval. All Christians should be a hindrance to evil wherever they are. When we permit evil to prevail it will only worsen, and if we are not cautious we could be influenced by it. Christians should neither cover up evil deeds nor compromise with evildoers at home, at church, in the workplace or wherever we find ourselves: *"Have no fellowship with the unfruitful works of darkness, but rather even reprove them."* (Ephesians 5:11 NHEB.)

Many Christians do not act against wrongdoing because of the fear of hurting others or of what others will do to them. The obligation of any Christian is first to God. We must not allow this fear to keep us from doing what is right. *"For if I were still pleasing people, I would not be a servant of Christ."* (Galatians 1:10 NHEB.)

Also, before reporting and rebuking people for their wrong deeds, we should first examine our motives. Are we doing this out of our selfish interest? Or are we doing it out of love – to rescue someone from the wrong way and its consequences? If our reason is not for love, then our motive is wrong. The motive of an act is what determines its purity. Correcting a wrong deed should not come from a heart seeking to take advantage of the misdeed to bring down the person or elevate ourselves. It should not come from a heart laden with pride, jealousy, anger, malice or any other inordinate motive. When the aim of reporting or rebuking is to ridicule or harm a person, the person reporting has missed the Christian virtue of love and compassion. Our intention in acting against a misdeed should be to prevent evil and restore the erring offender in love: *"Let all that you do be done in love."* (1 Corinthians 16:14 NHEB.)

It is the will of God that wrongdoing should not prevail in this world, and it is the responsibility of every Christian to enforce this will. Our action of standing for God in a godless world and in the face of daring consequences could also be instrumental in turning many to righteousness.

(For more on Integrity, see Chapter 4, Topic 2)

TOPIC 5: HANDLING REVELATION: JOSEPH'S DREAM – A CASE STUDY

GENESIS 37:5–11

The storm of discord gradually brewed like a cloud gravid with rainfall. It was a storm that had been ignited by the preferential love of their father, Jacob. Their brother Joseph had been gifted with a coat of many colours; then came the dreams that further infuriated them. It was a revelation that cast a shadow of inferiority on their future. Joseph's naivety in revealing his dreams to his brothers set in motion a cycle of mischievous intents and unlocked other doors of hostility.

Amid this hostile atmosphere, one might wonder what could have been if Joseph had handled his dreams appropriately. One could

126

wonder if the hatred and jealousy that clouded his brothers' minds would have been circumvented if Joseph had applied discretion to the revelation of his dreams. It is safe to say that his brothers' hatred and bitterness towards him, which led to their selling him to slavery, could have been averted if he had been appropriately guided to disclose his dreams to his father first before exposing them to his jealous brothers.

Some people opine that Joseph's disclosure of his dream to his brothers and their subsequent reaction was the only way God's plan for Joseph could be fulfilled. They argue that if Joseph had not informed his brothers of his dreams he would not have been sold to slavery, nor would he have landed in the quarters of Potiphar and been thrown into the prison that paved the way to the fulfilment of his purpose. Their position, however, ignores the fact that God is not limited by having a means to achieve His purpose; His sovereignty allows Him to utilise several ways to bring His plans into realisation. God will not require a person to sin for His plan to come to fruition. There is always wisdom in applying discretion in handling divine revelations.

Beyond any doubt, divine revelations bring with them a plethora of information that may be difficult for people to understand. This information might also require wisdom in conveying it. According to thefreedictionary.com, a dream is a series of images, ideas, emotions and sensations occurring involuntarily in the mind during certain stages of sleep. While they can sometimes be entertaining and fun, they can also be frightening and bizarre. Though they can be induced by desires, they can also be engendered by fear, medication or stress. Unlike regular dreams, dreams that are revelations from God, like Joseph's, are not generated from stress or induced by desires. Divinely inspired dreams and other forms of revelations are means by which God communicates to people. They are one of the chosen means by which God reveals His plans, will and purpose to us.

In situations in which we perceive we have received divine messages through dreams or other forms of revelations, wisdom demands that we handle such information with discretion and be guided by the word of God. Proverbs 3:21–23 admonishes us, *"My son, let them not depart from your eyes. Keep sound wisdom and discretion: ^{22}so they will be life to your soul, and grace for your neck. ^{23}Then you shall walk in your way securely, and your foot won't stumble."* (NHEB.) The ability to know when and how to divulge a piece of information is a trait many people lack. Just because God revealed to us that we would ascend to a podium of greatness or that someone would experience a certain fate does not necessarily mean He expects us to broadcast it without restraint or wisdom. When revelations are passed across from God to us, the effects may be grievous if wrongly handled. If we elect to abandon discretion regarding revelations we could expose ourselves to untoward experiences. When we fail to apply discretion to sensitive revelations concerning other people we may end up causing them pain instead of doing them good.

It is essential to consider that not all revelations from God to us concerning other people are to be divulged to them directly or immediately; neither are all revelations meant for public consumption. When Jacob was informed about Joseph's dreams, his decision to retain the information in his mind demonstrated discretion. While he attempted to manage the situation by rebuking Joseph, the deed was already done and the brothers had taken it to heart. His brothers hated him even more because of the dream and would have murdered him but for Reuben's timely intervention. *"They saw him afar off, and before he came near to them, they conspired against him to kill him. ^{19}They said one to another, "Look, this dreamer comes. ^{20}Come now therefore, and let's kill him, and cast him into one of the pits, and we will say, 'An evil animal has devoured him.' We will see what will become of his dreams.""* (Genesis 37:18–20 NHEB.) They later agreed to sell him into slavery in a foreign land and claimed that he had been devoured by a wild animal, causing their father immense grief. Considering that some may not possess the capacity or maturity to handle certain information, it is wise to weigh it, understand the impact, devise the best possible approach, and choose the right time to relay the information if necessary.

For revelations that have to do with others, we must endeavour to show tact and wisdom, as did Nathan. When approaching David about his sins of adultery and murder, Nathan delivered the revelation God gave him by gently approaching him and relating David's actions through a story. It was a wise approach that eventually elicited repentance from David rather than a hostile reaction. 2 Samuel 12:13 says, ***"David said to Nathan, "I have sinned against the LORD." Nathan said to David, "The LORD also has put away your sin. You will not die."***" (NHEB.) For every revelation God gives us, we can always ask Him for wisdom on how to handle it to avoid falling into pitfalls that could be sources of grief to ourselves or others. James 1:5 says: ***"But if any of you lacks wisdom, let him ask of God, who gives to all liberally and without reproach; and it will be given to him."*** (NHEB.)

TOPIC 6: LESSER SIN

GENESIS 37:25–28

Often, we tend to categorise sin and consider one worse than another. Many people subscribe to the idea of lesser and greater sins. They presume that different degrees of punishment will be apportioned to varying degrees of sins. They may not steal but lie. They may not kill yet they harbour anger in their hearts against another. They may not practise witchcraft yet they often rebel against God. Since their sins are subtle and seemingly less grievous in a practical sense, they condemn those who commit apparent grievous sins.

Sin is sin and has no measuring apparatus except the righteous scale of God. Even if the physical consequences differ, every unrepented sin – unrighteous thoughts, actions, words or lifestyle – regardless of its magnitude, violate God's word. As such, all sin is evil, dishonours God and attracts the same consequence – death. Romans 6:23 says: ***"For the wages of sin is death..."*** (NHEB.)

Examining the passage under consideration, murder, back then in Judah's days, was considered evil even before the law was given.

It seemed as though Judah's conscience would not accept the murder of his brother, his flesh and blood, but he was more comfortable with the lesser evil of selling Joseph off into slavery to the Ishmaelites. Judah knew it was wrong to kill Joseph and conceal his blood so he modestly objected to his murder. However, he suggested a seemingly lesser act of wickedness, saying, *"Come, and let's sell him to the Ishmaelites, and not let our hand be on him; for he is our brother, our flesh. His brothers listened to him."* (Genesis 37:27 NHEB.) Ironically, he sounded like a saint among his brothers. For Judah, selling his brother to slavery and deceiving his father was a lesser sin than killing him.

Consider a man who thinks it is alright to steal from the rich rather than the poor. Or a woman who feels justified for fornicating with a bachelor instead of a married man. Many people live their lives by this principle. The thing about lesser and greater sin is that the lesser evil is never the most appropriate option. The woman who preferred fornicating with a bachelor over an affair with a married man had a third option: no sexual activity before marriage. The thief had a third option: not stealing at all. Picking one sin over another does not make it right in the sight of God. To a moralist, the idea of perpetrating a lesser evil compared to a greater one could be soothing.

The human's conscience is a tricky tool; its flexible nature makes it both a means to save and destroy because it conforms a person to a sense of conduct – what is perceived as right or wrong. So in a way we make our consciences what we want them to be. The flexibility of the conscience can make a person accept that committing a seemingly lesser sin is the right thing to do.

As Christians, when our consciences start accepting the principle of lesser sins there is trouble. When we categorise sin, we put ourselves on the judgement seat of God. All sin, big or small, regardless of our perception, is disobedience to God to whom we must give an account. 2 Corinthians 5:10 says: *"For we must all appear before the judgment seat of Christ; that each one may receive the things in the body, according to what he has done, whether good or bad."* (NHEB.)

Jesus died and saved us from sin. Accepting the call to salvation means we rid ourselves of the old man and are born again. If your conscience starts contemplating, contrasting and accepting one sin over another, then a purge is needed. We need to turn to the Lord for help through prayer and, in some cases, fasting. The blood of Christ cleanses and purifies our consciences from acts that lead to death so that we may serve the living God. It gives us the grace to live holy and righteous lives. If you are struggling with sin, Christ invites you to be washed in His blood.

The accurate determinant of the rightness of an act is the word of God. Culture, norms and trends should not be our guide to what is wrong or right. Our consciences must be influenced by an accurate knowledge of God's word. Therefore, God's word must be engraved on the tablets of our hearts and we must obey the commands of God as written in His word.

One common denominator of all those who practise evil is their destination: *"But for the cowardly, unbelieving, abominable, murderers, sexually immoral, sorcerers, idolaters, and all liars, their part is in the lake that burns with fire and sulfur, which is the second death."* (Revelation 21:8 NHEB.) So, to the question, is there a lesser sin? We should try asking ourselves: since the unbelieving and liars will end up at the same place as sorcerers and murderers, should evil be categorised into lesser versus greater evils? Our focus should always be on pleasing the One who gave the commands, for all disobedience to Him is sin. Categorising sin into greater or lesser could leave room for compromise in our hearts and mar our relationship with God.

CHAPTER 13

TOPIC 1: GOD'S DISDAIN FOR WICKEDNESS

GENESIS 38:6–10

From the moment Adam and Eve disobeyed God, sin was introduced to the world. Sinfulness is something belonging to human nature and is considered part of human existence. Humans are tempted every day, and the lure to evil is seductively endearing.

Humans can be categorised into two groups: the righteous and the wicked. The righteous represents a group whose lifestyles are patterned after the word of God. For the wicked, however, the inclinations of their heart often tilt towards the perpetuation of evil. Acts of wickedness which range from murder, oppression of the poor, robbery, etc., categorically negate God's word.

There were two brothers from the same parent and both were recorded to be wicked in the Lord's sight. The life of Judah's first son, Er, was terminated by God due to his wickedness. What this wickedness consisted of we are not told. We only know it was evil enough for God to have carried out an immediate judgement on him. Judah's second son, Onan, also trod the lane of wickedness, by refusing to provide an heir for his brother as the custom required. We find from this account that, long before the mosaic law, it was an established custom that a man's brother would take his wife if the older brother died without a son. The first son of the second marriage was considered the first husband's child and would carry on his lineage. The marriage to one's brother's wife later appeared in the mosaic law, as seen in Deuteronomy 25:5–6: *"If brothers dwell together, and one of them die, and have no son, the wife of the dead shall not be married outside to a stranger: her husband's brother shall go in to her, and take her to him as wife, and perform the duty of a husband's brother to her. [6]It shall be, that the firstborn whom she bears shall succeed in the name of his brother who is dead, that his name not be blotted out of Israel."* (NHEB.) Onan was not coerced into marrying Tamar, after all. He could have objected, but he did not. While the responsibility of providing a son for his late brother did not appeal to Onan, the sexual gratification of the marital arrangement did. This act portrayed a lack of concern for his late brother's lineage and incurred God's judgement – death.

In the scriptures God's displeasure for wickedness can be noticed. In Noah's time and in the days of Sodom and Gomorrah the degree of wickedness was such that every single component of thought was evil. The fact that God annihilated the entire human race – except for Noah and his family – and destroyed the cities of Sodom and Gomorrah – except for Lot and his family – should provide us with a vivid insight into God's displeasure for wickedness.

God's aversion to wickedness is rooted in His nature. God's nature of holiness and righteousness makes wickedness repulsive to Him. For a God who radiates with an aura of purity, the perpetration of wickedness is no doubt unsightly. Since God has established instructions to guide our actions, any act of wickedness represents rebellion and disobedience.

God's disapproval of wickedness is also because wickedness affects humanity negatively. Think of those robbed of their possessions or someone who lost their loved ones to the cruel hands of assassins. Think of how unpleasant it would be for God to constantly witness man's inhumanity to man.

While God unequivocally detests wickedness, He also earnestly desires the repentance of the wicked. He does not just pass judgement without giving man the opportunity to amend his ways. Ezekiel 18:23

says: *""Have I any pleasure in the death of the wicked?" says the Lord GOD; "and not rather that he should return from his way, and live?""* (NHEB.) God does not just sit and wait for people to commit an offence and then bring judgement on them; He offers them the opportunity to turn from their wicked ways as He did for the Ninevites. Most of the time, people who end up at the receiving end of God's judgement die after spurning opportunities to repent. It is only when people who have been sailing on the sea of wickedness turn to the path of righteousness that they experience the salvation of their soul.

Likewise, as God's children, since God takes no delight in wickedness and sin, it is incumbent upon us to *"Abhor that which is evil. Cling to that which is good."* (Romans 12:9 NHEB.) Christ died to give us dominion over sin. His death broke the chain of sin that leads to damnation. The heart is the source of evil and wickedness. The only way the product of our hearts can be pleasing to God is by purging our hearts with the blood of Christ and being reborn into a new man ruled by the Spirit. We must continually allow the word of God to guide our actions and prevent us from carrying out acts of wickedness.

As much as it can be said that God has given us His grace to live above evil, it must also be noted that for children of God who allow themselves to slip in the swamp of wickedness, God extends His whip of discipline. Whenever we succumb to the temptations of evil, just like a loving father would discipline his erring child, our heavenly Father disciplines us. Hebrews 12:5–6 says: *"My son, do not take lightly the discipline of the Lord, nor lose heart when you are corrected by him. ⁶For whom the Lord loves he disciplines, and punishes every son he accepts."* (NHEB.) Discipline is to mould us into better people. If someone does not love you they couldn't care less about what becomes of you. But God loves us and He is very interested in keeping us in His fold.

Our reaction to wickedness done to us must be Christlike. It is never Christlike to wish for the death of others, no matter the wrong they may have done to us. Rather than repay evil with evil, we are to reciprocate with good for evil done to us. Despite the torture Christ faced on His journey to Calvary, He still found the strength to forgive when He prayed, *"Father, forgive them, for they do not know what they are doing..."* (Luke 23:34 NHEB.) Jesus could have prayed for the destruction of His enemies, but He did not. Our act of forgiving and repaying good with evil can be an evangelising tool to draw people to God.

Conclusively, we live in the era of grace, and as such, many people are quick to mistake God's patience with humanity for slackness. Grace should not be mistaken for the leeway to tread the path of rebellion without restraint, for God's expectation of us in this dispensation is higher: *"Anyone who disregards the Law of Moses dies without compassion on the word of two or three witnesses. ²⁹How much worse punishment, do you think, will he be judged worthy of, who has trodden under foot the Son of God, and has counted the blood of the covenant with which he was sanctified an unholy thing, and has insulted the Spirit of grace?"* (Hebrews 10:28–29 NHEB.) God is not slow to bring judgement upon the ungodly. Instead, He is patient with us, desiring that no one should perish and that we all shall come to repentance (2 Peter 3:9). Nonetheless, His patience should not be taken for granted. God still disdains wickedness, and the unrepentant will have their abode in the eternal lake of fire.

TOPIC 2: CHRISTIANITY AND TRADITION

GENESIS 38:6–11

Tradition is a practice upheld and believed by a group of people. It is birthed by the belief system of a people and is binding on every group member. Organisations and societies uphold different traditions; there are bound to be traditions wherever humans are. What people believe typically translates into their actions, and to act in a contrary manner is an outright rejection of such beliefs and could lead to punishment and, in some cases, ostracisation from the group.

The general objective of traditions is to ensure that the standards, customs or beliefs which guide a people are not lost or diluted.

When God picked one man, Abraham, through whose lineage the Saviour would be born, He called him from his people and tradition and began to teach him a new way of life. God intended that from this one man the whole world would come to know the right way to live. He said: *"For I have known him, to the end that he may command his children and his household after him, that they may keep the way of the LORD, to do righteousness and justice; to the end that the LORD may bring on Abraham that which he has spoken of him."* (Genesis 18:19 NHEB.) Before God called Abraham, people had traditions by which they lived. Some of these traditions bordered on idolatry, spiritism and divination, which were a rebellion against God, while others concerned morals and interpersonal relationships. God called Abraham from his traditions and customs and gave him and his descendants a new way of life. However, He permitted and instituted in the law certain traditions which were acceptable to Him until He perfected His salvation plan for the world.

Genesis 38:6–11 records the death of Judah's first and second sons. The first son, Er, died by God's judgement after committing an unnamed evil. Er died without a child and his brother Onan was supposed to marry his wife, Tamar. According to their tradition, the first son of Onan and Tamar was to be named for Er. This practice would ensure that the dead brother's name was carried on by the son who would be his heir. If we scale this tradition with the knowledge Christ has revealed to us, the tradition is not binding on the New Testament believers. Yet God responded to the wickedness that was done by Onan in desecrating that tradition. Onan took advantage of the provisions in the tradition to gratify his sexual desires with his brother's wife without an intention to fulfil his responsibility to his dead brother, so God took his life as well. Although the tradition was not originally commanded by God, it was later institutionalised by Him as a law for the Israelites. *"If brothers dwell together, and one of them die, and have no son, the wife of the dead shall not be married outside to a stranger: her husband's brother shall go in to her, and take her to him as wife, and perform the duty of a husband's brother to her. ⁶It shall be, that the firstborn whom she bears shall succeed in the name of his brother who is dead, that his name not be blotted out of Israel."* (Deuteronomy 25:5–6 NHEB.)

Today, there are traditions in practice in many parts of the world that are not scriptural yet are not contrary to God's word. As long as a tradition does not contradict God's word we can identify with it. However, some traditions put us against God and lead us to do those things God has warned us not to do. We should avoid any tradition that requires us to revere any deity apart from the one true God, or that encourages injustice, barbarism and immoral conduct. Christians, therefore, should be careful to have a good understanding of the intent of traditional practices wherever they find themselves. In times of ignorance, God overlooked (Acts 17:30–31), but we cannot hide behind the cloak of ignorance anymore, for the truth has been revealed to us. It is better to reject the traditions of men than to disobey the commands of God. During His earthly ministry, Jesus emphasised the importance of God's word over men's traditions. *"He said to them, "Full well do you reject the commandment of God, that you may keep your tradition. ¹⁰For Moses said, 'Honor your father and your mother;' and, 'Anyone who speaks evil of father or mother, let him be put to death.' ¹¹But you say, 'If anyone tells his father or mother, "Whatever profit you might have received from me is Corban, that is to say, given to God;"' ¹²then you no longer allow him to do anything for his father or his mother, ¹³making void the word of God by your tradition, which you have handed down. You do many things like this.""* (Mark 7:9–13 NHEB.)

Jesus' teachings set a template by which we can screen and discard every tradition which poses a danger to our salvation. The following questions are important in determining the interface or crossing point between Christianity and our traditions: does the tradition make unbelievers mock our profession as Christians? Do we trivialise any command of God by adhering to the tradition? Does the practice measure up to Jesus' standard for our soul's salvation? If a young believer joins us in that practice, will it pose any danger to his salvation? When we answer these questions honestly the traditions that matter will stand out. When traditions help our hearts to draw near to the living God and are tools for living rightly, they are acceptable. But when they distract our hearts from God's real purpose or the faithful adoration and worship of God, it is necessary to re-evaluate and desist from practising or giving our consent to such. If we trade the truth about God for the images manufactured in human minds, or make void the word of God, we will lose the most valuable thing – the salvation of our souls.

Christians have a different tradition from the world and this tradition is founded in Christ. When we become born again, our lifestyles must conform to our newfound life in Christ, and those practices of the world which are not in conformity with the word of God must be disregarded. Ephesians 4:21–24 says: *"if indeed you heard him, and were taught in him, even as truth is in Jesus: ^{22} that you put away, as concerning your former way of life, the old self, that grows corrupt after the lusts of deceit; ^{23} and that you be renewed in the spirit of your mind, ^{24} and put on the new self, who in the likeness of God has been created in righteousness and holiness of truth."* (NHEB.)

To obey Jesus' command of making disciples of all nations, we would have to move across ethnic groups. Hence, to make people from different ethnic groups become followers of Jesus as we travel to other parts of the world, we will have to learn about their cultures and practise those that conform to God's word. Apostle Paul practised this principle as recorded in 1 Corinthians 9:19–23: *"For though I was free from all, I brought myself under bondage to all, that I might gain the more. ^{20} To the Jews I became as a Jew, that I might gain Jews; to those who are under the law, as under the law, not being myself under the law, that I might gain those who are under the law; ^{21} to those who are without law, as without law (not being*

without law toward God, but under law toward Christ), that I might win those who are without law. ²²To the weak I became as weak, that I might gain the weak. I have become all things to all people, that I may by all means save some. ²³Now I do all things for the sake of the Good News, that I may be a joint partaker of it."
(NHEB.) As occasion demanded, he became like a Jew, like a Gentile or like the weak for one purpose: to make more disciples for Christ – without going against the word of God. Practising our host communities' traditions is one act of love that can influence them to come to Christ, provided such traditions are not against God's word.

When we go to places where the people still hold on to unwholesome traditions we should not treat them as outcasts. We who have seen the light and known the truth should reach out to them with love to show them the light of the gospel of Christ by the life we live and the preaching of the word of God with emphasis on salvation. Christians have the responsibility to shine as lights for others to see the right path. It is essential to pass on God's standards to future generations; therefore, our responsibility is to correct the wrong we see in our traditions. This should be done with care and the wisdom of God.

TOPIC 3: JUDAH, TAMAR AND THE MESSIANIC LINE

GENESIS 38:11–30

Look at some of the most precious stones and metals, beautiful and worth fortunes. Now, take a step back and ask them about their journey. Those charming pieces would tell you they came from the earth's dirt and places ordinary eyes would not see. Many of their kinds are still wallowing there; some could be exposed already, but people do not know what they can become down the line. As they become jewellery or ornaments, no one dare put dirt close to them. However, they cannot wish away the fact that they had dirt in their lineage. Some people would see the filth accompanying Judah and Tamar's story as a smear on the posterity of Judah, to which Christ belongs. It is a lesson that God can make us into what He purposes, irrespective of our lineage or past.

Judah had three sons and the first married Tamar. Because of his wickedness, God killed this first son and at the time of his death he was without a son. The second son had to marry Tamar according to tradition. God also killed him for sleeping with Tamar with the wicked intention of ensuring that Tamar did not become pregnant. Judah held back his last son and deceitfully told Tamar to go back to her father's house and wait for the boy to grow up. Judah's action was based on the fear that his third son might die as his brothers had done. When the boy grew up, Tamar realised that Judah did not intend for his last son to marry her so disguised herself as a commercial sex worker and tricked Judah into impregnating her. This widow of two brothers, who had no offspring, gave birth to twins through her father-in-law. One of those twins was Perez, from whom King David descended, and from David's lineage came Jesus. *"A record of the genealogy of Jesus Christ, the son of David, the son of Abraham. [2] Abraham was the father of Isaac, and Isaac the father of Jacob, and Jacob the father of Judah and his brothers, [3] and Judah was the father of Perez and Zerah by Tamar, and Perez was the father of Hezron, and Hezron the father of Ram"* (Matthew 1:1–3 NHEB).

This story of Judah and Tamar is smeared with deceit and counter-deceit. Many people would be quick to condemn Tamar for sleeping with her father-in-law to conceive. Judah would not be guiltless either because of his deceit, insensitivity and rash judgement and no excuse would be suitable to exonerate them from blame. In Tamar's days, 'playing the prostitute' as a betrothed woman was punishable by death; if Tamar had been found to have slept with someone other than Judah she would have been killed. Considering this, you would understand that if Jesus' ancestry were to be determined by human beings people like Tamar would not even be shortlisted, but God overlooked the mud surrounding her story. Tamar and Perez would later be referred to in prayers and blessings. The people of Bethlehem blessed Boaz and Ruth thus: *"Let your house be like the house of*

Perez, whom Tamar bore to Judah, because of the offspring which the LORD shall give you of this young woman." (Ruth 4:12 NHEB.)

Tamar's story is not an encouragement for us to resolve challenges with sinful methods, nor are we to follow Judah's example of deceit and of having a casual sexual relationship. It is reassurance that if God can allow Christ to come through Judah and Tamar's line, our not-so-clean lineage and past ceases to matter in Christ. Know that if someone reneges on their promise to us, as Judah did to Tamar, we must not act contrary to God's word in seeking redress. Instead, it is better to suffer loss financially, emotionally or materially than to shipwreck our faith and risk losing our soul's salvation. *"For it is commendable if someone endures pain, suffering unjustly, because of conscience toward God. [20] For what glory is it if, when you sin, you patiently endure beating? But if, when you do well, you patiently endure suffering, this is commendable with God."* (1 Peter 2:19–20 NHEB.)

People can struggle with their past; it can haunt their consciences and make them think they are undeserving of anything good. We must know that whatever our history God can still build a purposeful and marvellous future from it. Whatever your story, if you accept Christ as Lord and Saviour, old things are past: *"Therefore if anyone is in Christ, he is a new creation. The old things have passed away. Look, new things have come."* (2 Corinthians 5:17 NHEB.)

Paul was one of those who persecuted the church but today we all know him as one of the foremost apostles. In his writing to Timothy he attributed his calling as an apostle to God's mercies: *"And I thank him who enabled me, Christ Jesus our Lord, because he counted me faithful, appointing me to service; [13] although I was before a blasphemer, a persecutor, and insolent. However, I obtained mercy, because I did it ignorantly in unbelief. [14] The grace of our Lord abounded exceedingly with faith and love which is in Christ Jesus.*

¹⁵ The saying is faithful and worthy of all acceptance, that Christ Jesus came into the world to save sinners; of whom I am chief. ¹⁶ However, for this cause I obtained mercy, that in me first, Jesus Christ might display all his patience, for an example of those who were going to believe in him for everlasting life." (1 Timothy 1:12–16 NHEB.)

To be used by God requires us to be born again – to leave our sinful lives behind and make ourselves available for Him. Through our Lord Jesus Christ, the grace of God is exceedingly abundant for the forgiveness of our sins and for our salvation. Romans 5:20–21 says: *"where sin abounded, grace abounded more exceedingly; ²¹ that as sin reigned in death, even so grace might reign through righteousness to everlasting life through Jesus Christ our Lord."* (NHEB.) Grace is not a licence to sin. Instead, it gives us the opportunity to start afresh in obedience to God. It restores what sin had stolen. No matter how grievous our sins might seem, if we come to Jesus with contrite hearts He will be gracious to us and forgive all our sins. 1 John 1:9 says: *"If we confess our sins, he is faithful and righteous to forgive us the sins, and to cleanse us from all unrighteousness."* (NHEB.)

God is always ready to transform our lives if we submit to Him; our past does not matter. He can remake us into new beings prepared for noble purposes. Today there is hope for people with questionable backgrounds because God can make a valuable servant out of anyone, regardless of their lineage or past, and give everyone a glorious future. When we come to Christ we should not give our background a chance to hinder our purpose in God.

TOPIC 4: RASH JUDGEMENT

GENESIS 38:12–26

Rash judgement is drawing conclusions on a matter without careful consideration of the information or evidence available.

Here is Judah, condemning a woman to death for an act of prostitution in which he was an accomplice. After his wife's demise Judah had gone up to Timnah to shear his sheep. There, he had an affair with Tamar, his daughter-in-law, who disguised herself as a prostitute. Judah had sent Tamar to her parent's house under the guise of making her wait for Shelah, his youngest son, to grow up. But in reality he was cunningly dismissing her to prevent Shelah from dying as his other brothers. The next he heard of Tamar was when he was told she was pregnant. Interestingly, Judah felt entitled to express his grievance that his daughter-in-law had become pregnant through prostitution, neglecting his error in reneging on his promise to marry Tamar to his youngest son. That was why Tamar played the prostitute – she took matters into her own hands.

Judah wanted Tamar to be killed but his verdict was rash. When the event leading to the pregnancy unfolded, ***"Judah acknowledged them, and said, "She is more righteous than I, because I did not give her to Shelah, my son.""*** (Genesis 38:26 NHEB.) What if the daughter-in-law did not have evidence of her sexual affair with him? Judah would have demanded Tamar be killed for an offence to which he was an accomplice. Standing at the pinnacle of Judah's wrong attitude towards Tamar was his error in not asking Tamar's side of the story.

How often do we inadvertently make rash judgements, making assumptions when we really know nothing about others or their situations? We sometimes go as far as to treat them poorly as a kind of punishment or create stringent rules they must follow because of our rash judgement of their behaviour, while claiming our actions are right. If we can be considerate and patient and verify information or analyse situations we will save ourselves from the error of making rash judgements.

The error of rash judgement may leave us with immense regret, which will haunt us in the long run. Naturally, everyone wants to be treated well; we want people to forgive us when we err. We expect people to consider our circumstances and understand why we make certain decisions or take specific actions. We also desire others to treat us as humans, even though we are full of imperfections. Yet we are not in the habit of extending the same gesture to others. Jesus said in Matthew 7:12, *"Therefore whatever you desire for people to do to you, do also to them; for this is the Law and the Prophets."* (NHEB.) If we expect others to forgive us, overlook our errors and tolerate our weaknesses we should endeavour to do the same to others.

Love should be the deciding factor that rules our decisions. When we allow love to reside in the confine of our hearts, our reaction towards the wrong done to us or evil reports about others will be tempered with compassion. We will give the benefit of the doubt rather than condemn. Our judgement will be such that it is not only devoid of rashness but also of bias. Often, incomplete or false information about a person is disseminated just to defame the person's character or by a sheer act of gossip, especially in our modern society, in which information dissemination is speedy and easy. We risk condemning ourselves before God if we rush to a conclusion without proper investigation and analysis of the situation.

If we compare Judah's action to that of Joseph concerning Mary, the mother of Jesus, we will find a contrasting character on display. Judah was quick to pass judgement on Tamar, but in Joseph's case we see how much consideration he gave to Mary's welfare. If Joseph had been rash in judging Mary he would have exposed her to public disgrace. Instead, he planned to send her away discreetly for her protection. That was not all: before he took his final action the Bible records that *"he thought about these things…"* (Matthew 1:20 NHEB.) It was during this period of thinking that an angel appeared to him to give him further direction.

Joseph's attitude in this case is a standard we should aspire to. Joseph kept room for love, no matter how hurt he might have felt. We must learn not to be rash in passing verdicts. Instead, in love, we should look to our interests and the interest of others: *"each of you not just looking to his own things, but each of you also to the things of others."* (Philippians 2:4 NHEB.)

Outside of love are hatred and a judgemental spirit. Without love, we are liable to get caught up in the wind of rash judgement. We should, therefore, uphold love as our banner and let it guide us into making the best decisions at all times.

CHAPTER 14

TOPIC 1: THE EFFECT OF A CHRISTIAN'S PRESENCE

GENESIS 39:1–23

One distinctive characteristic of a child of God is the positive impact he makes wherever he finds himself. As lights of the world, children of God possess the illuminating capacity to beam their light anywhere they tread. But this light can only be illuminated when we act in consonance with the word of God.

Joseph was a light in Potiphar's house, the prison and in the whole of Egypt. His presence made a positive difference everywhere he found himself. Two factors played their parts in this. First, the favour of God was on him. Second, he was diligent and trustworthy in carrying out his duties. The effect of this perfect combination was the physical manifestation of God's blessings upon Joseph's work, which did not go unnoticed by his master: *"His master saw that the LORD was with him, and that the LORD made all that he did prosper in his hand."* (Genesis 39:3 NHEB.) A few decades before this time, a similar observation was made about his father, Jacob, while serving in Laban's house. *"Laban said to him, "If now I have found favor in your eyes, stay here, for I have divined that the LORD has blessed me for your sake.""* (Genesis 30:27 NHEB.) Thus, just as God blessed Laban on Jacob's account, so was Potiphar a beneficiary of God's blessings due to Joseph's presence. To serve as a positive influence, to spread God's blessing in our workplace or community, we need to embrace the habit of diligence.

The effect of our presence as Christians can only be felt when the presence of God is within us. The presence of God cannot be with a person who resorts to compromise when a sinful opportunity to improve living conditions presents itself. Joseph feared and acknowledged God in everything he did and God's presence was with him. The effect of a Christian's presence is not measured by material gains but by his fear of God reflected in his general conduct. We stand out because of the presence of God in our lives. But we will only have this presence if we seek Him. Azariah said to King Asa in 2 Chronicles 15:2, *"The LORD is with you, while you are with him; and if you seek him, he will be found by you; but if you forsake him, he will forsake you."* (NHEB.)

When the Lord is with us we can make a difference in any environment we find ourselves. Our lifestyles can make people testify that indeed God is with us. Like Joseph, we have the first part covered – the favour of God upon us. But the second part of diligence and commitment is entirely up to us. Wherever we find ourselves there should be a difference. We should be known and respected for our godly virtues such as patience, truthfulness, love, self-control and fairness. We are not to engage in unhealthy competitions nor exhibit eye service. *"Be careful that you do not do your righteousness before people, to be seen by them, or else you have no reward from your Father who is in heaven."* (Matthew 6:1 NHEB.) Dedication to our work should be out of reverence for the Lord. Apostle Paul wrote: *"And whatever you do, work heartily, as for the Lord, and not for people, [24]knowing that from the Lord you will receive the reward of the inheritance; for you serve the Lord Christ."* (Colossians 3:23–24 NHEB.)

Most believers desire God's blessing yet abandon the responsibility that would bring that blessing to fruition and also make them a blessing to others. Such people engage in a marathon of prayer yet make laziness a perpetual habit. They expect maximum pay with minimum effort or promotion from their employers, which is unmerited, then accuse God of turning deaf ears to their prayers when their expectations are not met. Proverbs 10:26 says: *"As vinegar to the teeth, and as smoke to the eyes, so is the sluggard to those who send him."* (NHEB.) Rather than illuminating their work environment with God's blessings and a godly lifestyle, such people remain dormant because of their laziness and nonchalance. We cannot experience the manifestation of the power of God if we neglect playing our part.

It must be understood that slothfulness portrays a negative example of Christians to unbelievers. If we continuously indulge our eyes in sleep or engage our mouth in a verbal joyride, what kind of character will we portray to people other than a negative one? It is then binding on us to demonstrate a work ethic that exemplifies commitment, industriousness and proactiveness and that fosters reliability. All these qualities distinguished Joseph and made him exude positivity. This earned him the confidence of Potiphar, who entrusted the care of his house to him, of the prison keeper, who entrusted the prison responsibilities to him, and of Pharaoh, who entrusted the governance of Egypt to him.

While it is admirable to be pious in our lifestyles we cannot positively influence an environment because we merely profess to be Christians. Like Joseph, we too have a role to play by being diligent in carrying out responsibilities. The effect of our presence should be such that people will look at us and acknowledge our heavenly Father.

(For More on The Effect of a Christian's Presence see Chapter 5, Topic 4)

TOPIC 2: THE RIGHT KIND OF FEAR

GENESIS 39:7–9

Man was created as a pure being and functioned in harmony with God's will and purpose. Man's first recorded expression of fear came after his disobedience and, thus, he ran from God instead of approaching Him for help. Adam said to God in the cool of that fateful day: *"I heard your voice in the garden, and I was afraid, because I was naked; and I hid myself."* (Genesis 3:10 NHEB.)

In our walk with God, the right kind of fear makes us obey God and live our lives to please Him. This is reverential fear. But there are kinds of fear that could make us sin against God or run away from Him instead of going to Him. Fear of others is one of the common factors that lead human beings into sinning against God. The fear of tomorrow leads many to steal and covet to secure a better future for themselves; the fear of harm leads many to turn to other gods for protection; the fear of punishment leads many to deny the truth. All these are dishonouring to God. However, when someone stands out in integrity and refuses to sin against God out of fear, God takes cognisance of that person.

Not many slaves would ignore the risk of directly rejecting Potiphar's wife's persuasion in the way that Joseph did. Many would accept her persuasive suggestion. But Joseph would rather fear God than his master's wife. Joseph was respectful to her as the mistress of the house; he stated that although he had liberties in the house, those liberties did not extend to her. Joseph told her that the reason he was rejecting her sexual advances was his fear of God: *"How then can I do this great wickedness, and sin against God?"* (Genesis 39:9 NHEB.) By implication, Joseph showed that he respected men but honoured and feared God; he could have easily said, "What if we get caught" and Potiphar's wife would have given him a million assurances on how and why they would not. His decision showed he feared God more than man; this is spiritual maturity.

Sin should be viewed as disobedience against God; societal opinions of evil acts are secondary. It is wrong to first see sin in the light of what people say or what physical punishment it will attract. The right kind of fear is the one that motivates us to take action that is honouring to God and reject any suggestion that leads us to disobey Him: *"To man he said, 'Look, the fear of the Lord, that is wisdom. To depart from evil is understanding.'"* (Job 28:28 NHEB.)

Either we fear God and face rejection and punishment by man or fear man and risk our salvation. The fear of God should inspire a child of God to refuse sin, even if that means standing against the most powerful people. It was the fear of God that made men like Peter and other disciples face powerful men in their time and say boldly: *"We must obey God rather than people."* (Acts 5:29 NHEB.)

Many have refrained from sinning for all the wrong fears. The fear of punishment and the shame of being caught is what keeps some from stealing; others are faithful partners because they fear divorce if found out. There are many more such fears. If these reasons are the foundation on which someone bases their abstention from sin, that is not holiness. When those reasons no more present themselves, the person falls like a pack of cards.

If we display the wrong kind of fear towards sin, we give the devil the opportunity to convince us to sin. When we refuse to steal money because we could get caught, the devil will present us with a method to go about it without being caught. When we refuse to fornicate because of pregnancy, the devil will quickly suggest different methods of contraception. Losing fellowship with God is worse than any other consequence a child of God will experience due to sin. When David realised his sin in the case of Bathsheba, after Nathan's confrontation, it was not the punishment he was afraid of but the loss of fellowship with God. He wrote in his psalm: *"Do not throw me from your presence, and do not take your holy Spirit from me. [12]Restore to me the joy of your salvation. Uphold me with a willing spirit."* (Psalm 51:11–12 NHEB.)

For many people death is their greatest fear, but the fear of God should free us from that. Jesus came to deliver those in bondage of the fear of death. Hebrews 2:15 says, *"and might deliver all of them who through fear of death were all their lifetime subject to bondage."* (NHEB.) If you are still struggling with the fear of man, death or physical consequences of sin over the fear of God, Christ is the way of freedom from that bondage. Submit yourself to Him, purge your heart and mind with the word of God, and Christ will give you the power to say "No" to sin, not because you are afraid of man or death, but because of your love for God.

TOPIC 3: HANDLING SEDUCTION

GENESIS 39:7–20

"My son, if sinners entice you, do not consent." (Proverbs 1:10 NHEB.)

It is natural to have a sexual urge but it is a sin to satisfy it through ungodly means. Couples can satisfy their sexual cravings within the confines of marriage, while the singles must exercise self-control till their marriage. Doing otherwise by whatever means or for whatever reason is sinful.

The case of Joseph and Potiphar's wife is a story of two characters with conflicting interests. Whereas Joseph desired to honour God in everything, his mistress's interest was to gratify her desire, not minding who was hurt or dishonoured by her act. As a handsome young man, Joseph caught Potiphar's wife's lustful attention. She attempted to seduce Joseph to commit adultery to satisfy her sexual urge, but Joseph consistently declined. This led her to resort to force, which eventually resulted in blackmail and Joseph's imprisonment. Joseph had eliminated any weakness that might lead him to cave in to her seduction by placing God first. Note his initial response: *"How then can I do this great wickedness, and sin against God?"* (Genesis 39:9 NHEB.) Because of the fear of God, there was an extra strength within him to overcome and suppress the inordinate desire that would have led him to sin against God; nothing could have possibly changed his mind.

Joseph knew how to win the war against seduction, leaving a model for us to follow in handling seduction whenever it occurs. He considered God bigger and greater than anyone or anything. He also applied the ultimate caution of fleeing in the face of sexual immorality. Apostle Paul stated this principle in 1 Corinthians 6:18 as a precautionary measure against sexual immorality, saying: ***"Flee sexual immorality. "Every sin that a person does is outside the body," but he who commits sexual immorality sins against his own body."*** (NHEB.) Through experience we have realised that sin generally becomes offensive and disgusting to us when God is paramount and His word is the reason for our actions. Seduction loses power when we see God as more precious and deserving of our reverence and His word as true and worthy of our obedience. When God is our priority sin is relegated to nothing and will eventually find its way out of a life which does not accord it recognition.

Seduction to various forms of sexual immorality is not scarce, be it at our homes, workplaces, churches, schools, social gatherings and even on social media. To overcome it will require self-discipline and, most importantly, godly fear with knowledge of the word of God. In our complex society, wisdom is requisite in handling seduction, for the Bible says, ***"The fear of the LORD is the beginning of wisdom…"*** (Proverbs 9:10 NHEB.) Without God, there is no human wisdom or philosophy that can stand the test of time or tame the fickle nature of man.

Handling seduction begins with handling oneself – self-discipline. Joseph had self-discipline and it held him firmly rooted in godly principles, to the extent of risking his life for it. Without self-discipline, man will be unable to draw a line between humour and propriety and may have no boundary for closeness with the opposite sex. Sometimes people use gifts, flattery and niceness as tools of seduction, but all these would not work against a child of God who has first learnt to overcome his flesh by subjecting it to the will of God.

Self-discipline also entails saying "no" and standing by it, no matter the pressure or persistence of others. Our conviction concerning sexual immorality should not be swayed by anything nor weakened over time. Potiphar's wife did not try to seduce Joseph just once, and Joseph did not say "no" just once. His first "no" remained "no" to the end. She kept trying, but Joseph kept refusing. Note this: *"she spoke to Joseph day by day..."* (Genesis 39:10 NHEB.) We need to be resilient against all forms of seduction because the seducer might not give up when we say "no" the first time. When you give room for a bit of compromise you will be vulnerable and exposed. Samson gave up the source of his strength due to Delilah's persistence. *"It happened, when she pressed him daily with her words, and urged him, that his soul was troubled to death. ¹⁷He told her all his heart..."* (Judges 16:16–17 NHEB.) If we cannot act swiftly by fleeing from seduction we may eventually be defeated due to excessive pressure.

Leaving the seduction environment – such as the workplace or any other place that links a person and the seducer – may sometimes be necessary if your refusal and respectful rebuke are without effect. To a slave such as Joseph leaving the job was not feasible; even so, he fled from the woman.

It also takes self-discipline not to be an object of seduction by consciously selecting the kind of thoughts we permit to settle in our minds, our choice of dressing, our way of life and the choice of our words when communicating. To have self-control we must order our steps with the word of God with emphasis on salvation, disapproving those things contrary to God's word or inconsistent with the Christian faith. Self-control is a fruit of the Spirit and is brought to life by obedience to the word of God.

With God is the power to overcome sin, and in His word is the means to live blamelessly. When we rely on the word of God for direction it will keep us from sinning against God. The psalmist wrote: *"In my heart I have hidden your word, that I might not sin against you."* (Psalm 119:11 NHEB.)

Joseph went to prison because of his stance and we may sometimes suffer loss or damage in standing firm for God. Nevertheless, we should be comforted by God's promise for overcomers: *"He who overcomes will be arrayed in white garments, and I will in no way blot his name out of the book of life, and I will confess his name before my Father, and before his angels."* (Revelation 3:5 NHEB.) Life is a battleground on which we face temptations to sin daily, and we are expected to overcome them. God has given us all we need to overcome and, therefore, we must not allow temptation or persecution to rob us of our salvation.

CHAPTER 15

TOPIC 1: STRENGTH OF CHARACTER IN ADVERSITY

GENESIS 40:1–8

A person's character is a combination of those distinctive internal qualities that make them different from others; these qualities reflect actions, reactions and feelings. A person's character can be seen or analysed by using their behaviour. People could display deceptive behaviours to mislead others – for instance, a miser giving money ostentatiously. But like a mirage those perceptions disappear as we draw near and a person's true character eventually unveils on closer observation or in tough seasons. Adversity is usually one of those conditions that test someone's strength of character, the consistency of a person's behaviour over time, irrespective of the circumstances.

Adversity brings out a person's true character. Just as the strength of a brand of car can be tested by exposing its prototype to high-speed crashes, tough climatic conditions and other harsh conditions, the strength of someone's character is, most of the time, best determined in adversity. For instance, faith and obedience, which form part of a believer's character, can remain as mere verbal confessions until adversity shows up.

There are some afflictions in life that God, in His sovereignty, will remove from our path, and there are others we will have to persevere through by His grace. Affliction can either refine us, make us spiritually mature or ruin our characters: *"If you falter in the time of trouble, your strength is small."* (Proverbs 24:10 NHEB.)

Joseph stands as a model for Christians passing through trials. At a young age he was denied the comfort of his home and his father's love because he was sold to slavery by his brothers. While in slavery he was falsely accused and sent to prison because of his faithfulness to God in refusing to sleep with his master's wife. It must have seemed at that point that all had gone from bad to worse for him. What is noteworthy is that Joseph never sinned, and the presence of the Lord was with him all through the severe challenges he faced. Rather than cave in to the enticement of sexual pleasure or do a 180-degree spin to a life of sin, he demonstrated strength of character by refusing to act against God's word or crumbling under the weight of adversity.

The peace and calm Joseph expressed in trying times is what God gives to those who trust in Him: *"You will keep him in peace, in peace whose thoughts are fixed on you, because he trusts in you."* (Isaiah 26:3 NHEB.) Joseph's calm in prison made him think less about himself and more about others, and as a prisoner he became a source of encouragement to his fellow inmates. This was why he became concerned when he saw the sad countenance of the king's officials. In truth, Joseph could have allowed himself to be crushed by the weight of depression and despair, transferred aggression and bitterness at his fellow inmates or directed the multitude of blames on God, concluding that holiness was not rewarding after all. But he did not. Instead, during what could be considered one of the lowest points in his life, Joseph demonstrated admirable concern for and responsibility towards his fellow inmates' welfare. Had Joseph allowed the circumstances surrounding him to affect his disposition towards life he would have missed the opportunity life presented to him to interpret those officials' dreams that led to his interpretation of Pharoah's dream, which later led him to become second-in-command in Egypt.

There is the tendency for one to throw away all godly virtues and become disgruntled, bitter and angry at God and everyone around him, to use affliction as an excuse to sin or to embrace the path of sin as an escape route. But on the contrary Christians are to learn to be courageous, submit their will to God's sovereign will and be resolute in faithfulness, to trust God and maintain the strength of their character amid severe adversity rather than cave in to the pressure of affliction. James 1:2–4 admonishes, *"Count it all joy, my brothers, when you encounter various trials, ³knowing that the testing of your faith produces endurance. ⁴Let endurance have its perfect work, that you may be perfect and complete, lacking in nothing."* (NHEB.) It is easy to find people joyful and spiritually sensitive when all is going well, but those qualities tend to dwindle in challenging situations. Just as Jesus, though the Son of God, learnt obedience by the things He suffered, we ought to learn to obey God perfectly under the pressures of affliction. A man's character is unreliable and feeble until it has been tried in the furnace of affliction.

It is common to see people drowning in the sea of adversity when the storms of life rise against them. For instance, being falsely indicted in a fraudulent practice at a workplace could introduce adversity that could render an individual jobless or cause them to be imprisoned. It is the kind of situation that could make one cleave to depression and resentment. And when there seems to be no light at the end of the tunnel, the possibility of acting against God's word becomes more likely. At this point, a person ought to demonstrate the right attitude to avoid falling into the pit of disobedience. In showing the kind of attitude characterised by unwavering strength, resilience and integrity in the face of adversity, our strength of character is proven. It is essential to establish the fact that adversity is inevitable in life. Rather than view adversity as a punishment or as unfairness we should see it as a sequence of events working harmoniously for our best interest. Romans 8:28 says, *"We know that all things work together for good for those who love God, to those who are called according to his purpose."* (NHEB.) Therefore, we will be able to remain undaunted and uncompromising in the face of challenges when we repose our trust in God.

We cannot successfully navigate the waves of adversity if we allow our circumstances to overwhelm us and affect our relationship with Christ. Just as Joseph refused to allow his circumstances to affect his obedience to God, the strength of our character as God's children is proven when we make choices and exhibit behaviours that align with God's word. Only when we study God's word – the Bible – with emphasis on salvation will we find the strength to remain undaunted, uncompromising and unwavering in times of adversity. Our knowledge of God and our relationship with Him based on that knowledge determines the strength of our character. Someone with poor knowledge of God who does not have a strong relationship with Him will not mind fluctuating between integrity today and compromise tomorrow. Daniel 11:32 says, *"but the people who know their God shall be strong, and take action."* (NHEB.) Daniel prophesied concerning a man of lawlessness who would seduce with flatteries; only the people who know their God shall be firm in character to resist such flatteries.

Jesus, in Matthew 7:24–27, using the illustration about two men who built their houses – one on a rock and the other on the sand – taught us that if we follow His teachings we will remain steadfast in the face of adversities. *"Everyone therefore who hears these words of mine, and does them, will be compared to a wise man, who built his house on a rock. ²⁵And the rain came down, the floods came, and the winds blew, and beat on that house; and it did not fall, for it was founded on the rock. ²⁶And everyone who hears these words of mine, and does not do them will be like a foolish man, who built his house on the sand. ²⁷And the rain came down, the floods came, and the winds blew, and beat on that house; and it fell—and great was its fall."* (NHEB.) The storms and the rains revealed the strength of both houses. We are admonished to be like the wise man who built his house on the rock by rooting ourselves in the word of God without compromise, for only then can we overcome the storms of life.

TOPIC 2: DREAMS AND INTERPRETATION

GENESIS 40:5–22

*W*hat started as an exchange of words between two friends soon degenerated into a fierce fight. Apart from insults hurled at each other, injuries were grievously inflicted. When onlookers finally succeeded in stopping the fight, it was discovered that one of them had accused the other of attacking her in her dream the previous night. She confronted her friend the following morning and accused her of sorcery; the result was an embarrassing scene. Without fully understanding the principles of dreams, interpretations and applications, people are bound to get confused. (Johnny, 2022.)

A dream is a series of images in a person's mind during sleep akin to the mind imagining things during waking hours. The mind frequently comes up with a series of images and events during sleep; this is a natural phenomenon.

Sometimes God steps into the natural process of dreams and makes someone have dreams that are not the workings of the mind. God does this, sometimes, to provide solutions to challenges or give directions, instructions or messages about future events. Satan can also send dreams to people, just as he sends thought waves into human minds.

In the passage, two imprisoned servants of Pharaoh had dreams that were quite disturbing. The dreams turned out to be messages about future events. Joseph, who was endowed with the gift of interpretation of dreams, interpreted their dreams. From Joseph's statement: *"Do not interpretations belong to God?..."* (Genesis 40:8 NHEB), we see that interpretation of dreams belongs to God, but that He can use men to help people who need His help in that way. As it turned out, the interpretations Joseph gave the two prisoners were accurate. Typically, many dreams which carry messages make the dreamers worried if they do not have the interpretations of their dreams. However, with interpretation comes an understanding of what the dream stands for.

In the Old Testament God ministered to people through dreams and visions and especially to the prophets. Daniel was one of the prophets God endowed with the divine ability to interpret dreams: *"Now as for these four youths, God gave them knowledge and skill in all learning and wisdom: and Daniel had understanding in all visions and dreams."* (Daniel 1:17 NHEB.) Today, the Holy Spirit is resident in every believer and ministers directly to them. God chooses whichever way He wishes to relay a message to His children. It could be through dreams or any other means. When we dream and such a dream is a message God wants us to understand, the Holy Spirit will guide us to understand the dream's meaning. Therefore, we should not be worried about the dreams we do not understand but commit them to God in prayers for Him to take control. However, if we are close to a believer whom we know to have the gift of interpretation of dreams, it is not out of place to seek counsel regarding our dreams. But if we do not know any such person, we should be contented to commit the dream to God.

Prophet Joel in Joel 2:28 prophesied about a time when God would pour out His Spirit upon all flesh. *"And it shall come to pass afterward, that I will pour out my Spirit on all flesh; and your sons and your daughters will prophesy, and your old men will dream dreams, and your young men will see visions."* (NHEB.) That time in which prophet Joel spoke about is now, but it behoves us to be sensitive to the Spirit of God to avoid being victims of wrong interpretations of dreams.

Our understanding of the scripture should influence our reaction toward our dreams. Our knowledge of the word of God helps us know how to subject messages received through prophets, teachers, dreams and all other mediums to scriptural checks and balances. If we have dreams or revelations that require us to go against the word of God we should ignore the dreams or revelations and always obey the word of God. The Bible remains the basic foundation in our relationship with God and the tool to keep ourselves in check.

Giving specific instructions on how to interpret dreams could be misleading. One formula does not fit all. People should be wary of any formula that offers a general interpretation of every possible dream. They should also avoid those formulas that provide a specific interpretation of certain items and their colours, the meaning of certain fruits, the interpretation of seeing people of certain age brackets and other generalisations.

It is possible that dreams, though correctly interpreted, may not come to pass as interpreted. Several factors could be responsible for that. One of the most common factors is intercession. Intercession can change the negative outcome of a dream. Whatever the case may be, we should not be enslaved by dreams and their meanings but should remain steadfast in faith and obedience to God's word.

(For more on Dreams, see Chapter 12 Topic 5)

TOPIC 3: KINDNESS AND EXPECTATION

GENESIS 40:5–23

For many, acts of kindness are like depositing money in a bank or making an investment, with the expectation of getting back what they deposited or even something more. Unfortunately, we often allow ourselves to be embittered by the unfaithfulness of others. We expect so much from humans – to always remember, to be fair, to be honest and to exhibit all virtues – forgetting that man has fallen from the position of perfection. Having expectations from people is not bad; the problem is that humans naturally tend to fail or renege on their commitments. Whenever we face such disappointments bitterness, resentment and pessimism can follow.

In prison, Joseph expressed kindness to prisoners by being concerned about their lives. He did not spend his time in bitterness and self-sorrow over his mistreatment by Potiphar's wife. Instead he created time to interact with other prisoners to find out how they were faring.

His concern over Pharaoh's servants' unease that particular day made them reveal the cause of their sadness to him – they each had a dream but did not understand what it meant. By divine assistance, Joseph was able to interpret their dreams. He requested that the chief butler remember him when he was reinstated and mention him to Pharaoh, stating that he was in prison for no crime and desired to be free. He had wished that the butler would remember him when he left prison, but the Bible records, *"Yet the chief cupbearer did not remember Joseph, but forgot him."* (Genesis 40:23 NHEB.) Note that God's divine arrangement paved the way from the prison for Joseph; it was not really thanks to Pharaoh's butler.

It should be noted that Joseph's request was not a condition for carrying out good deeds for the butler. Kindness is one way of expressing love. As love is pure and selfless, genuine kindness involves lending a hand and expecting nothing in return. If our act of kindness is not done with expectation we are less likely to feel any sense of disappointment if it is not reciprocated or is paid back with evil. We display kindness each time we go out of our way to help others. However, despite the sacrifice we make, those we help can still forget us when we are in need, even when they are in a position to help. Our hope and confidence should always be in God – the rewarder of men. When our hope is in God, we will not be surprised nor feel bad whenever we are repaid with ingratitude or evil for our kindness: *"It is better to take refuge in the LORD, than to put confidence in man."* (Psalm 118:8 NHEB.)

Conditional kindness defeats the essence of kindness. The Shunammite woman showed kindness to Elisha with a pure motive, and God rewarded her. She expressed kindness by taking care of Prophet Elisha whenever he passed by, without expecting favour from him. After some time, Elisha decided to requite the Shunammite woman's kindness by asking what she would want him to do for her. The woman replied that she was contented. When he discovered she did not have a child, he declared to her saying: *"At this season, when the time comes around, you will embrace a son..."* (2 Kings 4:16

CHAPTER 15

NHEB), and God blessed her with a son according to the word of Elisha. Also, Jesus taught us a lesson on kindness using the story of the Good Samaritan. The good Samaritan showed kindness from a compassionate heart to a man who was left half-dead by thieves, with no expectation of kindness in return. Jesus instructed that we emulate such kindness (Luke 10:30-37).

On the other hand, when we receive kindness from others it is wise to appreciate and return it when an opportunity arises, even when the person does not request it. Elisha used the Shunamite woman's childless condition to reciprocate her kindness, and that was an expression of gratitude. However, we should be careful not to be tempted to show kindness only to those who are kind to us, nor to go against the word of God in our bid to show gratitude for some kindness shown to us.

In Luke 17:17–18, Jesus expressed His displeasure at an act of ingratitude from nine lepers who did not return to glorify God after receiving their healing. *"Jesus answered, "Weren't the ten cleansed? But where are the nine? 18 Were there none found who returned to give glory to God, except this stranger?""* (NHEB.) They were not expected to pay for the healing but to show appreciation by returning to give glory to God. We should cultivate an attitude of gratitude to God and give Him the worship and honour He deserves for His kindness and compassionate love towards us by living in obedience to His word.

In conclusion, we should not be discouraged when people we show kindness to forget us or reward our good with evil. Remember the words of Christ: *"love your enemies, and do good, and lend, expecting nothing back; and your reward will be great, and you will be children of the Most High; for he is kind toward the unthankful and evil."* (Luke 6:35 NHEB.) When our actions are based on pleasing God, our expectations will no longer be on man; rather, our expectations will be the treasures reserved for us in heaven. The Bible encourages us in Colossians 3:2: *"Set your mind on the things that are above, not on the things that are on the earth."* (NHEB.)

CHAPTER 16

TOPIC 1: JOSEPH'S ELEVATION: GOD'S INVOLVEMENT

GENESIS 41:1–46

We often slide into misperception, wondering why God allows us to go through phases of trials. Amid trials, our finite minds push us to forget that the infinite God is in control and that His purpose plays a vital role in whatever His children are passing through. His involvement may appear to us in some circumstances as passive, especially when situations appear to be unpleasant, but the reality is that He is very much involved. In some instances He allows events and knits them together to fulfil His purpose for our lives.

While Joseph had to endure a series of unpleasant experiences, God demonstrated His involvement by using all the seemingly unfavourable events to fulfil His plan for him. God's involvement could easily be noticed when Joseph was given a divine revelation of his future through dreams. Just when his brothers thought they could truncate his destiny with their evil plot of murder and malicious act of selling him to slavery, God wove together their deeds like a piece of fabric, sewing every piece into the fulfilment of His plans for Joseph. From Potiphar's wife's false accusation to his wrongful imprisonment, God was with Joseph. God was actively involved in his elevation, from meeting with Pharaoh's servants to his interpretation of Pharaoh's dreams and elevation to second-in-command in Egypt. It signifies the fact that his elevation was not a coincidence but God's orchestration.

"Wait for the end of the story" or "The end will justify or validate" have been age-long sayings. In the affairs of men, God has both an earthly and an eternal plan for our lives. Sometimes He uses the wickedness of people to accomplish that plan and other times He uses another route. Never underestimate the fact that God can use your life's unpleasant experiences for your good, the good of others and for His eternal glory. God sees these events in the broader and higher context of His purpose for His children. We can make the above assertion because that was what Joseph said to his brothers in Genesis 50:20: *"As for you, you meant evil against me, but God meant it for good, to bring to pass, as it is this day, to save many people alive."* (NHEB.)

The detailed narrative of Joseph's life is about God, who guided Joseph through the valley of the shadow of death and landed him with good at the end of the tunnel. This is a reminder to all who look to Him that no matter what they are experiencing, sweet or bitter, good or evil, no matter how long it lasts, they ought to repose their faith in God, ask what He would have them learn and not grumble or be embittered by their unpleasant experiences. God had been in the background acting and though He did not reveal it to Joseph, Joseph kept faith. Let us analyse the event: what would have happened if the king had woken up in the morning and waved the whole dream away, or if his servants had been able to interpret the dream? This is God's hand and not a coincidence. Joseph told Pharaoh, *"Apart from God an answer of peace shall not be given to Pharoah."* (Genesis 41:16 NHEB.) So it was God's involvement that proffered the solution to the king's need, leading to Joseph's promotion.

Joseph's story is a striking illustration of how God's purpose can be found in our difficult situations. Sometimes in our lives things happen that are beyond our control. As children of God we can learn from Joseph. If we could understand that there is a reason for God allowing difficult situations in our lives, we will be able to go through it and become refined and stronger in faith. There is often a misconstruing of God's silence as inactiveness in the face of adversity, which may push us from the mountain of hope to the pit of discouragement. It may make us seek solutions contrary to God's word, which in turn severs our relationship with Him. There are times when it might seem that God is distant or inactive in our lives, but for His children His involvement is never detached or passive. These words of Paul should give us comfort in the face of adversity: *"We know that all things work together for good for those who love God, to those who are called according to his purpose."* (Romans 8:28 NHEB.)

In light of this scripture, the account of Mordecai's elevation in Esther Chapters 7, 8, 9 and 10 is another story that finely illustrates God's involvement in the affairs of those that are His. From the rise of Esther to the position of queen, to the fall of Haman, the handwriting of God was evident in Mordecai's success story. Esther, a Jew, becomes queen in a foreign land. Through her, Mordecai exposes an attempt on the king's life which later plays a role in his elevation. Working behind the scenes we can see the hand of God in using Haman's ploy to destroy Mordecai and the Jews for the good of Mordecai. As a result, Mordecai came to own the very estate of the man who plotted to kill him and won an honoured position in the king's court. Who else can the glory go to if not the Almighty God?

Regardless of how challenging adversities may seem, we must retain our trust in God and not give up. Rather than questioning and blaming God for any unpleasant situation we must trust His will. Like Joseph, who did not act against God's word, we must remain faithful in our relationship with God no matter how good or bad our circumstances might seem. We are not to use the trials we face in life as an excuse to sin against God, and neither are we to embrace sin to escape them. We must remain faithful even if being faithful costs us our lives or deprives us of earthly benefits. If we lose anything for the sake of our faith in God we actually lose nothing.

Joseph's elevation was the handiwork of God and should serve as a reminder that God is very much involved in our lives and is working all things together for our good. So let our hearts' desire be, "Lord, help me to be patient during my times of trial", "Help me to grow wise and strong while I am waiting", "Make me an instrument in your hands", "Enable me to use the lessons I have learnt to keep others from following the wrong steps", "Give me love and patience to wait until your plan for my life is unveiled in your perfect timing."

TOPIC 2: ACKNOWLEDGING GOD

GENESIS 41:15–16

It is a common proclivity for a natural man to haughtily ascribe his achievements or ability to do certain things to himself. In contrast, a spiritual man with a humble spirit recognises his limitations. With a grateful heart he acknowledges God as the source of whatever he is, whatever he can do or whatever he has done. This was the mentality of Apostle Paul when he duly acknowledged God, saying: *"by the grace of God I am what I am. His grace which was bestowed on me was not futile, but I worked more than all of them; yet not I, but the grace of God which was with me."* (1 Corinthians 15:10 NHEB.)

Joseph came to a point in his life at which he had the opportunity to choose between ascribing his ability to interpret dreams to God or self. Joseph chose the former over the latter, thereby acknowledging God. Under what circumstance did this happen? Pharaoh had two dreams, the kind of dreams that overwhelmed his spirit with perturbation. He was at his wits' end. He did not know how his dreams could be deciphered, especially when the hope of getting the interpretation through the magicians and wise men was dashed. Amid his nervousness, the chief butler raised Pharaoh's hopes when he recommended Joseph to him as a man with the ability to interpret dreams.

Joseph's response when brought to Pharaoh is worth emulating by all and sundry. In the first part of his response he recognised his limitation and inability to interpret Pharaoh's dreams. He understood that he could have no spiritual capability to interpret any dream without God. By this, Joseph silenced any pride that might want to rear its ugly head in his human nature. He refused to assign to himself credit that belonged to God. The other part of Joseph's response ascribed all glory to God. He said, *"Apart from God an answer of peace shall not be given to Pharoah."* (Genesis 41:16 NHEB.) Joseph acknowledged God as the One who would interpret Pharaoh's dreams rather than himself. Acknowledging God in this manner demonstrated his total reliance on God in using him as a vessel to interpret Pharaoh's dreams.

It takes a degree of humility for the gifted or anointed ones to recognise that they can do nothing without God. A person may be endowed with the gift of interpretation of dreams; however, unless the Holy Spirit reveals the meaning of any dream to them, they will by themselves do nothing whatsoever. When King Nebuchadnezzar asked Daniel if he could reveal his dream and its interpretation, Daniel immediately recognised the human inability to unfold such a mystery and that only the living God could do so. Daniel 2:26–28 says, *"The king answered Daniel, whose name was Belteshazzar, "Are you able to make known to me the dream which I have seen, and its interpretation?" ²⁷Daniel answered before the king, and said, "The secret which the king has demanded is such that no wise men, enchanters, magicians, nor soothsayers, can show to the king; ²⁸but there is a God in heaven who reveals secrets, and he has made known to king Nebuchadnezzar what shall be in the latter days. Your dream, and the visions of your head on your bed, are these""* (NHEB). With this, Daniel acknowledged God just as Joseph had done.

As Christians we need to understand that we are nothing without God and that all we are or will ever be is owed to His grace bestowed on us. No matter how fervently an anointed person may pray for the sick, unless the Lord heals the sick, that person can actualise no healing by his human power. In Acts 3:4–8, Peter, through prayer in the name of Jesus, healed the lame man at the Beautiful Gate.

"Peter, fastening his eyes on him, with John, said, "Look at us."
⁵He listened to them, expecting to receive something from them.
⁶But Peter said, "Silver and gold have I none, but what I have,
that I give you. In the name of Jesus Christ the Nazorean, get up
and walk." ⁷He took him by the right hand, and raised him up.
Immediately his feet and his ankle bones received strength.
⁸Leaping up, he stood, and began to walk. He entered with them
into the temple, walking, leaping, and praising God." (NHEB.)
When people in attendance were gazing at him as if it were by his
power that he had accomplished the miraculous act, Peter immediately
redirected their attention. He acknowledged Jesus – the mighty name
through which the lame man was made whole. This is the right
attitude every anointed vessel should emulate. Even if the grateful
people try to praise you or ascribe glory to you after performing any
miraculous act, God should be promptly acknowledged as the One
who brings about the remarkable phenomenon. By doing this, God is
glorified through us.

At any point in our walk with God, we must never think that we can
do anything without Him. It must be imprinted in our minds that we
can only do what Christ strengthens and enables us to perform
through the Holy Spirit – *"I can do all things through him who
strengthens me."* (Philippians 4:13 NHEB.) Without Christ, we can
do nothing of ourselves. It is easy for some people to disregard this
truth and instead bask in the delusion of self-glory. Many people
attribute their successes, promotions, achievements and prosperity,
for example, to their abilities, merits or efforts, while neglecting
the source of all things, God, thereby disregarding the biblical
injunction that says, *"In all thy ways acknowledge him…"* (Proverbs
3:6 NHEB.)

The implication of taking the glory due to God is often horrible.
Time and again, God has demonstrated that He does not take it
lightly when anyone ascribes to himself glory that is due to Him.
In Daniel 4:33–34, King Nebuchadnezzar prided himself as the
builder of Great Babylon. God spoke to him directly from heaven,

turned him into a beast, and a beast he was for seven years. When he came to his senses he realised his arrogance and acknowledged God's sovereignty in the affairs of humanity. *"The same hour was the thing fulfilled on Nebuchadnezzar: and he was driven from men, and ate grass as oxen, and his body was wet with the dew of the sky, until his hair was grown like eagles' feathers, and his nails like birds' claws. [34]At the end of the days I, Nebuchadnezzar, lifted up my eyes to heaven, and my understanding returned to me, and I blessed the Most High, and I praised and honored him who lives forever. For his dominion is an everlasting dominion, and his kingdom from generation to generation."* (NHEB.)

God detests a proud person. But God, being merciful, gave him a second chance. Note that not every proud person will have the same story as King Nebuchadnezzar. Another example of an arrogant person is King Herod. After giving an oration, people praised him to the skies saying, *"The voice of a god, and not of a man."* (Acts 12:22 NHEB.) While they were still praising him, an angel struck him dead because he did not attribute glory to God. God makes it clear in Isaiah 42:8 that He is unwilling to share His glory with anyone or anything. *"I am the LORD. That is my name. I will not give my glory to another, nor my praise to engraved images."* (NHEB.)

Joseph understood that he was just a vessel through which God manifests His power and wisdom, so he could not take credit for what was not his. But many are like King Nebuchadnezzar and King Herod: they are quick to ascribe their achievements in businesses, ministries, marriages or careers to their abilities or wisdom. It is pride that will move someone to share or take God's glory for himself. The inherent nature of pride in a natural man is more than willing to tempt him into basking in self-glorification. When a person allows pride to brew within him he gets to a point at which he is no longer poor in spirit, feels adequate in his strengths and detaches himself from God's control. His end is usually fatal. The thing about pride is that it clouds a person's vision and makes them puff up until they fall into destruction. No wonder Proverbs 16:18 says: *"Pride goes before destruction, and a haughty spirit before a fall."* (NHEB.) When pride blindfolds a person it gives them a sense of self-sufficiency and self-glory, and its purpose is clear as crystal – to destroy his soul.

Pride is not one of the fruits of the Spirit and so must not be exhibited by any child of God. Instead, we must study God's word and allow it to dictate the course of our lives. We are to allow it to enable us to walk in humility before God and man. We understand by the knowledge of God's word that acknowledging God for everything we have and everything He uses us to accomplish is well-pleasing to Him.

TOPIC 3: PLANNING FOR RAINY DAYS

GENESIS 41:25–49; 53–57

Check all the great success stories in life, and one secret that cannot be missed is the importance of planning – those who neglect to plan for the future prepare for themselves a recipe for failure and regret.

It is indeed wisdom to save and plan for the future. It is the idea of saving and planning that the writer of Proverbs pointed us to when he wrote: *"Go to the ant, you sluggard. Consider her ways, and be wise; ⁷which having no chief, overseer, or ruler, ⁸provides her bread in the summer, and gathers her food in the harvest. ⁹How long will you sleep, sluggard? When will you arise out of your sleep? ¹⁰A little sleep, a little slumber, a little folding of the hands to sleep: ¹¹so your poverty will come as a robber, and your scarcity as an armed man."* (Proverbs 6:6–11 NHEB.)

Planning is a basic function that involves deciding how to deal with a situation that we may encounter in the future. It borders on logical thinking and rational decision-making. It entails what is to be done, when it is to be done and how it should be done. After Joseph interpreted Pharaoh's dream he proffered a solution to the problem. He helped Pharaoh identify the coming famine that could affect the entire nation and recommended a policy that entailed storing the harvest during the years of plenty and setting out procedures for distribution during the drought. He assessed current resources and developed a strategy for managing those resources during the lean years. Joseph gathered up food during the seven years of plenty, so much so that they were like the sand of the sea.

Joseph's strategic planning and execution stand as a model for any individual, family, community or nation. It demonstrates several key principles that are just as applicable today as they were during Joseph's days in Egypt. Everyone needs to plan in case of rainy days. Rainy days refer to periods of unforeseen difficulty or lack. One cannot leave one's life to chance or fate: it leads only to a crisis. Many who do this end up shifting blame or venting their frustration on others or God; they fail to place themselves as the primary cause of their problems. Planning for rainy days is necessary as we go through life; it will assist us during unexpected storms of life. Not all seasons in life will be filled with roses and sunshine. There might come trying moments, and how these affect us is dependent on how much we prepare during the good times. It is truly wise to make hay while the sun shines, for in so doing we will be adequately ready on rainy days.

Everyone wants to live comfortably but few get to do the needful. You can have dreams in life but a dream without a plan is only a wish. Saving your finances can only get you so far but making the right investments and involving yourself in trustworthy and profitable business ventures will not only help you survive rainy days but thrive through them too. There is always that sense of insecurity and uncertainty that makes people afraid to leave their comfort zones; they fear that if they do and get involved in a venture it will only lead to disaster. It should be understood that there is no reward without some element of risk, and as children of God fear is not our watchword; instead we are to pray to God, seek His guidance, commit our plans to Him, ensure we are investing in a credible venture and trust that the Lord will direct our path. Proverbs 3:5–6 says: ***"Trust in*** *the LORD with all your heart, and do not lean on your own understanding. ⁶In all your ways acknowledge him, and he will make your paths straight."* (NHEB.)

Many people go through life hindered by ignorance, complacency and procrastination. They act as though there will always be an influx of money. They feel as if their current job is secured. Some live with the excuse that their income is not sufficient in the first place, and others subscribe to the procrastinating mentality of "I will save in the future." In the same vein, the "You only live once" mentality propels some people's financial indiscipline into spending on unnecessary items. The result of all this is that, when storms and crises hit, such people are sucked into lack and desperation. On the flip side, planning for rainy days offers many benefits, including peace of mind. While others are running helter-skelter looking for respite, we will live comfortably and happily because we were wise enough to do the needful.

Some people tend to misconstrue the scriptures and blame God for things they caused themselves. They exhaust their finances and make no reservation and investment for tomorrow. They quote Matthew 6:25–28 as a negation of planning for their future; after all, Christ says we should not worry about tomorrow. *"Therefore I tell you, do not be anxious about your life, what you will eat or what you will drink; or about your body, what you will wear. Is not life more than food, and the body more than clothing? ²⁶See the birds of the sky, that they do not sow, neither do they reap, nor gather into barns, and your heavenly Father feeds them. Are you not of much more value than they? ²⁷And which of you, by being anxious, can add one cubit to his height? ²⁸And why are you anxious about clothing? Consider the lilies of the field, how they grow. They do not toil, neither do they spin"* (NHEB). Jesus in no way discouraged the wisdom of planning; instead, He intended to take our hearts from the fire of anxiety and place it on God. While we are to put our hope in God, it does not translate to discouragement from planning, saving and investing for our future.

God provides for the ant but it still goes out to grab and save, and His word teaches us to learn from ants concerning planning for the future. We cannot be lazy and short-sighted about our future and expect that all will be well. It is advisable to prepare for the future and it is unwise to be nonchalant about it. We may be comfortable today but tomorrow may be a different story. If we have not made plans to deal with tomorrow's difficulties we will have to deal with regrets and discomfort.

The core of the matter is that we must endeavour to rely on God to guide us concerning planning issues. When we make it a habit to depend on His wisdom during moments of prosperity we will undoubtedly have no cause for panic during times of scarcity.

TOPIC 4: DIVINE WISDOM

GENESIS 41:33–39

Wisdom is the attribute of exercising sound judgement or possessing the proper knowledge in handling any issue, to attain the best possible end. It is the ability to make the best decision in every situation. Divine wisdom could be said to be God's interface with humans that unravels mysteries that the human intellect cannot unravel and provides solutions to alleviate the challenges we encounter in our endeavours. When we are confronted by life's issues and are unclear on what decision to make, God's wisdom is always available when we ask Him in trust.

Joseph manifested divine wisdom when he stood before Pharaoh and in his leadership and administrative roles in Potiphar's house and prison. The successes of Joseph's leadership and administrative duty as second-in-command in Egypt were proof of his wise decisions and actions. The interpretation of Pharaoh's dreams indicated that there would be seven years of surplus harvests, followed by seven years of famine. Since wisdom is the correct application of knowledge, Joseph wisely advised Pharaoh to save in the years of abundance and reserve the food for the period of famine. Pharaoh was pleased with Joseph's wise counsel, saying, *"Can we find such a one as this, a man in whom is the Spirit of God?"* (Genesis 41:38 NHEB.) Pharaoh acknowledged the exceptionality of the wisdom and Spirit of God in Joseph and recognised the uniqueness of Joseph's wisdom and his discerning capability. Subsequently, he exalted him to the position of second-in-command in Egypt.

God's wisdom is indispensable for a successful Christian walk; it is essential for personal living and crucial for effective human interactions. Without divine wisdom, living unwisely is inevitable. Therefore, we should desire divine wisdom.

The best approach to providing solutions to life's problems is to solve them by the wisdom of God. God's wisdom helps us proffer appropriate and effective solutions to spiritual and secular matters; these solutions can either be for groups or individuals. Divine wisdom is available to all who have a healthy relationship with God. The wisdom expressed by Joseph was a direct result of his relationship with God.

Daniel was another biblical character endowed with divine wisdom. His wisdom was evident from his youth during king Nebuchadnezzar's reign to his leadership and administrative role as one of the three administrators during the reign of King Darius. Through wisdom, he managed the resources at his disposal judiciously and distinguished himself among other leaders, and in consequence King Darius made plans to exalt him to be the overall head. Daniel 6:3 says, *"Then this Daniel was distinguished above the administrators and the satraps, because an extraordinary spirit was in him; and the king thought to set him over the whole realm."* (NHEB.)

Aside from the limitations of human knowledge, it is also carnal and appeals to the human senses and emotions. It is selfish and seeks ease and self-gratification, unlike God's wisdom, which reflects God's will and desire in every situation. God demands that we seek His wisdom, and only in Him will we find fulfilment. And speaking of God's wisdom, where can it be found? Job 28:13 says, *"Man doesn't know its price; Neither is it found in the land of the living."* (NHEB.) This implies that one has to die to this world and be born again in Christ to find true wisdom. 1 Corinthians 3:19 says, *"For the wisdom of this world is foolishness with God..."* (NHEB.)

The right way to open up the treasure store of divine wisdom is through God's word and total dependence on the Holy Spirit. When we study the word of God with emphasis on salvation, meditate on its precepts and live a life of obedience, yielding to the leading of the Holy Spirit, we open ourselves to the fountain of divine wisdom that will give us uncommon skills and insight. The more intimately we walk with God and allow His word to govern our lives, the wiser we become.

Ultimately, the fear of God is the beginning of wisdom. A man begins to be wise when he begins to fear God. *"The fear of the LORD is the beginning of wisdom. All those who do his work have a good understanding. His praise endures forever."* (Psalm 111:10 NHEB.) When we become aware of spiritual realities – about righteousness and sin, the temporariness of this present world and eternal life with God – we are on the path of divine wisdom. This will propel us to live with the consciousness of our obligation to the Creator.

Right association can also enhance our wisdom. Proverbs 13:20 says: *"One who walks with wise men grows wise, but a companion of fools suffers harm."* (NHEB.) Right associations have been avenues through which wisdom is gained or enhanced. But more importantly, divine wisdom can only be acquired from a divine source. Jesus is and will remain the veritable source of divine wisdom. For example, the disciples of Jesus had issues with the religious leaders that bordered on the defence of the gospel. In the process of the disciples' explanation, the religious leaders observed that they had been with Christ. *"Now when they saw the boldness of Peter and John, and had perceived that they were unlearned and ignorant men, they were amazed. They recognized that they had been with Jesus."* (Acts 4:13 NHEB.)

It is costly to base our lives on human wisdom. In Matthew 7:24–27 Jesus describes the one who lives by God's word as a wise man who builds his house on solid ground that can withstand the rain and the wind. However, the man who does not live his life by divine wisdom – God's word – is described as a foolish man who built his house on sand. When the wind and the rain came the house crumbled. *"Everyone therefore who hears these words of mine, and does them, will be compared to a wise man, who built his house on a rock. ²⁵And the rain came down, the floods came, and the winds blew, and beat on that house; and it did not fall, for it was founded on the rock. ²⁶And everyone who hears these words of mine, and does not do them will be like a foolish man, who built his house on the sand. ²⁷And the rain came down, the floods came, and the winds blew, and beat on that house; and it fell—and great was its fall."* (NHEB.)

Only those who are born again and live by the wisdom of God have their eternity secured. When we build our lives on divine wisdom we will withstand the wiles of the devil and the world's system.

CHAPTER 17

TOPIC 1: FULFILMENT OF JOSEPH'S DREAMS

GENESIS 42:6–9

One famous saying that is often used as a consolation whenever people are going through difficult moments is: "There is light at the end of the tunnel." This is a statement of hope to hold on to. But what happens when it seems as if there is no end to that tunnel? Or what if the darkness in the tunnel feels darker at every stride? How then can one deal with this overcast situation? One positive thing one can do is trust God and rest on His unfailing promises. This will not only keep hopes alive but also satiate a person's heart with peace, even when what is hoped for seems delayed or does not happen in the manner expected.

The story of Joseph is intriguing. His journey to greatness began with divine dreams that gave him a glimpse of his glorious future. Despite this, the challenges encountered as he moved from one phase of his life to another were turbulent. He was the apple of his father's eye – his father loved him above all his children. This preference did not sit well with his siblings and they hated him for this very fact. But that was not all, Joseph, in his naivety, added insult to injury when he told his brothers about his dreams of being a ruler over them. Many years later, while he faithfully pleased God in everything he did at every place he found himself, Joseph's dreams finally came true: his brothers indeed bowed to him, and he ruled over them. The fulfilment of Joseph's dreams was never straightforward. It was marred by myriad trials and challenges. Joseph was almost killed by his brothers, was sold as a slave and was falsely accused by Potiphar's wife and sent to prison. Against all the odds, every effort to thwart God's purpose for Joseph proved abortive because he stayed and lived within the confine of God's will. In the long run, all the unpleasant experiences were divinely orchestrated to bring Joseph into the glorious future he once dreamt about. Sometimes the most difficult times in our lives may be the pathway to our expected end.

In the same vein, when a glimpse of our future regarding God's purposes for our lives is revealed to us through His written word – the Bible, dreams, trances or other godly channels, our minds should be set on God's word to guide our paths in obedience. And we should have confidence in God's ability to bring it to pass at His appointed time.

The path that leads to the fulfilment of God's purposes may often run uphill – be characterised by oppositions, trials or temptations. Though we might have had a glimpse of what the Lord has in store for us, while looking at our present condition everything might look gloomy due to challenges. One thing is certain though: there is always hope in the future for a child of God, no matter how bleak it may look at the moment, so we are never to be discouraged. If we read through the scriptures we will find that the paths that great servants of God walked before God's purpose for their lives came to fruition were not devoid of challenges. God took them through hills and valleys to prepare them for the great tasks He had for them. The way of the Lord is beyond human understanding and is unsearchable. We just need to trust Him and walk at His pace as He leads the way. Isaiah 55:9 says, ***"For as the heavens are higher than the earth, so are my ways higher than your ways, and my thoughts than your thoughts."*** (NHEB.)

As God's children, we are the apple of His eye. He loves us, and it is a love unparalleled by any expressed between humans. And as a loving and caring Father, He wants the best for us. This does not, as earlier stated, make us immune to challenges. Sometimes when He takes us through storms, fear creeps in and we are tempted to lose hope in Him. At such a point we should remain firm in God, always bearing in mind the words of Isaiah 41:10, *"Do not be afraid, for I am with you. Do not be dismayed, for I am your God. I will strengthen you. Yes, I will help you. Yes, I will uphold you with the right hand of my righteousness."* (NHEB.) With these words of encouragement giving up should never be our decision. Even when every other thing fails in this life God's purpose for our lives will never fail, provided our manner of living pleases Him. Therefore, rather than lose heart, we should keep trusting God to fulfil His purpose for our lives while at the same time living in constant obedience to His word.

When all godly efforts to change the unpleasant experience we are currently going through have been exhausted we should submit ourselves entirely to God's sovereign will. The mentality of getting what we want at all costs without being sensitive to God's will is not Christlike. As such, we are to remain steadfast in faith no matter what the severity of our present challenges.

While on the journey towards the fulfilment of God's purpose for our lives we must be very sensitive not to be pressured into taking any step that is detrimental to the salvation of our soul, irrespective of the challenges that come our way. During these trying moments, the devil might deceptively offer us counterfeit things to deprive us of the fulfilment of God's purpose for our lives; the most important thing the devil will go for is the salvation of our soul, but we are not to succumb. If Joseph had yielded to the sexual advances from Potiphar's wife he could have forfeited the fulfilment of God's purpose for his life and his relationship with God. Not everything that looks glittery is precious. *"There is a way which seems right to a man, but in the end it leads to death."* (Proverbs 14:12 NHEB.)

God is not pleased when we compromise our faith in Him by allowing challenges to move us to display actions that do not align with His word. Even when everything seems contrary to His purpose for our lives we must prioritise our fear towards God and obedience to His word above everything else, just as Joseph did. We should be content to have God as the hope for our ultimate purpose – the salvation of our souls. This is the light at the end of the tunnel.

TOPIC 2: GUILTY CONSCIENCE

GENESIS 42:21–23

The horrific deed of their past infiltrated their memory. The images of the unpleasant treatment meted out to their brother televised on the screens of their minds. They had been cruel and ruthless. They had subjected their brother, Joseph, to the agony of the pit. And even though he pleaded for mercy, with hearts hardened in hatred they sold him off to slavery. It was all done in a bid to hinder the fulfilment of his dreams. But here they were, thrown in an Egyptian prison, distressed and guilt-stricken and everything seemed like poetic justice to them; they felt as though they were reaping the reward of their action. So they said to one another: *""We are certainly guilty concerning our brother, in that we saw the distress of his soul, when he begged us, and we wouldn't listen. Therefore this distress has come upon us." ²²Reuben answered them, saying, "Did I not tell you, saying, 'Do not sin against the child,' and you wouldn't listen? Therefore also, look, his blood is required.""* (Genesis 42:21–22 NHEB.)

We all possess an inherent sense of what we believe is right and wrong, and our different beliefs and norms influence this moral guide. This inner sense is called conscience, and it evaluates our every thought, word and deed. The conscience serves as the moral compass of every man. As a moral compass, the conscience has a flexible nature as it pertains to different individuals. Its flexibility means that one person can feel guilt for a particular action but the next person might not. One person feels guilty after fornication but another does not. One person feels guilty for lying but the next person does not. It can be said that for those who are not God's children the beliefs that form the basis of their conscience or what they believe to be right and wrong may differ from God's standard. For instance, someone who steals from the rich to help the poor may consider themselves as doing a kind deed and may receive applaud from people, but stealing, barring any moral justification, is something God disapproves of. The flexibility of the conscience also allows someone, who initially felt guilt for wrongdoing, not to feel guilty about it after some time if that person continues in it. Against these backdrops, the conscience itself cannot be an appropriate guide unless that conscience conforms to the principles of God's word.

The conscience of people who have not experienced the new birth is prone to perceiving the world's standard as acceptable. Some of the things they see as the usual way of life are evil in the sight of God, but their consciences may not condemn them when they indulge in those sinful ways. If such people continue in that way of life, their end is explicitly stated in the scripture. Proverbs 14:12 says: ***"There is a way which seems right to a man, but in the end it leads to death."*** (NHEB.)

Sin is supposed to bring with it feelings of shame and guilt. Guilt can erupt from a sense of wrongdoing; however, it is supposed to be radically God-centred. True guilt is the crushing sense of contrition at the thought of having despised the Almighty by living against His words and counsel. Godly sorrow makes a Christian better; every believer who has acted in disobedience to God's word and experienced God's forgiveness can testify that godly sorrow makes a Christian better.

For our conscience to be a trusted moral guide we must endeavour to form our conscience by God's word, entirely influenced by the Holy Spirit. Daily renewal of our minds with the word of God affects our words and actions so that we conform to Christian norms and values; societal norms that contradict God's word are expunged from our hearts. Through this, our conscience becomes perturbed whenever we go against God's word, which now shapes our norms and values.

Like Joseph's brothers, those who are culpable of wrongdoings tend to be ridden with a guilty conscience, which is sometimes accompanied by the fear of reckoning. This guilt can lead to panic, terror and anxiety. It is as Proverbs 28:1 says: *"The wicked flee when no one pursues; but the righteous are as bold as a lion."* (NHEB.) Throughout history, people have desperately wished that they knew how to escape a guilty conscience. Many have gone to the extreme of committing suicide to escape the torments of their guilt. Judas Iscariot's suicide after betraying Jesus attests to this fact: *"Then Judas, who betrayed him, when he saw that Jesus was condemned, felt remorse, and returned the thirty pieces of silver to the chief priests and elders, ⁴saying, 'I have sinned in that I betrayed innocent blood.' But they said, 'What is that to us? You see to it.' ⁵He threw down the pieces of silver in the sanctuary, and departed. He went away and hanged himself."* (Matthew 27:3–5 NHEB.) Others could go as far as inflicting injury on themselves to appease their guilty conscience, but that is not the way out. To all those struggling with guilt, rest can be found only in one place – the feet of Christ. The Master's arms are wide open, and He lovingly calls us: *"Come to me, all you who labor and are heavily burdened, and I will give you rest."* (Matthew 11:28 NHEB.)

The devil may try to use our wrongs to build a prison of guilt from which we cannot escape. But we should take solace in the fact that if our hearts are crushed by guilt and our peace is lost, Christ is ready to purify our conscience by His word. Therefore, we should not lose hope but rise and stand forgiven in His perfect love. Jesus' conversation with the adulterous woman should further give us hope that He is ready to forgive us of all our trespasses if only we come to Him with contrite and penitent hearts. Jesus said to her: *""Woman, where are they? Did no one condemn you?" ¹¹And she said, "No one, Lord." And Jesus said, "Neither do I condemn you. Go your way. From now on, sin no more.""* (John 8:10–11 NHEB.) The same assurance given to this woman extends to all who are guilty of wrongdoing. Jesus does not condemn us; He invites all who are guilty laden into His rest.

Acknowledging our wrongs and accepting that the blood of Christ takes away sin is the first step to dealing with our guilt. The consciousness of our forgiveness and justification through the blood of Christ should spur the desire within us to make right the wrongs done to others. It should bring about a willingness to make restitution where necessary. We should take to remembrance the words of our Lord: *"If therefore you are offering your gift at the altar, and there remember that your brother has anything against you, [24] leave your gift there before the altar, and go your way. First be reconciled to your brother, and then come and offer your gift."* (Matthew 5:23–24 NHEB.) Christ commands reconciliation. It is paramount to believe that Christ can forgive sins but it is also imperative, as long as it is within our power, to seek the forgiveness of those we wronged and restitute if possible.

There is a peace that comes from being guilty of nothing; indeed, as the saying goes, "There is no pillow as soft as a clear conscience." But, on the other hand, a guilty conscience denies us peace of mind and instead plagues us with many sorrows and anxieties. For this reason we should always strive to keep our conscience clear and guiltless before God and man. Apostle Paul wrote, *"This being so, I also do my best to always have a clear conscience toward God and people."* (Acts 24:16 NHEB.)

(For more on Guilty Conscience, see Chapter 7, Topic 1)

TOPIC 3: RASH DECISIONS

GENESIS 42:29–37

There are times in life when we find ourselves tempted to abandon the process of reasoning and caution for a decision laced with rashness. While making a rash conclusion might seem wise momentarily and may, in some instances, achieve an immediate goal, it can make us grapple with consequences that could leave us drowning in regret.

A man once told his daughter, "Before you speak to someone, first speak the words into your hand, then put the words in your ear; listen how it sounds in your ear; if it is okay, you can then speak the words to someone else."

This is a theatrical way of advising: "Think before you speak." This is not just a check for angry words; it also checks against careless words of immense consequences.

A cursory look at the words of Reuben and the certainty of his declaration calls for examination. He said to his father Jacob, **"Kill my two sons, if I do not bring him to you..."** (Genesis 42:37 NHEB.) It is an utterance that one will consider bizarre and rash. Why would he make his children the collateral choice of his promise? If he was so confident he could have mentioned any other valuable option, including himself, but he chose to put his children's lives in harm's way. Why was he so confident in himself and his ability? How sure was he that he would bring Benjamin back home safely, especially if one considers that he hadn't planned to leave Simeon behind the last time? It was a long journey; what is the certainty that nothing would happen on the way? He was offering Jacob the lives of Jacob's two grandsons as collateral for Jacob's son. It is understood that Reuben was concerned about the safety of Benjamin but he did not consider human limitations. He should have learnt from his experience regarding what happened to Joseph: although he had wished to return Joseph safely to his father, he could not. He must have desired that Simeon was not detained in Egypt, yet he could do nothing about it. These are the possibilities Reuben should have considered. In such a situation the ideal thing to say is "The God we serve will grant us a safe journey back." To be so confident in himself as to offer his sons' lives is an action without thorough consideration. **"Do you see a man who is hasty in his words? There is more hope for a fool than for him."** (Proverbs 29:20 NHEB.)

The wise carefully think before they act, carrying out actions with knowledge and proper consideration. They do not say or do anything hastily or irrationally. Wise people weigh up all available facts and possible outcomes before deciding, approaching a concern with wise judgement and thoughtful discretion. Proverbs 13:16 says: *"Every prudent man acts from knowledge, but a fool exposes folly."* (NHEB.) As children of God, we have a choice. We can be open to information, increase our understanding, try to curtail assumptions and, most importantly, ask God for direction on how to go about a matter without making mistakes and not putting other people's lives up as collateral. Decision-making or drawing a conclusion on any issue is delicate. To have a good and correct outcome, one must be careful in weighing up every possible way that would not be detrimental to one's life and those of others.

Jephthah the Gileadite returned victorious from war and as he did so his daughter appeared and rejoiced to see her father. Unknown to the daughter, Jephthah had sworn unto God that whatever comes out first to meet him would be offered to God. Judges 11:35 records: *"And it happened, when he saw her, that he tore his clothes, and said, "Alas, my daughter. You have brought me very low. You have become a stumbling block in my sight. And you are among those who trouble me. For I have given my word to the LORD, and I can't break it.""* (NHEB.) Standing before his only daughter, Jephthah would realise that he had not considered all possibilities, leaving him with regret and grief. This should be a great lesson. It is wisdom to ponder carefully on our actions before taking them. This will save us a great deal from the negative implications of wrong decisions.

We are not to allow pressure or emotions to make us do things that we will regret in the long run. Instead, we ought to consider certain factors even though our decisions may seem right at the time. Will our actions be beneficial to us in the long run? Will it have a negative implication on others? And most importantly, is it an action that God is pleased with or approves? When we ponder our words and actions we significantly reduce the chances of making wrong decisions.

Some people have found themselves plagued by unnecessary grief and regret because of decisions that were made rashly. Others find themselves wedged into a tight corner or situation due to promises they never fully thought out before making. There are times, as Christians, when we face difficult situations and may not know which decision is right. At such times, it is advisable to seek the word of God concerning the issue or seek counsel from mature Christians who can point us in the right direction. When we show complete dependence on God our know-it-all attitude will disappear. We will rely more on the wisdom from above and will escape the troubles that result from a rash decision. James 1:5 says: ***"But if any of you lacks wisdom, let him ask of God, who gives to all liberally and without reproach; and it will be given to him."*** (NHEB.) When we trust, obey and walk in line with God's word, seeking His direction in all we do, then we can be sure that He will help us in moments of decision-making.

(For more on rash decisions, see Rash Conclusions in Chapter 6, Topic 4 and Rash Judgement in Chapter 13, Topic 4)

CHAPTER 18

TOPIC 1: GIFTS

GENESIS 43:11–14

"You have bereaved me of my children. Joseph is no more, Simeon is no more, and you want to take Benjamin away. All these things are against me." (Genesis 42:36 NHEB.) This was the expressed fear of Jacob. He could not imagine losing another child. For this reason he was unwilling to let Benjamin go with his brothers to Egypt, as requested by the Egyptian ruler. However, as the severe famine persisted in the land, Jacob needed food for his family and with no other choice had to reconsider his decision. Though Jacob had no idea that the Egyptian ruler was Joseph, he knew that for his family to survive the famine he had to comply with the condition of the ruler. But he did something noteworthy: he did not permit Benjamin to go with his brothers to Egypt without sending gifts to the ruler. Jacob selected the best fruits of the land with other gift items and sent them to the Egyptian ruler. Above all, he spoke some words of hope, sought God's mercy for the release of Simeon, who was detained, and for Benjamin, because of his fear of the unknown.

This was not the first time Jacob was involved in gift-giving. He gave gifts to Esau in a bid to pacify his anger. Also, he gave bountifully gifts of high quality and immense worth. Gifts can help pacify someone we offend. Jacob understood the significance of sending gifts in a bid to soothe the soul of whoever he would have a direct or indirect meeting with. We can take a cue from Jacob in this regard and apply it to our relationships with others. Gifts, when given with pure motives, are not bad. In actuality, offering gifts is one of the necessary acts of commitment to any relationship.

The gifts in the giver's hands are given with different purposes and manifold motives. However, for a Christian, the purposes must be godly, the intentions must be pure and the occasions must be proper. Some give gifts to honour, appreciate or congratulate people, others to pacify anger, while others still give gifts as an expression of love for their spouses, children, parents and friends. Gifts can be given to express one's appreciation of somebody's kindness, to open doors or to give someone access to important people. Proverbs 18:16 says: *"A man's gift makes room for him, and brings him before great men."* (NHEB.)

The problem is that when it comes to giving gifts many people have subconsciously focused their actions on those they expect to gain from, forgetting the most crucial aspect of gift-giving. Gifts should not only be given in situations where there is a possibility of gaining something in return; our gifts are needed by the orphans, the poor, the homeless and other less privileged people. This path of Christian living is characterised by love and care and a willingness to bear other people's burdens. When we give gifts to people who cannot repay us God is not only pleased with such sacrificial acts of giving, He will also reward us with treasures in heaven. Proverbs 19:17 says: *"He who has pity on the poor lends to the LORD; he will reward him."* (NHEB.) Our gifts can open doors for us but when we give to the poor who cannot repay us, God becomes our rewarder. He can open doors for us which no man can open. If you give to please others, they may forget you or repay you with evil, but you can never go unrewarded in this life or in the life to come when you give to please God.

It does not matter whether you have a lot to give or a little; it is the motive behind giving the gifts that matter. For giving to be considered to have the right motive it must be neither to impress onlookers nor take advantage of the less privileged; it should be a generous act of kindness and love from a compassionate heart. This will go a long way to making a difference in the recipients' lives, and you never can tell how far such small acts of kindness can go in bringing a soul to Christ.

Giving gifts with pure motives as an expression of love is an act of godly living; this should be an inherent part of every child of God at all times.

TOPIC 2: AWOOF

GENESIS 43:19–23

A young man walks down the street, sees a purse, stoops and picks up the purse. On opening it he discovers wads of money. The first words that come out of his mouth are "Thank God." A taxi driver, worried over his mother's medical condition and the cost of surgery, finds a bag filled with money in the back seat of his vehicle and cries out, "Thank you, Lord, for your blessing." This is the paradoxical way in which humans sometimes relate to God. We say God is all pure and fair yet at the same time we are not hesitant in attributing the wrong things to Him.

"Awoof" is African slang – it means an item stumbled upon that is not earned. The two people in the illustrations found what one would consider an awoof but instead of attributing it to a person's mistake they attributed it to the orchestration of God. Such people may hide behind the concept "The Lord works in mysterious ways", but someone who knows God truly will know that He does not work in such a manner.

Jacob's children had gone to buy corn in Egypt and on their return had discovered that all the money they took to Egypt was back in their sacks. When they told Joseph's steward about the surprise, he replied, *"Peace be to you. Do not be afraid. Your God, and the God of your father, has given you treasure in your sacks..."*

(Genesis 43:23 NHEB). Although the steward made this statement in deceit, knowing fully of Joseph's ploy, there is a lesson we can learn from it when considering people's reactions to free things. People are fond of attributing events that are not of God's orchestration to God's way of attending to their needs.

Everything has a price in life. If you desire success or growth figure out the price then pay it. Every successful person has a "price story" to tell. One cannot achieve success in life without sacrificing something. This is the key and not awoof. The principle of success for God's children is working with our hands, which is followed by God's blessings upon the works of our hands. He can also make us beneficiaries of favour and gifts, but He has not chosen the awoof path to shower His blessings on us. The Almighty, who is fair towards all and sundry, does not work that way. We should not expect Him to inconvenience others so that we will be comfortable. We should not expect Him to deprive others of their money so that we can be all smiles. When our source of happiness constitutes a source of sorrow to our fellow human beings we have not shown the kind of love Christ teaches. What is awoof to you may be a source of agony to another, but when we see things that do not belong to us and return them, as did the brothers of Joseph, we have achieved two things: brought joy to the person involved and glory to God by our display of honesty.

There is an interesting and hypocritical side to awoof. When people are culprits they wave their hands in the air, giving testimonies and singing "Hallelujah", but when they fall victim they pray for the worst for the culprits. In life, it is always a beautiful thing to put ourselves in others' shoes. Sometimes, asking ourselves some honest questions brings reality to the fore. What if I was the victim? What if this was my company's money or my child's school fees? How would I feel about it? Jesus made a remarkable statement in Matthew 7:12: ***"Therefore whatever you desire for people to do to you, do also to them; for this is the Law and the Prophets."*** (NHEB.) Looking at our actions through other people's eyes will go a long way to addressing how we deal with situations such as the issue of awoof.

Believers have a name and an identity to protect and treasure. Rather than praising God and calling things awoof it behoves our honesty and integrity to consider those suffering loss. What you praise God for might be a source of sorrow to another person. As those who represent Christ our reaction to accidentally encountering monetary or material items must be such that it leads us to take the proper measures by inquiring and returning the items to the owner or reporting the discovery to authorities. Our image as God's children as well as our soul's salvation must propel us into taking appropriate action in such situations. Think of how unbelievers perceive Christianity when Christians display honesty and goodwill in a world plagued by wickedness. We not only portray a good image of Christianity but are unconsciously sowing seeds in the hearts of others as well. We might just win a soul for Christ by our display of love so, rather than selfishly take things as awoof, let the love of Christ and love for our neighbour be the propelling factors behind our actions.

CHAPTER 19

TOPIC 1: WISDOM IN RECONCILIATION

GENESIS 44:1–34

One saying commonly used in persuading people to forgive those who hurt them is "Forgive and forget." While this can be essential in dealing with grievances, it may, at times, not be as easy as it sounds. That said, we may not literally forget before we forgive or forget after we forgive. True forgiveness is exhibited when the thought of the wrong done to us does not cause a feeling of resentment and a desire to seek vengeance. Forgiveness is required of all believers. However, even though we forgive, there are many situations in which the application of wisdom is necessary for reconciliation. The application of wisdom in reconciliation is an act that is necessary to test the character of someone who offends us and to be able to help such a person in overcoming their weakness.

Joseph put his brothers through a series of tests to test their character. These tests did not mean that Joseph had not forgiven them and neither were they a means to get even with them. If he had not forgiven them he would probably have had them permanently incarcerated the moment he saw them. His motive in putting them through this seemingly rigorous process and interrogation was to discern the characters of those who had been cruel to him. It was wise for him to exercise caution and not immediately trust people who had conspired to kill him and then sell him to slavery. His approach ultimately proved productive, as his brothers' sincerity in the interrogation process ensured his reunion with them was without reservations about their characters.

Despite their cruel treatment of him Joseph's decision to forgive his brothers and apply wisdom in the reconciliation process is worthy of emulation, but for us, our motive should be to help our offenders overcome their weaknesses and encourage them on to the path of salvation. In truth, extending forgiveness to those who have hurt us can be challenging. Even when they are our loved ones, the pain and betrayal can run so deep that forgiveness may not be easy. However, as Christians, forgiveness is mandatory, not optional, irrespective of the gravity of the offences committed against us. We are commanded in Ephesians 4:32 about this: *"And be kind to one another, tenderhearted, forgiving each other, just as God also in Christ forgave you."* (NHEB.) It must be sunk into our consciences that forgiveness must not be dependent on the remorsefulness – or lack of remorse – of the offender nor must it be conditioned on whether the person who hurt us seeks forgiveness. Joseph did not wait for his brothers to ask for forgiveness before forgiving them from his heart. In like manner, our reaction towards our offenders must be forgiveness, whether they are deserving or not.

As much as we must forgive those who have hurt us, the expectation is that reconciliation is done with wisdom. We have been commanded to forgive, but that does not mean we should throw all caution to the wind in reconciliation. It does not mean we should put ourselves back in harm's way or put the person in a position whereby they will easily be tempted to commit the same offence again and risk the salvation of their soul. We should also follow up on the person to see and help them outgrow that weakness, bringing them back on the path of salvation. In reconciliation, wisdom is required in dealing with our offenders, especially when trust is broken. Without doubt, trust is a cord that holds a relationship together. Without trust, we cannot feel safe or confident around others. When those you love betray you trust is easily eroded. When those you expect to be faithful disappoint you trust tends to vanish. Therefore, in reconciling with those who have offended us, be it through betrayal, disloyalty or infidelity, it is crucial to do so with the application of wisdom. In applying wisdom, we should put in place necessary measures to prevent a reoccurrence of the offence.

One such measure is helping a person prone to a weakness and who has caused us pain to grow out of such behaviour. This can mean assigning the person a different responsibility. For instance, a domestic who was caught stealing money may continue stealing if we forgive them yet retain them in a position in which they are still exposed to money. As good as forgiving such a person is, we can also help them deal with their weakness by teaching them the gospel and assigning to them a different role within the household to save them from that weakness until we observe genuine repentance in them. The same approach can be adopted in church gatherings. For example, an usher who steals offerings should be forgiven and corrected and transferred to another department in which they will have no dealings with money.

While applying wisdom is essential, even after forgiving others, we must be careful not to adopt measures that cause resentment to surface. Whatever action we take to rebuild trust or whatever approach we adopt to fix a relationship marred by betrayal or deceit must be done with love.

TOPIC 2: RASH CONCLUSION

GENESIS 44:3–10

There is always a risk of jumping to conclusions without recourse to careful thought. It is a danger that can bring unimaginable regret or leave in its wake a trail of consequences not just for ourselves but for others too.

This fact was one that Jacob's children did not sufficiently consider in their desperation to prove their innocence. In what seemed like a drama being acted out, Jacob's sons found themselves playing to Joseph's script, a script that was nothing more than a test. They had left Egypt that morning, euphoric and all smiles. They had the grains, they had Simeon, and most importantly no harm had come to Benjamin. As a bonus, they had enjoyed a sumptuous meal the previous day. Their trip could not have gone any better. But a twist came to spoil the fun. As they rode their donkeys away from the city Joseph's steward caught them up. He brought the news that his master's cup had been stolen. His accusation stung like the sting of a bee. It was impossible! None of them could have been that irrational to have stolen the Egyptian master's cup. In their desperation to prove their innocence, they were driven into making a rash statement that boxed them into a tight corner: ***"With whoever of your servants it be found, let him die, and we also will be my lord's bondservants."*** (Genesis 44:9 NHEB.) In truth, none of them was guilty, but the cup was found in Benjamin's sack. What if the threat from Joseph's camp was real? What if their vow was taken seriously? Needless to say, they would have suffered the consequences for their rash proclamation. They were fortunate that the whole experience was a test.

(For more on rash conclusions, see Rash Conclusions in Chapter 6, Topic 4, Rash Judgement in Chapter 13, Topic 4 and Rash Decision in Chapter 17, Topic 3)

TOPIC 3: COMMITMENT TO RESPONSIBILITY

GENESIS 44:18–34

It is one thing to promise to be held responsible for a particular task or an anticipated occurrence and another to remain committed to this responsibility. Many are quick to make promises on the spur of the moment then cave in when confronted with reality. People generally break their commitments because they might gain some form of undue advantage or out of fear of loss, harm or inconvenience. Whenever we make a promise or give our word it becomes our responsibility to fulfil it. It takes strength of character to remain undauntedly committed to our responsibility in the face of severe circumstances. Judah exhibited such strength of character.

Judah had earlier committed himself to take full responsibility for whatever might betide Benjamin. This he did in his plea to win

Jacob's approval to permit Benjamin to follow them to Egypt as requested by Joseph, who was yet to reveal himself to them. Jacob granted his request after due consideration. While they were returning to Canaan, Joseph's silver cup was found with Benjamin after being strategically planted by Joseph's steward in an attempt to detain him. Judah then recounted his word given to his father and his responsibility to ensure the safe return of Benjamin at all costs, pleading for Benjamin to be released and offering himself as a slave instead. Judah, who once suggested that Joseph be sold into slavery, now presented himself as a slave in place of Benjamin. He took responsibility for Benjamin's safety, and he was faithfully committed to keeping the promise made to his father, even to his detriment. Judah's act is worthy of emulation by everyone who is heavenly-minded: *"¹LORD, who shall dwell in your sanctuary? Who shall live on your holy mountain? ⁴In his eyes a vile man is despised, but he honors those who fear the LORD. He keeps an oath even when it hurts, and doesn't change it."* (Psalm 15:1,4 NHEB.)

Commitment is the decision or state of being devoted to a particular cause, and responsibility is the state of being accountable. Both commitment and responsibility are obligations; they cannot be separated from each other. Therefore, commitment to responsibility could be seen as a decision or obligation to be accountable to a particular cause no matter the inconveniences that may be suffered as a result. There is no extent to which people committed to a responsibility will not go. They do not see quitting as an option and are bent on fulfilling their responsibilities no matter what the challenges faced on the way.

Like Judah, Ruth had taken on the responsibility of standing by her mother-in-law after the demise of her husband. Her commitment to this responsibility was so well executed that people acknowledged her as better than seven sons to Naomi. *"He shall be to you a restorer of life, and sustain you in your old age, for your daughter-in-law, who loves you, who is better to you than seven sons, has borne him."* (Ruth 4:15 NHEB.)

Judah and Ruth took on responsibilities but sometimes God bestows responsibilities on us. We ought to treat our God-given responsibilities with similar regard. God called Moses and charged him with the responsibility of leading the children of Israel to the land of promise, and his commitment to this responsibility is worth noting. At one point the Israelites had sinned against God, and God was willing to destroy them and make a great nation out of Moses. Moses interceded on their behalf, pleading with God to forgive them, and asking that if God would not forgive them his name be blotted out of God's book. Another person who demonstrated tremendous commitment to his God-given responsibility was Apostle Paul. Christ had handed him the responsibility of preaching the gospel to the Gentiles and he remained committed to this responsibility even in the face of severe difficulties. At some time in his ministry he said, *"except that the Holy Spirit testifies in every city, saying that bonds and afflictions wait for me. [24] But I make my life an account of nothing precious to myself, so that I may finish my race, and the ministry which I received from the Lord Jesus, to fully testify to the Good News of the grace of God."* (Acts 20:23–24 NHEB.) The Bible is replete with examples of great men who were committed to their responsibilities like Peter and the rest of Jesus' apostles, including Stephen, who was martyred, and Luke, who was Paul's companion.

As Christians, we ought to exhibit the utmost commitment to our responsibilities. Note that our commitment to responsibility must cut across every aspect of our lives. We should be devoted to meeting our obligations in every aspect of life. For instance, a Christian should not be more committed to church activities than to his marriage or his children. Likewise, a Christian should not be more passionate about his job or career than to his walk with God. Our commitment to responsibility must be all-encompassing because God desires that we are found faithful and accountable in every aspect of our lives. He has given us several responsibilities in life, and only those committed will accomplish their duties. Whether or not we will live fruitful lives depends on our attitude towards our responsibilities. We must always bear in mind that a fulfilled life requires sacrifices; therefore, we must be determined to undergo any inconveniences in making our lives worth living.

The salvation of our souls is also not without obligation. God offers no one any form of salvation without responsibility on their part. God has freely provided His Son as atonement for our sins; even so, the salvation of our souls comes with a cost – total surrender. Although we are saved by faith in the sacrifice of Christ, this faith must be accompanied by a life of absolute obedience to God, for faith without works is dead: *"You see that a person is justified by works and not by faith alone."* (James 2:24 NHEB.) To find God we must follow the Way – Christ Jesus. Whoever will follow Christ must deny themselves – they must take up their cross and be willing to bear all the shame and persecution associated with identifying with Christ, and then follow Him wherever He leads: *"He said to all, "If anyone desires to come after me, let him deny himself, take up his cross daily, and follow me. ²⁴For whoever desires to save his life will lose it, but whoever will lose his life for my sake, the same will save it.""* (Luke 9:23–24 NHEB.)

We are to live in constant communion with God. Relationships deepen and grow when we are willing to commit time and energy to foster them. Commitment to Bible study and discipleship is essential for spiritual progress. Beginning the race is not all there is to the race. We must finish it and finish well. Without personal commitment, our love and passion for God will die out on the way and we might not get to the end of the race. The children of Israel unanimously agreed to serve the Lord at Sinai on their journey to the Promised Land, *"All the people answered together, and said, "All that the LORD has spoken we will do." Moses reported the words of the people to the LORD."* (Exodus 19:8 NHEB.) But Hebrews 3:16–19 gives a somewhat contrasting and ironic report of their end. *"For who, when they heard, rebelled? No, did not all those who came out of Egypt by Moses? ¹⁷With whom was he displeased forty years? Was not it with those who sinned, whose bodies fell in the wilderness? ¹⁸To whom did he swear that they would not enter into his rest, but to those who were disobedient? ¹⁹ We see that they were not able to enter in because of unbelief."* (NHEB.) Let them be an example for us on the need to remain committed. We must be careful not to be like the son in the parable of the two sons in Matthew 21:28–32, whom the father requested to go to work in the vineyard and he responded positively, saying, "I will go, sir" but then disobeyed his father. When we choose to travel the narrow path we must be committed to reaching the end of it.

We are responsible for making disciples, training them in spiritual matters and building them up to spiritual maturity. Matthew 28:18–20 says, *"Jesus came to them and spoke to them, saying, "All authority has been given to me in heaven and on earth. ¹⁹ Therefore go, and make disciples of all nations, baptizing them in the name of the Father and of the Son and of the Holy Spirit, ²⁰ teaching them to obey all things that I commanded you. And look, I am with you every day, even to the end of the age.""* (NHEB.) We also have the responsibility to be the light of God and worthy ambassadors of His kingdom in a world engulfed in darkness. We are not only to preach the gospel; our lives must reflect the teachings of Christ contained in the Bible. Our lifestyles must bear witness to what we preach. The growth and revival we desire in the body of Christ and the world at large cannot happen without a firm commitment to our God-given responsibilities.

CHAPTER 20

TOPIC 1: REALISING GOD'S PURPOSE FOR OUR LIVES

GENESIS 45:1–8

The deep-rooted effects of trials have a strange way of altering people's perspectives on how they look at life. They sometimes breed a pessimistic or doubtful drive that makes people see the world in a negative light. They also serve as an element that can stop people perceiving and realising God's purpose for their lives.

Though unpleasant, a trail of challenges could be the path God allows us to tread for His purpose to be fulfilled. When we understand that He makes all things work together for our good we will be motivated to discover God's purpose for us rather than focus on the negative side of the process. Joseph realised this after experiencing a series of trials before gaining his position as the second-in-command in Egypt. Joseph was shown a glimpse of his future in a dream he had at a young age. It was a future that would ensure his elevation, his family's survival and their posterity. He had not fully understood that then nor did his brothers. They saw a brother who seemed a threat rather than a helper. And when they conspired to consign him to a life of slavery it must have felt like the end of his dreams and the termination of his purpose, as revealed by their statement: ***"We will see what will become of his dreams."*** (Genesis 37:20 NHEB.) In the wake of what he encountered – the misery of slavery, the seduction and the elevation from prison to the palace – Joseph understood the purpose of his challenges. The aggregate of his life's experiences was not some kind of punishment or life's unfairness but a process to attain his purpose.

This understanding made him realise that all his brothers' actions, though evil in intention, were swayed in his favour by God who placed him in his position of purpose. This realisation made it easy for him to extend forgiveness to them.

Like Joseph, everyone has a purpose attached to their lives. No one was designed by God merely to occupy space. God's purpose for mankind varies from person to person. For Esther, her elevation to be queen of a great Persian kingdom helped save the Jews from the genocidal plot of Haman. Speaking to Esther, Mordecai said, *"Who knows if you haven't come to the kingdom for such a time as this?"* (Esther 4:14 NHEB.)

The quest to discover and fulfil our life's purpose is best embarked on from an early age. Unfortunately, it seems that some people are contented to go through life without realising their purpose or fulfilling it. Some who would have become one of the best at imparting knowledge to people waste their lives on frivolities. Others who would have become trailblazers in different careers end up struggling in other career paths because they fail to discover their purpose. Only when we have discovered our purpose will we be able to complete the kind of exploits God has designed for us. The first step in realising God's purpose in our lives is to live our lives according to the will of God. The knowledge of God's purpose for us can be obtained through different means. For some, God can reveal His purpose by placing a burden in their hearts and through this, He can lead them towards a particular task, as was the case with Nehemiah, who rebuilt Jerusalem's walls. *"I arose in the night, I and some few men with me; neither told I any man what my God put into my heart to do for Jerusalem; neither was there any animal with me, except the animal that I rode on."* (Nehemiah 2:12 NHEB.) For others, God can make known to them His purpose in other ways, for example through His audible voice, dreams, visions or trances.

God can also lead us through circumstances to discover our purpose, as was the case with Joseph. Every event in his life led him to the fulfilment of his purpose. We should interpret our circumstances through the lens of God's purpose. Understanding our divine purpose during adversity helps us see the accurate picture of such adversity: as a process and not a destination; to see people as instruments, not enemies. As it was for Joseph, there may be rough places and paths that God allows us to go through. We must never let seemingly bad situations weigh us down or make us bitter. Instead, we must come to the realisation that tough times could be God's way of working all things for our good and bringing to fulfilment His purpose for our lives. With that realisation, nothing will happen in our lives that will be seen as a misfortune or coincidence. We must remain diligent by making the most of whatever situation we find ourselves in, whether pleasant or not.

To fulfil our purpose in challenging circumstances we must never allow ourselves to be overwhelmed to the extent of going against the word of God. Indulging in sin is one way to prevent ourselves from discovering and fulfilling God's purpose for our lives. Imagine if Joseph had allowed his experiences to make him yield to the advances of Potiphar's wife. If that had been the case, he would have enjoyed the temporal pleasure of such acts but would most likely not have realised or fulfilled the purpose of God for his life. As God's children, we must not see sin as an escape route or a means to ease ourselves of the inconveniences of the path of purpose that God has ordained for us.

It must, however, be said that although God has a specific purpose for everyone, He also has a general purpose for all men – the salvation of their souls. *The Lord is... patient toward you, not wishing that any should perish, but that all should come to repentance.* (2 Peter 3:9 NHEB.) Our individual purpose will amount to nothing if we fail to achieve this one purpose in the course of our earthly pilgrimage. Our entire existence will be meaningless if this purpose is not attained. As such, we must prioritise our soul's salvation in all we do. We must endeavour to live in complete obedience to God's word. Only when we follow God faithfully every step of the way will He unravel His specific purpose for us.

TOPIC 2: RIGHT ATTITUDE TOWARDS OUR ADVERSARIES

GENESIS 45:1–28

*A*s the old professor was wheeled into the medical director's office he suddenly motioned his wife to stop pushing the chair. His wife could not understand her husband's sudden apprehension on seeing the medical director. The old professor, who had wanted to thank the director for waiving all his bills, could not even raise his face to look at him. His wife noticed a teardrop and his chest heaving in a sob. She turned to the director, asking a million questions with her eyes. The young man smiled and shrugged. Then, not able to stand the emotion-laden scene any longer, he motioned for the woman to wheel the old man home. As she swirled the wheelchair around the old man muttered, "I am sorry, my son, please forgive me." The director responded: "Prof, it's okay; we will talk later."

Inside the car, the old man turned to his still-bewildered wife. "Do you know, I had that man's life and destiny in my hands as his lecturer in medical college? Instead of moulding it, I frustrated his life to the point that he left the university. I never set my eyes on him again until this afternoon. Yet for three days I laid unconscious in his hospital." He grabbed his wife. "That man had my life in his hands, and he spared it. (Johnny, 2022.)

When we are hurt by others we are faced with two options: taking the path of bitterness and resentment – spending our lives brooding over the hurt done to us and plotting our revenge – or taking the path of forgiveness. The first path might initially seem right and feel good due to the Adamic nature of mankind, but when we are saved – come to the knowledge of Christ – we realise that the second path is the path of wisdom. The difference between these two paths is that the first makes us slaves to our toxic emotions, keeps us perpetually hurt and the wound fresh on the inside, while the second sets us on a journey of healing and recovery.

Joseph chose the second path. His attitude towards his brothers, who had sold him into slavery, was noble. His brothers had fallen into his hands and he had the opportunity to take revenge, but at that point, despite such opportunity, he displayed an admirable attitude. *"Joseph said to his brothers, "Come near to me, please." They came near. "He said, I am Joseph, your brother, whom you sold into Egypt. ⁵Now do not be grieved, nor angry with yourselves, that you sold me here, for God sent me before you to preserve life.""* (Genesis 45:4–5 NHEB.) After that, Joseph nourished them, gave them gifts such as clothing, loaded their donkeys as much as they could carry and arranged for the whole family to relocate to Egypt.

Joseph responded to his brothers' betrayal and cruel actions with love and forgiveness. What was his motivation? Where did this attitude originate? Joseph knew and feared God; he understood that God is all-powerful and controls the affairs of man, so he looked beyond his brothers and their actions and acknowledged that it was part of God's plan. Though God did not ordain nor prompt their evil actions, He turned them for His purpose.

We may never display this kind of attitude if we do not understand Christ's love and forgiveness. No matter what we pass through in life, we should not spend our lives resenting people or fighting those who have wronged us. When Jesus looked at the people who condemned Him to death, He acknowledged their ignorance and prayed for their forgiveness. An understanding that those who carry out evil actions against us might actually be ignorant of what they are doing will make it easier to relate with them and forgive them.

King David was another fellow in the Old Testament who had the right attitude towards an adversary. Saul had tried to kill David and hunted him to take his life, but when David had the opportunity to kill him he spared his life twice. Killing Saul would have seemed like a shortcut to the throne David was destined to have, but he understood that that was not the way God had destined him to have the throne and that killing Saul would have been a sin against God. His attitude is worthy of emulation; Saul said to David, *"You are more righteous than I; for you have done good to me, whereas I have done evil to you."* (1 Samuel 24:17 NHEB.) Stephen in the New Testament also displayed a proper attitude when he prayed for forgiveness for those who stoned him: *"He kneeled down, and shouted out, 'Lord, do not hold this sin against them.' When he had said this, he fell asleep."* (Acts 7:60 NHEB.)

In dealing with ill-treatments from others, we should know that whatever we go through might be God's design for our growth. He may have a bigger plan for us, but our resentment can thwart it. Therefore, rather than blaming others for our misfortune, we should trust God, who can make all things work in our favour. Joseph understood that, and remarked: *"As for you, you meant evil against me, but God meant it for good, to bring to pass, as it is this day, to save many people alive."* (Genesis 50:20 NHEB.) All their thoughts, plots and actions had only plunged him on the path towards the fulfilment of his purpose. If we truly trust in divine providence that all will be well at the end, we will understand that fighting others is only a distraction from our purpose.

Beyond a shadow of a doubt we cannot prevent anyone from being an adversary to us, but we can control our attitude towards the adversary. Our strength is not shown in how we negatively respond towards our adversaries; instead, it is shown in how we react positively. Attitude is important because it makes or mars our Christian testimony. It takes a positive attitude to achieve positive results. Do not let another person's evil make you evil. Romans 12:21 says: *"Do not be overcome by evil, but overcome evil with good."* (NHEB.) When we let our adversaries make us exhibit evil actions, they can be said to have been victorious over us. If we let the sinful actions of others overwhelm us to the point of displaying similar sinful acts such as envy, bitterness and hatred, then we are being overcome with evil. As with the professor and younger medical director, we can win over our adversaries with our good deeds. We can make them realise their evil and see the need to act appropriately when we repay their evil with good deeds.

Resentment. Vengeance. We all know those feelings. It is natural for the fallen man to hold a grudge and seek revenge. If Joseph had paid back his brothers in their own coin, many who heard of his ordeal would have excused him; that is the way of the world. Joseph lived long before Jesus, yet he lived the teachings of Christ: *"But I tell you, love your enemies, and pray for those who persecute you"* (Matthew 5:44 NHEB). This is the right attitude we should have in adversity and towards our adversaries. Let the words of Christ be our motivation and guide in our actions and reactions to our adversaries. By recompensing evil with good we would demonstrate the right attitude as God's children towards our adversaries and ensure our soul's salvation at the end of time.

CHAPTER 21

TOPIC 1: SEEKING GOD'S GUIDANCE

GENESIS 46:1–4

Making a choice to navigate through the path of life without seeking God's guidance could be disastrous. One thing is for sure, we are bound to falter in certain moments when we rely on our understanding rather than on God's leading. It stands to reason that one can never take a wrong turn when one depends on God, who created and understands the terrain of life. Psalm 37:23–24 assures us of this: *"The steps of a man are established by the LORD, and he delights in his way. ²⁴Though he stumble, he shall not fall, for the LORD holds him up with his hand."* (NHEB.)

In what could be described as a significant decision, Jacob's relocation to Egypt was assured with the aid of God's guidance. It was a move Jacob never imagined he would make for the reason he did. He had just received astonishing news: his beloved son was alive. He was not going there just to see him; he was going to live there. Amid the ecstasy and the craving to reunite with Joseph lay a fear of the unknown. Jacob knew decisions of this magnitude needed divine guidance and sought God's face through sacrifice when he stopped at Beersheba. God's response gave an insight into the state of Jacob's mind – he was apprehensive about his relocation to Egypt. *"Do not be afraid to go down into Egypt, for there I will make of you a great nation."* (Genesis 46:3 NHEB.) God's response to him was as reassuring as it was soothing. Jacob need not fear; God guaranteed. His quest to reunite with his long-lost son had God's backing just as much as it had His presence and guidance. Indeed, no believer can be confused or apprehensive with these kinds of reassuring words from a God, who delights in ordering the footsteps of His children.

God's guidance in our lives could be understood as His direction, advice, instruction, counsel or approval concerning a situation. It is God's method in aligning our lives, step by step, with His ultimate plan and purpose. There are several means by which God guides us. God can communicate with us by a direct audible voice as He did with the young Samuel (1Samuel 3:1–14). God can guide us through dreams as in the case of Joseph, whom God directed to flee from Bethlehem because of Herod's plan to kill Jesus (Matthew 2:13), through visions as was seen in Ananias' case when God directed him to Paul to pray for the restoration of his sight (Acts 9:10–16), and through trances as in Peter's case when God prepared his mind for meeting Cornelius, a Gentile (Acts 10:9–29). God can guide us by providence or circumstance, as in the case of King Saul, whose father's donkeys suddenly went missing; in seeking for those donkeys, Saul encountered his purpose (1 Samuel 9, 10:1–2). God can also guide us through the inner witness of the Holy Spirit. This could be an inner conviction, a burden or an assurance regarding a particular decision. Hence, when we yield ourselves to the voice of the Holy Spirit within us, He will nudge us on the right path. In addition, it should be noted that God's word – the Bible – remains the fundamental means by which God guides His children. Through God's word, messages from all other means of revelation can be validated. Through His word, we have an indisputable medium through which to obtain guidance from God in every facet of our lives.

There are certain times when we are faced with uncertain situations, when the conviction to act confuses our feelings with God's leading. For instance, we might have the burden of leaving a lucrative job to go into full-time ministry and are confused about whether it is God's leading or not. In such a case, we need to seek the face of God in prayer or/and seek counselling from a mature believer. In another scenario, we might have the opportunity of a lucrative job but the job will require us to carry out activities against God's word. We can be sure that such leading is not from God since it would require us to act contrary to His word as contained in the Bible. This is why we need to be acquainted with God's word. When our minds are renewed by His word we are able to discern God's good and perfect will for our lives. Romans 12:2 says: *"but be transformed by the renewing of your mind, so that you may prove what is the good, well-pleasing, and perfect will of God."* (NHEB.)

In our journey through life we will be faced with situations that require a decision that could make or mar our lives – where to live, where to work, or who to marry, for example. In moments such as these, we ask questions: How can I know if this is God's will or not? While it is natural to be held by the grip of hesitation, turning to God provides us with an assurance of guidance that will lead to the right decision.

However, the nature of man is such that the dependence on our intellect, wisdom, experience or friends' advice often leads us to sideline God in our decision-making process. Little wonder why some end up on career paths they do not find fulfilling, marriages that make them miserable and situations in which they do not derive joy. Often lost in the recesses of our hearts is the fact that no one can provide guidance as accurately as God because no one is infallible. Asking and relying on divine guidance is a sign of acknowledging our limitations and dependence on God. Obtaining guidance from the One who sees the end from the beginning will undoubtedly keep us one step ahead in life. Seeking divine guidance is a formula that can help us live according to God's will and purpose. When we see God as the ultimate source of direction we can rest assured of His leading. Proverbs 3:5–6 says: *"Trust in the LORD with all your heart, and do not lean on your own understanding. ⁶In all your ways acknowledge him, and he will make your paths straight."* (NHEB.)

Those who seek God's guidance with a sincere heart will find it. God wants to take you by the hand, not twist you by the arm.

God does not impose His will; He will only lead those who desire it and who are willing to be led. We can demonstrate our willingness to get guidance from God by making Him the Guide of our lives. David narrates God's guidance over his life by describing himself as a sheep and God as his Shepherd. *"The LORD is my shepherd; I lack nothing."* (Psalm 23:1 NHEB.) God can only be our Shepherd if we are His sheep. God will not lead those who are stubborn or reject His leading in matters that pertain to life and eternity. The sheep as an animal is meek and defenceless; it is vulnerable on its own and its survival depends on the guidance and protection of the shepherd. Like the sheep, we ought to rely solely on God for leading and protection. We must seek Him for direction in making decisions in every facet of our lives. When we let Him hold our hands He will lead us aright and keep us in perfect harmony with His will for our lives.

TOPIC 2: FULFILMENT OF JOSEPH'S DREAM

GENESIS 46:1–34

Walking with God often seems like a tedious and confusing task. It is seemingly not easy following Him on the journey of life without having the urge to run faster, go back or stop the journey halfway. However, all He expects is that we obey, believe and walk in line with His word. In the end, we will arrive at the place He wants us to be, and His glory will be seen in us.

There were two dreams, two dreams that enflamed the fury of Joseph's brothers like adding fuel to the fire. When he narrated the first dream his brothers asked, *"Will you indeed reign over us? Or will you indeed have dominion over us?..."* (Genesis 37:8 NHEB.) Ultimately, that first dream came to fulfilment. The second dream of the sun, moon and 11 stars bowing to him depicted his authority over his family. Genesis 46 records the fulfilment of that dream. The house of Israel relocated to Egypt, where Joseph was the second-in-command, and they all lived under his leadership.

God has a specific purpose for everyone; this is one truth that cannot be refuted. However, how this purpose is disclosed to each individual is solely determined and dependent upon God's sovereignty. For instance, God can lead a person through life's circumstances just as He did for Joseph or He can expressly unveil His purpose for a person just as He did for Jeremiah. Jeremiah 1:5 says, *"Before I formed you in the belly, I knew you. Before you came forth out of the womb, I sanctified you. I have appointed you a prophet to the nations."* (NHEB.)

In point of fact, the fulfilment of God's plans for our lives is a process we have to follow. It is easy to think that realising God's plans for our lives will be easy. However, the journey may not be devoid of trials and challenges; it may not be as smooth as we may envisage. We could encounter bumps along the way, bumps that will shake the foundation of our trust and challenge the pillars of our faith in God. Joseph faced his own bumps and his dreams became a rose with thorns. He plucked the rose in the end, but did not do so without suffering the piercing pain of the thorns.

Just after he had his dreams of greatness, a conspiracy to kill him arose, with one singular purpose, *"Look, this dreamer comes. ²⁰Come now therefore, and let's kill him, and cast him into one of the pits... We will see what will become of his dreams."* (Genesis 37:19–20 NHEB.) He was not killed but was sold into slavery after much deliberation. That was not the end of his plight. Troubles followed him to the land of Egypt with his resolve not to sleep with Potiphar's wife landing him in prison.

The psalmist in Psalm 105:18–20 briefly describes Joseph's journey and the fulfilment of his purpose: *"They bruised his feet with shackles. His neck was locked in irons, ¹⁹until the time that his word happened, and the LORD's word proved him true. ²⁰The king sent and freed him; even the ruler of peoples, and let him go free."* (NHEB.) Until the time for the fulfilment of Joseph's dream, he faced challenges and a test of his character. Joseph, however, showed an exemplary attitude during this process.

Also, Joseph was not obsessed with God's plan of greatness for his life. When we react to God's promises with obsession, we are sucked deep into worry and cynicism. Our obsession with the revelations and promises of God becomes an unhealthy fixation that tends to narrow our lives to fulfilling those promises. A life of wanting everything to work as fast as the speed of light puts us in conflict with God's timing and will. Our trust in God will be affected, and we may be lured by the devil to tow the path of sin to find a counterfeit version of God's plan. In that instance, we choose the path of sin by following the world's fleeting pleasures and strain our relationship with God and our eternal communion with Him. The ultimate promise a Christian must cling to is the promise of the salvation of his soul. This promise should be the centre of our focus. When we focus entirely on this promise our relationship with God will remain intact, despite possible delays in the fulfilment of God's plan for us.

Furthermore, the most essential ingredient in fulfilling God's plan is living in constant obedience to God's word. This is what God expects from us rather than obsessively focusing on how God will bring His plan to fulfilment. We must remain faithful and stay within the confine of God's will regardless of the challenges that may come our way during this process. Those trials and challenges are not to mar us; instead, they are meant to test and strengthen our faith in God. Besides, He will also use them to teach us to trust and depend on Him while He works things out to fulfil His purpose for our lives according to His will. The Lord, who has the blueprint of His purpose for our lives, will bring it to pass at His time. You only need to walk at God's pace while He orchestrates events and circumstances to bring His plans to fruition. Jeremiah 29:11 says: ***"'For I know the plans that I have for you,' says the LORD, 'plans for your welfare, and not for calamity, to give you hope and a future.'"*** (NHEB.)

It is binding on us to be conscious of our attitude when God eventually brings to fulfilment His plans for our lives. We should not be filled with pride, believing it is by our making. Also, we should not fail to glorify God by working in line with the purpose of God's plan for our lives.

God's plans for us are sure, but we may not be able to determine the time of their fulfilment. Therefore, consistent obedience to God's word is vital to ensure that His purpose for our lives is fulfilled.

CHAPTER 22

TOPIC 1: COMPETENCE

GENESIS 47:5–6

An African proverb says, "A developing child does not wait to see cooked yam to chew before his teeth are formed." The adage implies that preparations to chew the food should be done before the food arrives and not after. It teaches that skills and competence are to be developed in anticipation of opportunities, but that if one waits for the arrival of opportunities before one is trained, one will be unable to take advantage of them, or the opportunities will be taken by others who are more prepared.

The reunion of Jacob's family was finally complete. Joseph went ahead to introduce his family to Pharaoh, taking five of his brothers along. As Pharaoh received them, he made a request to Joseph: *"The land of Egypt is before you. Settle your father and your brothers in the best of the land. Let them dwell in the land of Goshen. If you know any able men among them, then put them in charge of my livestock."* (Genesis 47:6 NHEB.) An opportunity came knocking, but the question is, was any of them prepared to open the door? Of course, that question would be for Joseph and his brothers to answer. But do we not all have a similar question to answer? If an opportunity comes knocking, are we prepared to open the door?

King Solomon made a similar request to the King of Tyre: *"Now therefore send me a man skillful to work in gold, and in silver, and in bronze, and in iron..."* (2 Chronicles 2:7 NHEB.) The King of Tyre responded thus: *"Now I have sent a skillful man, endowed with understanding, of Huram my father's, [14]the son of a woman of the daughters of Dan; and his father was a man of Tyre, skillful to work in gold, and in silver, in bronze, in iron, in stone, and in timber, in purple, in blue, and in fine linen, and in crimson, also to engrave any kind of engraving, and to execute any design; that there may be a place appointed to him with your skillful men, and with the skillful men of my lord David your father."* (2 Chronicles 2:13–14 NHEB.) An opportunity came knocking and Huram-Abi was very competent in the task. This emphasises what Proverbs 22:29 says: *"Do you see a man skilled in his work? He will serve kings. He won't serve obscure men."* (NHEB.) Competence can take us to a place of highest honour.

Today, the problem with many people being stuck in the loop of inadequacy is not the lack of opportunity but of adequate preparation. Most of us treat opportunities as surprise guests we tell to wait outside while we prepare our homes for their visit. It is better to be ready for an opportunity than to have one and not be prepared.

Many complain about how unfair the world is, the scarcity of jobs and the struggle for survival. The truth is that opportunities keep presenting themselves every day, but mostly we do not recognise them.

One of the catalysts to a successful life in line with preparedness is versatility. Versatility is being competent in a particular field while having the capability of handling other ventures. For instance, nothing stops a person who has a first-class degree in law from being a fantastic caterer. Often, opportunities present themselves in various forms and it behoves us to be prepared for them.

In today's ever-changing world, versatility is essential for everyone. Our versatility enables us to adapt to the changing needs and demands of the society we live in; hence, Christians in the labour market should continually keep improving and updating themselves to be abreast of the economy's dynamism. We are to be determined in pursuing the necessary education and skill that will enable us to stand out from the crowd.

King Solomon was not looking for just anybody, likewise Pharaoh in our Bible passage; they were looking for men who were exceptionally skilled and competent. When we develop ourselves, our expertise will set us above the crowd. We might not look for opportunities; instead, opportunities will come looking for us. People do not celebrate mediocrity; neither do they search for those who are lazy. If we are willing to pay the price of utmost commitment to our personal growth and development, it will not be too long before we see the results. When opportunities meet our preparedness, we will shine exceptionally in our generation. Our success begins at the end of our complacency towards life. We should not be so concerned about what we do not have; instead, we should make the best of our resources. Success does not happen overnight; hence we should not be afraid to start small and be committed to our small beginnings. When we have a nonchalant attitude towards our small beginnings, hoping to be more committed when we achieve greatness, we might never achieve excellence. But if we are willing to do the little things with utmost commitment we will encounter better opportunities. Remember the words of Solomon: *"Whatever your hand finds to do, do it with your might..."* (Ecclesiastes 9:10 NHEB.) It is wisdom to add godly virtues such as humility, discipline, commitment and integrity to our competence.

As children and representatives of God here on earth we should endeavour to be competent in all we do. Our works and character should reflect the excellence and competence of God, our Father. That will be a testimony to the watching world. We should take heed to the admonition in 1 Thessalonians 4:11–12, *"and that you make it your ambition to lead a quiet life, and to do your own business, and to work with your own hands, even as we instructed you; [12] that you may walk properly toward those who are outside, and may have need of nothing."* (NHEB.)

Competence breaks socio-ethnic barriers. For Daniel, being a foreigner in Babylon did not matter; his competence was instrumental in elevating him to high honour in a strange land.

In our pursuit of competence we must never forget the pivotal role of God in our success equation. We must rely on God and depend on His aid, knowing full well that we can do nothing without Him. *"Unless the LORD builds the house, they labor in vain who build it. Unless the LORD watches over the city, the watchman guards it in vain."* (Psalm 127:1 NHEB.)

However, it is against God's will to use our skills and knowledge to perpetrate fraudulent acts. Thus, our areas of competence should be aligned with God's will. We are to carry out all our activities faithfully as unto God. Our competence should not be limited to our secular life. It should extend to our services to God and our responsibility in spreading the gospel of salvation.

TOPIC 2: DILIGENCE

GENESIS 47:13–26

The wise King Solomon wrote: *"The hands of the diligent ones shall rule, but laziness ends in slave labor."* (Proverbs 12:24 NHEB.) Diligence is a dedicated and consistent effort in accomplishing a task in the best way possible. It is to be hardworking, effective and efficient with available resources.

Diligence was one recurring element in the story of Joseph's journey from slavery to national prominence. In what many might have seen as a downturn, but which turned out to be a fulfilment of divine purpose, Joseph moved from being a slave supervising the affairs in Potiphar's house to being a prisoner overseeing the welfare of inmates in prison. After some years in prison, God helped Joseph interpret Pharaoh's dreams and Pharaoh gave him the responsibility of gathering food during the seven years of plenty and distributing the same during the seven years of famine. To that responsibility was added the authority of being the second-in-command to Pharaoh. Joseph applied the same diligence he applied in home management and prison management in managing the national affairs of Egypt in a critical season. Indeed, God was responsible for Joseph's elevation, but if he had failed to play his part by being diligent, his sustenance as the second-in-command in Egypt would have been jeopardised. Thus, God's favour and Joseph's diligence were the required mix for Joseph's success. He painstakingly carried out his duties and achieved the task that Pharaoh set out for him.

In the same way, the favour of God takes us to stepping-stones that should propel us to elevated positions, but we need to be diligent in our responsibilities to God and in our engagements, for the blessing of God to materialise and to maintain that position. Sadly, some people lose out along the way by acting in ways contrary to God's word. Without the fear of God, the stepping-stones that should have taken them up become sinking sand in which they are consumed.

Like Joseph, a diligent person working in a delegated capacity seeks to understand the will of the person who assigns him the responsibility and strategically gives attention to matters with top priority. By the monarchial system of his days, Joseph, even as second-in-command, was still Pharaoh's servant acting in a delegated capacity; his loyalty was to Pharaoh alone. The Bible says: *"Joseph gathered up all the money that was found in the land of Egypt, and in the land of Canaan, for the grain which they bought: and Joseph brought the money into Pharaoh's house."* (Genesis 47:14 NHEB.) The money he made was for Pharaoh; all the strategies he employed in his work favoured Pharaoh. Looking at his zeal, discipline and dedication we can learn how to be dedicated in duty and service to both our heavenly and earthly masters.

At work and in private life, Christians are expected to be hardworking and efficient. Paul wrote: *"For even when we were with you, we commanded you this: 'If anyone will not work, neither let him eat.'*

[11]For we hear of some who walk among you in rebellion, who do not work at all, but are busybodies." (2 Thessalonians 3:10–11 NHEB.) We must understand the work we are doing and who will ultimately benefit from it. Is God glorified in our work? Is our earthly benefit following God's standards? We must seek to answer these questions as we apply ourselves to our services. We must also know the system to put in place to efficiently complete our tasks. These are some of the things we must learn from Joseph. Diligence entails a willingness to work hard with a discerning focus, a sense of urgency, a vigilant carefulness with faithful perseverance.

We should note that without diligence, there can be no authentic leadership. Diligent people will sit with kings. Solomon wrote: *"Do you see a man skilled in his work? He will serve kings. He won't serve obscure men."* (Proverbs 22:29 NHEB.) Hard work in little things is a route to being bestowed with superior things. Therefore, we must give every assigned task our best shot, being conscious that we do not have all the time and will not get a second opportunity to live after we are gone.

Many Christians want to be great, but they do not want to be hardworking. Some delude themselves that they will be more diligent when handling greater responsibilities or when they own their businesses. They do not consider Christ's instruction in Luke 16:10,12: *"[10]He who is faithful in a very little is faithful also in much. He who is dishonest in a very little is also dishonest in much. [12]If you have not been faithful in that which is another's, who will give you that which is your own?"* (NHEB.) A close look at the life of Jesus shows that He was diligent. *"But he answered them, "My Father is still working, so I am working, too.""* (John 5:17 NHEB.) A Christian who is not diligent at his work – whether in business or private life – cannot say he is a true son of his Father.

However, we should not exhibit industriousness contrary to the word of God. Working hard in a job contrary to God's word might bring the desired reward but will negatively affect the most crucial thing in our lives, our relationship with God. In applying diligence to our Christian walk, Paul admonishes us in 2 Timothy 2:4–5, *"No soldier on duty entangles himself in the affairs of life, that he may please him who enrolled him as a soldier. ⁵Also, if anyone competes in athletics, he is not crowned unless he has competed by the rules."* (NHEB.) A Christian's first loyalty is to Christ. In our diligence, we must not become entangled in worldly affairs. Sinning, in the name of hard work, is not expected of us as God's children. Pleasing others is great, but it is only permissible to the extent that we do not displease God. Our main task is to please God – not others, nor ourselves. If we work hard at making a profit and that hard work is unduly impoverishing others, it goes contrary to God's love. If we claim to love God and turn around to take advantage of people in their times of need, we are not displaying Christlike character.

A closer look at Joseph's model will reveal certain things that Christians should not copy. Joseph's loyalty and allegiance to Pharaoh, his earthly master, was good, but as long as Pharaoh was happy with his work, Joseph was satisfied with it. It did not matter to him that the people, under his supervision, went into the famine period free citizens but became slaves to Pharaoh to get food at some point during the famine. The Egyptians used up their money, lands, livestock and everything they had, and all these went to Pharaoh. We should be careful to note that Joseph's diligence enriched his master but left most Egyptians as slaves without personal properties. Making money is great, but making it at the expense of the people you oversee – obtaining their wealth and enslaving them in the process – should not be named among Christians. Paul wrote to the Corinthians: *"I will most gladly spend and be spent for your souls. If I love you more abundantly, am I loved the less?"* (2 Corinthians 12:15 NHEB.) Instead of making money at others' expense, we are supposed to act for the benefit of the physical and spiritual welfare of the people we serve.

Applying diligence, whether in our spiritual exercises, relationships or economic lives, leads to excellence. Putting in diligence in our walk of faith leads to spiritual growth, a greater love for others, greater love for Christ and a greater understanding of the gospel and love of God for us.

TOPIC 3: BURIAL

GENESIS 47:28–31

Sunken in the depth of the sea or scattered as ashes
Right in the belly of the beast or rotten as debris in the forest
To dust, it returns
Laid in the grandiose of tomb or cast shabbily to a pit
Graced with pomp and dignity or attended with shame and neglect
Still, to dust, it returns
All that matters are choices made while alive;
All that soars are works done before death
The remains, to dust it returns. (Johnny, 2022.)

It was time for Jacob's departure, at 147 years old. Jacob had lived to a good old age, having seen his children all grown and his third generation amounting to a great number. But, in the comfort of the land of Egypt, nature came calling, so he prepared his house. He made Joseph swear to bury him with his fathers in Canaan. Possessing the land of Canaan was a promise transferred to him – a promise God made to Abraham. God had appeared to him in Bethel to reaffirm this promise, so Jacob was sure God would give the entire land of Canaan to his descendants. Because of this assurance, he committed Joseph with an oath to carry his body back to Canaan when he died. To Jacob's children, it was a tonic to remind them that Egypt was not their home – Canaan was.

Like Jacob, we shall all reckon with death while the coming of Jesus lingers, and our bodies will be put away somewhere, somehow and someday. To make plans concerning how or where we are to be buried is good; nonetheless, that should be the least of our worries. However, the destination of our souls after death should be our priority. True rest awaiting our souls is not in the grave or burial site. It is the supreme rest we shall have in being with God and enjoying His fellowship evermore at the close of time, where we shall no longer be plagued with sickness, troubles and afflictions, but dwell in the perpetual light and love of the Almighty. It is the rest we shall have in arriving finally at our home – our eternal Promised Land. Hence, the issue of the nature of our burial should not be overrated.

When a person dies, the real man, which is the soul, goes yonder. What is left lying in state is the body – dust – which should be appropriately disposed of to prevent contamination of the environment. Whether buried in the ground, kept in a cave or cremated, all these methods do not constitute any importance to the soul's salvation and are of no spiritual significance. Considering the hope of resurrection in 1 Corinthians 15:42–44, we realise that burial has to do with the body and not the soul: *"So also is the resurrection of the dead. It is sown in corruption; it is raised in incorruption. [43] It is sown in dishonor; it is raised in glory. It is sown in weakness; it is raised in power. [44] It is sown a natural body; it is raised a spiritual body. There is a natural body and there is also a spiritual body."* (NHEB.) How and where our bodies are sown does not really make any difference. From dust, we came, and to dust, we shall return. The location of the dust does not matter. Imagine if it did, those who died accidentally in plane crashes, capsized boats, who were burnt in fires or who died in other incidents after which their bodies could not be found or recovered would have no hope of being raised with a spiritual body.

Some people share a sentimental and cultural inclination regarding where they should be buried. Some cultures share the belief that burying the dead close by helps in guarding the living. Some other cultures believe that burying a relative in their hometown allows the person to rest with their ancestors. We know that these beliefs are not scriptural in light of the Christian faith. Therefore, we should hold our traditional beliefs loosely and our faith in God tenaciously. Human culture should not be the basis of our decisions and choices in life; rather, the word of God should be.

There is nothing wrong with desiring to be buried in your native land. However, if the process will inconvenience your family in terms of cost and risk, it is proper to spare them the trouble. It is wrong to refer to Jacob's request to be buried in Canaan as an indication that Christians must be buried in their hometowns. While Jacob might have made his request to be buried in Canaan due to God's promise to give the land to his descendants, making such a request regarding where we desire to be buried has no significance to our faith. Furthermore, with the position of Joseph as the second-in-command in Egypt, vested with wealth and authority, Jacob's request was not a burden to his children. We should be mindful of the rationale behind desiring to be buried in a specific place or in a particular manner. Our motives should not border on fear, superstition or pride.

Christians should always consider the wellbeing of the people they will leave behind, as is expected of them while alive. If we desire to be buried in a particular place or manner that may be financially demanding, we should ensure that adequate provisions have been made to lighten the burden on those we leave behind. However, it will honour God more if such money is dedicated to the welfare of the needy. Also, keeping a corpse for too long because of lack of finance for an extravagant burial does not portray the simple lifestyle a Christian is required to lead. Instead of wishing for an elaborate funeral, when the means are difficult to come by, or one that wastes resources, we should wish for our families to live in love and continue in the service of God. People should only be sorrowful for missing our presence on earth and not for the enormous inconveniencies surrounding our burial.

If we have an understanding of God's pronouncement in Genesis 3:19, *"For you are dust, and to dust you shall return"* (NHEB), we will not bother about what happens to this temporary covering. The real person is the soul. Since death is inevitable for all, we must live to ensure the salvation of our souls and that of our loved ones if possible. After death, the grace of God that brings salvation will no more be accessible. Each individual's earthly deeds will determine the eternal abode of the soul; as such, while we are alive, obedience to God should be our priority.

TOPIC 4: YOUR WORD, YOUR BOND

GENESIS 47:29–31

"I will do it." "I can do it." "I am capable of doing it." These are words that typically come out of our mouths when we commit ourselves to a promise. Yet few as they may seem, sometimes the fulfilment of such words is realised not with mere utterance but with sincere commitment. Words spoken in agreement as an assurance that the thing agreed upon will be carried out can be encouraging and can give relief to the person counting on those words to be put into action.

Jacob was old and about to die. He would undoubtedly die in peace after seeing his long-lost-son Joseph, who was now the second-in-command in Egypt. It was time to address his family before his death – to proclaim the future that awaited each of his children. But for himself, he had one final request: he wished to be buried in the cave of Machpelah, the burial site Abraham had purchased in which to bury his wife Sarah, and where Abraham, Isaac, Rebekah and Leah were buried. He requested the favour from Joseph, making him promise with an oath to bury him at Machpelah. It was a request within the powers of Joseph to fulfil and one Joseph could not refuse. This was the father he had never thought he would see again, the father who made him a coat of many colours and the father who showered him with nothing but care and affection. After Jacob's death, the words that came out of Joseph's mouth were a promise he was obliged to fulfil, and fulfil he did. Joseph proved that he was a man of his word in a way that is instructive for us and worthy of emulation.

Whether casually spoken or in a formal arrangement, one thing that can either win trust or distrust is our integrity in keeping our word. Unfortunately, we live in a society in which people do not treat their words with the weight of honesty they deserve. All spheres of human endeavour greatly suffer for want of integrity. The virtue of honesty is rare to find. How often do we affix our words in agreement to a request but fail to do what we have promised? Our society is plagued by a general epidemic of lies and falsehood. People no longer see their words as binding: they break their words at will, make promises they never intend to keep or break their marital vows at the slightest opportunity. Even among the many who profess to be Christians these traits are common, but this should not be the case.

The importance of integrity with our words cannot be separated from our walk with God. To trust the message of salvation from us, people must trust us to keep simple commitments. In several scriptures of the Bible, God instructs us to pay attention to the words we say. Vain and profane words should never be heard from a Christian. A Christian should say only good and useful things to the hearer. *"Let no corrupt speech proceed out of your mouth, but such as is good for building up as the need may be, that it may give grace to those who hear."* (Ephesians 4:29 NHEB.) He should be quick to hear but slow to speak. The one who can withhold himself from sinning with his words has found the key to perfect living. *"For in many things we all stumble. If anyone does not stumble in word, this one is a perfect person, able to bridle the whole body also."* (James 3:2 NHEB.) As Christians, the words we are to be mindful of include promises made to others. Promises devoid of hypocrisy and falsehood are consistent in a person whose heart is bereft of hypocrisy and deceit, for the mouth speaks out of the abundance of the heart. *"how can you, being evil, speak good things? For out of the abundance of the heart, the mouth speaks."* (Matthew 12:34 NHEB.)

Jacob demanded that Joseph swear that he would honour his request. In the olden times, oaths were used to ensure that what was spoken or agreed was fulfilled. It was common knowledge that a person who failed to fulfil a promise made in oath risked the wrath of God. Hence, promises or commitments made with an oath were trusted and reliable. However, in this dispensation, it is essential to note that oaths are no longer permissible. Jesus made this clear when He said: *"But I tell you, do not swear at all: neither by heaven, for it is the throne of God; 35 nor by the earth, for it is the footstool of his feet; nor by Jerusalem, for it is the city of the great King. 36 Neither should you swear by your head, for you cannot make one hair white or black. 37 But let your 'Yes' be 'Yes' and your 'No' be 'No.' Whatever is more than these is of the evil one."* (Matthew 5:34–37 NHEB.) In other words, swearing to fulfil a promise is unnecessary for Christians today and it is also prohibited. Since every word we speak could define us and affect our salvation, every promise we make is as good as backed by an oath. Therefore, it is erroneous for a Christian to back his words with an oath even if he intends to fulfil it with all sincerity. He only needs to say yes when he means yes and no when he means no; anything besides this is not from a pure heart.

Sometimes it may be better to avoid making promises altogether if there is the slightest probability that we would not fulfil them. Emerging with a solution to someone's problem is always more effective than making a promise. In making promises we should consider the circumstances first, weighing up all possible means to be sure we can keep our word. We do not know what may happen in the next splits of seconds, for only God knows the future. Therefore, while making a promise, it is better to say, *"If the Lord wills, we will both live, and do this or that."* (James 4:15 NHEB.)

There could be times when circumstances beyond our control force us to renege on our promise. Notifying the other party on time of our inability to fulfil our pledge at the expected time due to the prevailing circumstance is the right course of action. This will go a long way towards maintaining our integrity while we gain more time to fulfil our promise. We ought to be careful to fulfil our words and more careful not to promise what we do not mean to do. The psalmist asks the question: *"LORD, who shall dwell in your sanctuary? Who shall live on your holy mountain?"* (Psalm 15:1 NHEB.) Then he gives the answer to include: *"In his eyes a vile man is despised, but he honors those who fear the LORD. He keeps an oath even when it hurts, and doesn't change it."* (Psalm 15:4 NHEB.) This paints a picture of someone who would do whatever it takes to fulfil their word even if it incurs some form of hurt in the process. People must be able to trust us to fulfil what we have promised under any circumstance.

Trust, once broken, is difficult to regain. If those around us cannot trust us they might never believe anything we say, and this may give unbelievers an occasion to treat the name of the Lord with contempt. Therefore, let us live with the consciousness that the words we speak can have an eternal consequence on our soul's salvation. *"For by your words you will be justified, and by your words you will be condemned."* (Matthew 12:37 NHEB.)

CHAPTER 23

TOPIC 1: CARING FOR AGED PARENTS

GENESIS 48:1–2

The words "old age" elicit different pictures in the minds of diverse people. For many, they equate to a frail person dependent on aids for walking, hearing, seeing and sometimes feeding. The very thought of growing old can be scary for some because they have to depend on others for what they were doing for themselves when they were young. However, when one has the assurance that there will be loved ones who will help, the thought of growing old may not be that scary after all. There is an air of relief when aged people know they have people to care for them.

Ageing is a natural process. However, as one ages physical impairments and functional disabilities are bound to occur, resulting in increased dependency. This is when parents need care from their children or caregivers; hence, caring for aged parents becomes an essential task for us as God's children.

When news got to Joseph that his aged father was ill he dropped everything and visited his father with his two sons. He was concerned about his father and thought it wise to personally see him rather than send messengers. This act is noteworthy for believers regarding caring for their aged parents.

Nurturing aged parents is very sensitive, and children should be extremely careful about it, especially knowing that God places a high value on parental honour. Ephesians 6:1–3 says: ***"Children, obey your parents in the Lord, for this is right.*** *² "Honor your father and mother," which is the first commandment with a promise: ³ "that it may be well with you, and that you may live long in the land.""* (NHEB.) Unfortunately, there is a tendency for children to become so busy with life that they no longer bother about the wellbeing of their aged parents. Providing money and material needs is essential, but that is by no means the only care our aged parents need. They also need our visits and attention. We may not have the luxury of time or a flexible job, but we should care for them by endeavouring to maintain frequent contact. Considering that technology has made it possible for people to communicate visually and audibly, there can be no excuse not to be involved in their lives. By making time out to visit them, we can create an ambience of happiness and a collection of pleasant memories through our presence.

Caring for aged parents can be very challenging. Their behaviours and mannerisms might seem odd or out of place at this time, but we are to be patient with them, bearing in mind that they could be dealing with different forms of stress that accompany ageing. There are times when they might exhibit some childlike behaviours, but we should be tolerant and gentle in dealing with them. We have to equip ourselves with knowledge of the process of ageing and the challenges involved. We may need to read some books, talk to professionals or seek appropriate counselling from those who have had the experience before us. Regardless of our schedules, our involvement in their lives must remain active, consistent and compassionate, and all the while we must remember that we will one day be old like them and could need the same help.

The option of a retirement home or hiring a caregiver can be considered if the consistent physical presence of the children is not feasible. This option ensures that house chores and the feeding and health of aged parents are adequately taken care of. However, the retirement home or caregiver's services should not replace our responsibilities as children.

Paul admonished Timothy that while the church was to take care of widows who had no caregiver, children and other younger relations should look after their widowed parents, thus lessening the church's burden. *"Honor widows who are widows indeed. ⁴But if any widow has children or grandchildren, let them learn first to show piety towards their own family, and to repay their parents, for this is acceptable in the sight of God."* (1 Timothy 5:3–4 NHEB.)

It is worth pointing out that some people erroneously forsake honouring their parents in their attempt to display honour for God. In one of the erroneous traditions held by some Jewish sects, someone could declare that they had given to God what they were supposed to give to their parents, leaving them free of the obligation to the parents. This doctrine encourages people to be irresponsible towards their parents. In Matthew 15:3–6 Jesus took His time to correct this doctrine and rebuked its adherents. *"And he answered them, "Why do you also disobey the commandment of God because of your tradition? ⁴For God said, 'Honor your father and your mother,' and, 'He who speaks evil of father or mother, let him be put to death.' ⁵But you say, 'Whoever may tell his father or his mother, "Whatever help you might otherwise have gotten from me is a gift devoted to God," ⁶he is not to honor his father or his mother.' You have made the word of God void because of your tradition.""* (NHEB.) Jesus' rebuke implied that honouring parents also involves supporting them financially when they need it. Sadly, some people today ignorantly express such reprehensible attitudes as those Jesus rebuked. They give generously in their service to God but neglect caring for their parent. In our devotion to God we should not abandon our parents. Our worship of God is expressed by obeying His commands, which involves honouring and caring for our parents.

In caring for the physical needs of our aged parents, we should not neglect their spiritual needs as well. We should make it a duty to continuously pray with and for them.

TOPIC 2: CHILDREN: GIFTS FROM GOD

GENESIS 48:8–9

There are many things in life we trivialise which are of eternal consequence. One of them is how we perceive our little ones. Children are not merely a means of continuing man's existence on earth or our successors when we pass on; they are gifts from God, a gift to which God still retains ownership. Therefore, parents are caregivers to raise children for the Lord. Psalm 127:3 says: *"Look, children are a heritage of the LORD. The fruit of the womb is his reward."* (NHEB.)

A gift could be said to be a thing willingly and freely handed to someone. Children, as gifts, come with the responsibility of nurturing them. The way this responsibility is handled could have an eternal consequence for the parents. When Jacob saw the two children Joseph brought, he asked Joseph: *"Who are these?"* (Genesis 48:8 NHEB.) Joseph replied, *"They are my sons, whom God has given me here."* (Genesis 48:9 NHEB.) Joseph knew his children were from God. His perspective on the source of his children is the idea behind good parenting. When we realise children are God's gifts, our disposition towards them will change for the better.

Like Joseph, who acknowledged God as the Giver of children, Jacob made a similar statement to Esau when they reunited after many years: *"He lifted up his eyes, and saw the women and the children; and said, "Who are these with you?" He said, "The children whom God has graciously given your servant.""* (Genesis 33:5 NHEB.) Abraham, their father, was promised a son by God. God expressed His trust that the gift of children He was giving Abraham would be raised properly. He said in Genesis 18:19: *"For I have known him, to the end that he may command his children and his household after him, that they may keep the way of the LORD, to do righteousness and justice; to the end that the LORD may bring on Abraham that which he has spoken of him."* (NHEB.)

CHAPTER 23

God expects us to take care of our children, teach them His ways and guide them away from errors.

Many people's failure in realising that children are God's gift has led them to manage their children with less concern, thereby risking their relationship with God – the Giver. Parenting is not only about being a father or mother; it is the ability to raise a child who will be in character and attitude, a candidate of God's eternal salvation plan. We fail in parenting when we do not do all within the word of God to ensure that the children under our care do not become godless. A parent who condones a child who lives an ungodly lifestyle or earns their living through ungodly means will be answerable to God for raising the child inappropriately.

It is the responsibility of parents to train and mould the character of their children in a godly manner. Children come as empty or clean slates from God – innocent and dependent. They are not born with a belief or lifestyle of their own, and the foundation of their belief will be the things we teach them. We can give them a lifestyle by gradually shaping their attitudes and preferences. In a child's innocence, their mind is open to activities in the environment and the home they live in. As such, parents can influence the actions within the home and guard the children against negative influences from the environment. It is true that before society affects a child, the parents – biological or foster – play a more significant role in the child's character. Children do not only learn what parents teach them; they learn faster from what they see their parents do. Thus, parents teach their children by their character even without knowing. This learning by the children is taken into society and serves as the platform on which other learning is built. A child raised in fear of the Lord will have the strength of character to resist negative societal influences, while one who is not raised correctly will readily embrace whatever society offers. Such a child, without divine intervention, will become a tool in the devil's hands. The reason we have many children with ungodly attitudes is that many parents live ungodly lifestyles and are yet to realise that they have a divine responsibility towards the gift of children, which must be carried out in harmony with the word of God: *"Train a child in the way he should go, and when he is old he will not depart from it."* (Proverbs 22:6 NHEB.) Training here refers to a consistent moulding of a child's character in the way of the Lord, by discipline, daily studying of the word of God, praying together and living out the life for the child to see and practise from a tender age.

Many parents pursue wealth and fame, neglecting their role as parents, and may push their primary responsibility onto the educational system or nannies. Some give their children the best education and welfare but neglect the most important gift – the knowledge of God's word. Catering to the material needs of our children is very important and must not be treated lightly. About the one who would not cater for the material needs of his family, Apostle Paul wrote: *"But if anyone does not provide for his own, and especially his own household, he has denied the faith, and is worse than an unbeliever."* (1 Timothy 5:8 NHEB.) However, if we successfully cater to the material needs of our children but fail to guide them in their spiritual journey, we will have made a grievous mistake. A child could go hungry and will probably lack good formal education if the parents are financially handicapped. This is understood. But no child should go without the knowledge of the word of God for whatever reason. Doing the right thing first will give us the boldness to approach God to help take care of our children's material needs when the means are not forthcoming.

Note that a Christian parent who does not train their child in the way of the Lord cannot be excused if the child picks up bad habits from society. God will hold the parent accountable, as was the case of Eli. Eli's fault, for which God held him to account, was his failure to discipline his children and bring them up in the way of God. As a result, his children dishonoured God among the people, treated God's offering with contempt and slept with the women at the entrance of the tent of meeting. God judged the house of Eli by withdrawing the priesthood from it. Eli and his two sons died on the same day (1 Samuel 3, 4:1–18). Genuine love for our children means disciplining them and bringing them up in God's way.

Every child is a gift from God regardless of his physical makeup or circumstances surrounding his birth. Upon coming into the world, a child's first need is the parents' love, which should manifest in accepting the child the way they are and taking good care of them. No child should experience the trauma of rejection by parents because of deformity or other challenging physical problems, which, of course, are not the child's fault. A believer in such a situation should accept the child and love them dearly as God's perfect gift. Also, a child should not be mistreated because of an unpleasant circumstance surrounding their birth, such as unplanned pregnancy or pregnancy resulting from rape. Every child is a gift from God, unique and innocent at birth; it is left for us to raise children to be the best they can be.

The love we owe our children should not give room for indulgence. Pampering at the expense of discipline is not love. Discipline is one of the godly ways of child training. Proverbs 22:15 says, ***"Folly is bound up in the heart of a child: the rod of discipline drives it far from him."*** (NHEB.) Whenever they err, children should be promptly corrected and disciplined where applicable. Discipline will help them distinguish between acceptable and deviant behaviours. However, discipline should not be allowed to gravitate into abuse, for it will be disregarding God's gift. A disciplinary measure that leaves bodily injury on a child or crushes their self-esteem is abuse and not discipline. Many acts of unwholesome discipline end up destroying a child's life, making them resentful, critical and violent, instead of correcting them. Whether the child is biologically of the parent or not, we must assume the responsibility of good parenting. We should treat every child we come across in the same way we would treat our biological children.

Parents should realise that they cannot raise children in the way of God without first knowing God. They cannot teach children about God if they do not know God themselves, for parents must be living examples of what they teach their children. Hence, it is essential to become devoted to God, study His word and live by it. In that way, it will be easy to raise godly children, which we, as good stewards, will present happily to God.

When parents, either biological or foster, have the knowledge that children are God's own, they will see parenting as a divine assignment entrusted to them as stewards who will give an account of their stewardship to God on the last day.

TOPIC 3: GOING BACK HOME

GENESIS 48:21–22

Have you ever felt uncomfortable or that you do not belong in a particular place? Perhaps you have found yourself amid people having a coarse and obscene conversation and you felt like the odd person in that group. Or maybe you were invited to a party that turned out to be an arena of immorality and you could not bear but to leave because you felt so out of place there. That is how every true Christian feels in this world: uncomfortable, out of place and odd, because the prevalent lifestyle in the world contrasts with the Christian way of life. Christians are sojourners in this world, not citizens: *"For our citizenship is in heaven, from where we also wait for a Savior, the Lord Jesus Christ"* (Philippians 3:20 NHEB).

Egypt was not a place Jacob considered home. The instruction to take his corpse back to Canaan for burial and handing the portion of land he took from the Amorites to Joseph was motivated by his understanding that he was a foreigner in Egypt. Although God approved his stay in Egypt, and Egypt catered to his family's needs at the time, it was just for a while. He knew that their stay there was a temporary one. The land of Canaan was the Promised Land, not the land of Egypt.

Symbolically for us, the world represents our Egypt, a temporary abode as believers, and we are nothing but strangers in a foreign land – the world. We live in a world abounding with things that attract and distract us, which seem to create a feeling of comfort for those who belong to it. Talk about the pleasures of life: some people will not hesitate to abandon their identity as believers to pleasure themselves. Talk about wealth: what you see is some believers ignoring the pursuit of everlasting treasures in heaven for an inordinate and ephemeral quest for wealth on earth.

Behaving in the way the world behaves, talking the way the world talks, thinking the way the world thinks or dressing the way the world dresses does not portray our status as strangers in the world. Our yearning to return to our eternal home is undoubtedly suppressed when we conform to the world's values. Apostle Paul admonished us in Romans 12:2, saying: *"And do not be conformed to this world, but be transformed by the renewing of your mind, so that you may prove what is the good, well-pleasing, and perfect will of God."* (NHEB.) Jacob understood the temporality of dwelling in Egypt and the blessings of the Promised Land. As such, he did not want his children to get too attached to the extent that they forgot there was a better place awaiting them that was truly their home. Our status as strangers can only be noticeable when our actions conform to the word of God and when we make pleasing God our priority. A wise stranger who knows that he will return home will spend his resources laying treasures in his real home. Jesus, in the parable of the rich fool, refers to anyone who lays treasures for himself in this life and is not rich towards God as a fool. *"But God said to him, 'You foolish one, tonight your soul is required of you. The things which you have prepared—whose will they be?' 21 So is he who lays up treasure for himself, and is not rich toward God."* (Luke 12:20–21 NHEB.)

There is that one thing that can hamper our return home – sin. Sin will cause a separation between you and your Father and give you an alternative permanent home that will be filled with suffering and anguish rather than joy and happiness. Therefore, as you anticipate a pat on the back and a "welcome home child" from God, you must remember not to conform to the pattern of this world. There are things we should not be part of in this place we occupy. We ought to know the transient nature of this earthly dwelling. It is infested with sin and we must be careful because we have been given a garment as pilgrims that must not be stained.

We can only act like Jacob did if we genuinely believe in God's promises. The propensity to give a property as inheritance to Joseph in a land he was not inhabiting reflects someone with zero doubt that they will return. It was the same dogged certainty that Joseph shared when he made the Israelites swear an oath to take his remains back to the Promised Land when the Lord visited them. *"Joseph took an oath of the sons of Israel, saying, "God will surely visit you, and you shall carry up my bones from here.""* (Genesis 50:25 NHEB.) Jacob died without inheriting the land of Canaan as God had promised him, but he was unshaken in his faith that God would bring His promises to fulfilment. This was the kind of faith that the Patriarchs expressed and this is the kind of faith that every Christian should exhibit. Just as Jacob and Joseph believed God, a belief that was justified when God handed the Promised Land to the Israelites many years later, we are confident in God's fulfilment of His salvation plan for mankind, which He brought about by His Son Jesus Christ, and that all who believe in Him shall not perish but have everlasting life. Jesus also made it known to us that He goes to prepare a place for us and that He will come to take us there. *"And if I go and prepare a place for you, I will come again, and will receive you to myself; that where I am, you may be there also."* (John 14:3 NHEB.)

When we align our ways with the word of God our yearning and inner longing will be towards migrating to our Canaan – our eternal dwelling that abounds with joy beyond comprehension and glory beyond description. Nothing in this world should be held so dearly that we risk our salvation. Our involvement in the world's affairs should only be to the extent that it does not constitute harm to our souls. We are not to be yoked with unbelievers, for our culture, values and norms are of the heavenly home. The final possession of our heavenly home will be based on our actions while on earth. Therefore, we must be prepared at all times so that when our time to leave this world comes we, like Apostle Paul, can say: *"For I am already being offered, and the time of my departure has come. ⁷I have fought the good fight. I have finished the course. I have kept the faith. ⁸From now on, there is stored up for me the crown of righteousness, which the Lord, the righteous judge, will give to me on that day; and not to me only, but also to all those who have loved his appearing."* (2 Timothy 4:6–8 NHEB.)

CHAPTER 24

TOPIC 1: SIN AND ITS CONSEQUENCES

GENESIS 49:1–7

A man had been a drunk for the greater part of his life. In his 50s he repented and was forgiven. Soon after, he was diagnosed with liver malfunction and other alcohol-related ailments. He battled those ailments for the rest of his life. Was he forgiven of his sins of drunkenness? Absolutely! But he still faced the consequences of his past addiction. While it is certain that the man had been spared the eternal consequences of the sin of drunkenness, it is evident that he was facing the physical effects of his past misdeeds. We make choices every day of our lives and these choices have consequences. While some repercussions manifest instantly, others come much later in life; and others do not show up in this life.

Genesis 49 records the prophetic predictions of Jacob to his sons before he died. Jacob had gathered them to bless them and make pronouncements of what would be of their future generations. There must have been anxieties and expectations. The first seven verses centre on Jacob's first three sons – Reuben, Simeon and Levi. Incidentally, Jacob's first three sons had negative pronouncements due to their past deeds. Reuben had slept with Jacob's concubine Bilhah. Simeon and Levi massacred an entire community of Shechemites out of anger for Dinah's rape. All these had happened several years before the day of pronouncement. Yet, here they were: the day of reckoning had come and they had to learn the consequences of their actions. For Reuben, his passion – the uncontrolled emotions that led him to disrespect his father through his intercourse with Bilhah – earned him the curse: *"you shall not excel..."* (Genesis 49:4 NHEB.) For their act of massacre, Simeon's and Levi's descendants were to be scattered among the tribes of Israel. Simeon and Levi would live with the regret that they had plunged their descendants into undesirable consequences. They had made their choices and their descendants would suffer for them.

God made man a free moral agent – with freedom of choice. As with every other liberty, freedom to choose has its responsibilities. When Adam and Eve exercised that liberty by disobeying God and yielding to Satan's suggestions their action was not without repercussions. The immediate consequences were shame, fear and expulsion from the garden, followed by a life of toil and suffering. Their action had the eternal effect of plunging the human race into the bondage of sin, resulting in man becoming dead in sin. Paul wrote about the consequence of Adam's disobedience: *"Therefore, as sin entered into the world through one man, and death through sin; and so death passed to all people, because all sinned."* (Romans 5:12 NHEB.) Jesus, however, provided the remedy through His sacrifice on the cross. The human race, faced with the consequence of sin – death – is now offered God's gift – eternal life through Christ. *"For the wages of sin is death, but the free gift of God is everlasting life in Christ Jesus our Lord."* (Romans 6:23 NHEB.) Even with Christ's offer, man has the responsibility to accept and believe in Him as the Saviour and live according to His word. People who receive Him are spared the spiritual and eternal consequence of sin, which is separation from God and eternal abode in the lake of fire. The everlasting effect of sin is wiped away when one repents and forsakes sin. Judging by the eternal consequences of sin, it is only wise for us to abstain from it as advised in 1 Peter 2:11: *"Beloved, I urge you as foreigners and temporary residents, to abstain from fleshly lusts, which war against the soul"* (NHEB). The way to achieve this is to make the word of God part and parcel of our lives. When we read and apply His word, it will lead us on the right path.

Also, there are natural consequences of our actions, as there were for the former drunk living with subsequent ailments. People tend to confuse forgiveness with consequences and wrongly assume that natural consequences are wiped away with sin. Facing natural consequences does not mean that the person has not been forgiven; being forgiven does not necessarily mean that the person may not face the physical consequences of his action. Although God has the power to overturn natural consequences, He may choose not to. There are some physical repercussions God may, in His mercy, overturn. For example, a girl whose womb was damaged in the course of abortion may, after repentance, be content with bearing the consequence of living the rest of her life without giving birth. However, God can change her story despite scientific and natural barriers. God can step in to overturn consequences as He wills, but people should not take God and His grace for granted and expect God to overturn physical consequences at all times.

Misdeeds bring about personal consequences and may have consequences for other people too. 1 Chronicles 21:1–4 records David's sin of conducting a census. *"Satan stood up against Israel, and moved David to number Israel. [2]And David said to Joab and to the leaders of the people, "Go, number Israel from Beersheba even to Dan; and bring me word, that I may know the sum of them." [3]Joab said, "May the LORD make his people a hundred times as many as they are. But, my lord the king, aren't they all my lord's servants? Why does my lord require this thing? Why will he be a cause of guilt to Israel?" [4]Nevertheless the king's word prevailed against Joab. Therefore Joab departed, and went throughout all Israel, and came to Jerusalem."* (NHEB.) Although David was the one who ordered the census, even against the wise counsel of Joab, when the repercussions of his action came the entire nation suffered. David's punishment could be said to be the painful burden of guilt – seeing his people die for his misdeeds. As leaders – in whatever capacity – we should be mindful of what we do, for the negative impact of our misdeeds may spill over to the people under our leadership.

When faced with the physical consequences of our misdeeds, we should be careful not to circumvent those unpleasant moments by going against the word of God. When God allows us to face them, we should do so with humility, repentance and thanksgiving. In humility, we should accept our faults. In repentance, we should be remorseful for our actions and endeavour to make a change in our life. In thanksgiving, we should thank God for the lessons we can draw from our experience, which can benefit us and others. When we repent and live according to His word in thanksgiving, God can turn to good even those circumstances that we had concluded to be irredeemable. Let us not take the grace of God for granted – committing sin at will believing that God will forgive.

Experience, they say, is the best teacher, but the tuition can be very costly and our experiences may leave us with damaging effects, which is not the best teacher. If we have the privilege of seeing people suffer the natural consequences of their sin, we should learn from them instead of making our own mistakes.

Whether we face natural consequences of our actions or God steps in to turn things around, we should know that sin is repulsive to God, and that should be sufficient to discourage us from sinning. Each time we sin, God is saddened, and we risk losing fellowship with Him and spending eternity in hell if we do not repent. This should be enough discouragement to keep us from sin, and be a greater discouragement than the fear of any natural or physical consequences.

TOPIC 2: THE BLESSINGS OF THE SONS OF JACOB

GENESIS 49:1–28

As he lay on the bed, knowing he would soon leave this world Jacob veered into an episode of prophecy for his 12 sons. The words he uttered to them were both prophetic utterances and a series of blessings and curses. These blessings and prophecies were primarily figurative in form, and though they were made to Jacob's sons, they were not fulfilled in their time but in the lives of their descendants. Jacob's sons represented the future tribes of Israel, so the entire nation's fate was being pronounced in Jacob's last words.

A certain air of displeasure pervaded Jacob's words as the actions of some of his children were now brought into account. Reuben received a proclamation of failure and forfeited his rights as the firstborn because of his affair with his father's concubine. The initial praise from his father signifies the privilege Reuben would lose because of sin. *"Reuben, you are my firstborn, my might, and the beginning of my strength; excelling in dignity, and excelling in power."* (Genesis 49:3 NHEB.) Although Reuben committed the sin several years before that moment, it left an indelible mark on his posterity. He was entitled to a particular privilege or right as the firstborn son, which afforded him authority over the household in his father's absence and which was twice what was received by the other sons. But he lost this birthright to the sons of Joseph as a result of his sin. 1 Chronicles 5:1 affirms that: *"The sons of Reuben the firstborn of Israel (for he was the firstborn; but, because he defiled his father's couch, his birthright was given to the sons of Joseph the son of Israel; and the genealogy is not to be reckoned after the birthright)."* (NHEB.)

Reuben's life is a deterrent for engaging in sin, for no matter how long it takes, no sin goes unpunished unless we repent of it. It may initially appear that sin is adequately concealed, ignored by God, and that we may as well feel no immediate physical effect. Yet all of us will stand before God and be judged for our sins at the end of life.

Jacob's pronouncement on Simeon and Levi represented a judgement on their violent vengeance against the Shechemites. Jacob prophesied that Simeon and Levi would be scattered throughout Israel. Although Levi was later blessed by God with the office of the priesthood, and God became his inheritance, Jacob's prophesy was fulfilled in that Levi's descendants were scattered all over Israel, being allotted territories in the lands of the other tribes. *"The LORD said to Aaron, "You shall have no inheritance in their land, neither shall you have any portion among them. I am your portion and your inheritance among the sons of Israel.""* (Numbers 18:20 NHEB.) And Joshua 14:4 says, *"For the children of Joseph were two tribes, Manasseh and Ephraim: and they gave no portion to the Levites in the land, except cities to dwell in, with their suburbs for their livestock and for their property."* (NHEB.) Some have suggested that the decline in the number of Simeonites revealed by the censuses conducted at two different instances was a fulfilment of Jacob's prophecy. Numbers 1:23 says, *"those who were numbered of them, of the tribe of Simeon, were fifty-nine thousand three hundred."* (NHEB.) And Numbers 26:14 says, *"These are the families of the Simeonites, twenty-two thousand two hundred."* (NHEB.) The fact that their inheritance was within the inheritance of Judah is an indication of the fulfilment of Jacob's prophesy. Joshua 19:1 says, *"The second lot came out for Simeon, even for the tribe of the children of Simeon according to their families. Their inheritance was in the midst of the inheritance of the children of Judah."* (NHEB.)

The atmosphere in the room must have assumed a depressive dimension at this juncture. The first three sons had received curses instead of blessings. Then was Judah's time; he was the fourth in line. What would his fate be? Respite had its way as Jacob's declaration turned out to be a blessing for him. The blessings he received were no ordinary blessings. They were manifold. He was to be honoured by his kin. The metaphorical allusion of both a lion and the lion's cub signified the strength and courage of Judah's tribe and depicted the kingship and national prominence they would assume as a tribe. Judah became a leader and the strongest tribe among his brothers. *"For Judah prevailed above his brothers, and of him came the prince…"* (1 Chronicles 5:2 NHEB.) The last part of Jacob's prophesy for Judah was that the sceptre would not depart from him. Great kings, including King David, emerged from Judah and, ultimately, the earthly lineage of Christ – the everlasting King – is traced to the tribe of Judah. *"One of the elders said to me, "Do not weep. Look, the Lion who is of the tribe of Judah, the Root of David, has*

overcome so that he can open the scroll and loose its seven seals.""
(Revelation 5:5 NHEB.)

Zebulun was next in turn for Jacob's pronouncement. Jacob gave him the sea and its related trade. When the Promised Land was shared by lot, Zebulun's lot fell between the Mediterranean Sea and the Sea of Galilee, with its border stretching as far as Zidon. Jacob's prediction was fulfilled in Zebulun's geographical location. *"The land of Zebulun and the land of Naphtali, toward the sea, beyond the Jordan, Galilee of the Gentiles"* (Matthew 4:15 NHEB). It became a haven for ships.

Issachar's tribe later inherited the rich farmlands of Jezreel in Galilee to fulfil Jacob's prophecy. *"The fourth lot came out for Issachar, even for the children of Issachar according to their families. ¹⁸And their border was to Jezreel, and Chesulloth, and Shunem"* (Joshua 19:17–18 NHEB). Jacob prophesied that they would be a people given to agriculture. They would willingly oblige to all tributes levied against them by neighbouring tribes or foreign authorities who invaded them rather than leave their lands.

Of Dan, Jacob predicted he would be a judge and also compared Dan to a snake that would attack riders as they passed: a sneaky, tricky tribe that would cause the fall of the careless. Judges 1:34 lets us know that the Danites were pressed by the Amorites back to the hill country. *"The Amorites forced the children of Dan into the hill country; for they would not allow them to come down to the valley"* (NHEB). Judges 18 narrates how they set out to look for land. In the process, they displayed their snakelike nature. They came to Laish and saw the people there – how they lived quietly and safely without any defence. *"Then the five men departed, and came to Laish, and saw the people who were there, and how they lived in security, after the manner of the Sidonians, quiet and secure; for there was no one in the land possessing authority that might trouble them in anyway, and they were far from the Sidonians, and had no dealings with Aram. ⁸They came to their brothers at Zorah and Eshtaol, and their brothers said to them, "What do you say?"* [9] *They said, "Arise, and let us go up against them, for we have entered and journeyed in the land as far as Laish, and we saw the people how they lived in security, after the manner of the Sidonians, and they were far from the Sidonians, and they had no dealings with Aram. But arise, and let us go up against them; for we have seen the land, and look, it is very good. Will you do nothing? Do not hesitate to go and to enter in to possess the land.* [10] *When you go, you shall come to a secure people, and the land is large; for God has given it into your hand, a place where there is no want of anything that is on the earth.""* (Judges 18:7–10 NHEB.) Finally, the Danites sneaked behind and slaughtered the people, possessed their land and changed the name to Dan. Some have suggested that the prophecy that Dan would judge his people as one of the tribes of Israel was fulfilled during Samson's judgeship.

The declaration that came to Gad must have been depressing and relieving to him in equal measure. His tribe was going to have a warlike experience with times of failure and periods of success. Moreover, Gad would be continually plagued by neighbour enemies the Amorites. Jeremiah prophesied concerning the oppression of the people of Gad in Jeremiah 49:1: *"Of the children of Ammon. "Thus says the LORD: 'Has Israel no sons? Has he no heir? Why then does Malcam possess Gad, and his people dwell in its cities?'"* (NHEB.)

Asher was told he would enjoy a good soil that would provide quality delicacies to royalty and others alike. And it turned out that Asher's tribe later inherited the very fertile land of Carmel along the sea coast.

Much was not said about Naphtali and much is unclear about the fulfilment of Jacob's prophecy about Naphtali in the Bible. However, the imagery of an emancipated female deer breeding beautiful young deer connoted a future of appealing fertility. Naphtali is described as a free deer bearing beautiful fawns. The meaning of the prophecy seems to be that Naphtali would dwell in a rich and fertile territory bordered by the sea.

Then came Joseph, beloved of his father. Jacob, first of all, recounted the incredible manner in which God had rescued Joseph from his enemies, and then declared his blessings. The blessings of the heavens above, deep below, and the breast and womb all referred to the material blessings of fruitfulness that would characterise the future of Joseph's tribe. Given the right of the firstborn, God's blessings upon Joseph's tribe were manifested in the prominence of the tribes of Ephraim and Manasseh. The pronouncements on Joseph were mainly a recollection of what he had been through as a young man. However, Jacob blessed him with the blessing of the Almighty God. Joseph's tribe of Ephraim was the leading tribe in the Northern Kingdom. Joseph received the birthright of Reuben and his descendants became abundantly blessed: ***"The sons of Reuben the firstborn of Israel (for he was the firstborn; but, because he defiled his father's couch, his birthright was given to the sons of Joseph the son of Israel; and the genealogy is not to be reckoned after the birthright)."*** (1 Chronicles 5:1 NHEB.) They had tremendous numerical strength and political influence among their brothers. Joshua 17:17–18 records, ***"Joshua spoke to the house of Joseph, even to Ephraim and to Manasseh, saying, "You are a great people, and have great power. You shall not have one lot only; ¹⁸but the hill country shall be yours. Although it is a forest, you shall cut it down, and it's farthest extent shall be yours; for you shall drive out the Canaanites, though they have chariots of iron, and though they are strong.""*** (NHEB.)

Finally, the declaration for the last born, Benjamin, was issued in three folds. First, the comparison to a wolf symbolised a tribe known for its fierceness and courage. Second, devouring its prey in the morning and dividing its spoils in the evening was an indicator of a tribe with impressive military characteristics, as exhibited by Saul, Ehud and Jonathan. The Benjamin tribe showed a warlike character several times in their history. However, the other tribes almost wiped Benjamin out completely due to Benjamin's cruelty, as recorded in Judges Chapter 19 and 20. Benjamin became so few that Saul said they were the smallest of all the tribes in Israel: ***"Saul answered,***

"Am I not a Benjamite, of the smallest of the tribes of Israel?..."
(1 Samuel 9:21 NHEB.)

Jacob's prophecies to his children represented a declaration of their future according to their past actions and God's will. Thus, we can see how they came to fulfilment, including the promise of the Messiah, despite the number of years it took. We should, therefore, rest in God's promises and His words, knowing that they will all come to fulfilment if we continue in obedience.

TOPIC 3: THE BLESSINGS OF JUDAH

GENESIS 49:8–12

Having declared the future of his first three sons – Reuben, Simeon and Levi, the time had come for Jacob to bless Judah, his fourth son. Judah's blessing in connection to his descendants was second to none among his brothers. Judah means praise, and, just as his name implies, his father blessed him to be praised by his brothers. Judah's blessing means that his descendants, the tribe of Judah, would rule over the descendants of his brothers. As such, they would serve and reverence him because he was blessed to be great in honour and majesty. The fulfilment of this prophecy began in David when he ruled as king over the whole of Israel, and this continued with his son, Solomon, before the ten tribes were taken away from Rehoboam, Solomon's son, and transferred to Jeroboam, the servant of Solomon because Solomon sinned against God. Despite that, the sceptre was not taken away from the tribe of Judah.

Further, Judah's strength was compared to that of a lion in courage, might and boldness. His descendants were blessed with exceptional strength and might to enable them to prevail over their enemies in battles – as long as they remained obedient to God. The blessing in verses 11 and 12 describes the greatness of the physical prosperity of the tribe of Judah. As a royal tribe, Judah was incredibly blessed and this was evident in the greatness of King David, King Solomon and others.

Above all, Jacob prophetically blessed Judah saying: *"The scepter will not depart from Judah, nor the ruler's staff from between his feet, until Shiloh comes. To him will the obedience of the peoples be."* (Genesis 49:10 NHEB.) The sceptre refers to the royal staff of authority. Thus, rulership would remain within the tribe of Judah until Jesus, the Messiah to whom it rightly belonged, came, and the reign of His government would be eternal.

When Adam sinned, mankind's relationship with God was severed. Man lost the beautiful fellowship he had had with God. But in God's compassion and mercy, He did not leave man to desolation but devised a plan to restore man to Himself. This plan would require His Son – Jesus – to come into the world in human form and be offered as a perfect sacrifice for the sins of mankind. *"For him who knew no sin he made to be sin on our behalf; so that in him we might become the righteousness of God."* (2 Corinthians 5:21 NHEB.)

The Son of God needed to come as a human and thus, it had to be through a family line. Here is where Abraham came into play. God called Abraham out of his kin to become the father of many nations and to start the Messiah's line. Of Abraham's sons, God chose Isaac to continue the Messianic line. Isaac had two sons, Esau and Jacob, and even before their birth the mantle was placed on the younger son to continue the lineage of the Messiah.

As Jacob was blessing his children, Judah received a prophetic blessing regarding the coming of Jesus, the Messiah. It was a unique privilege for Judah to be the progenitor of the Messiah. The birth of Jesus into the family of Joseph of the tribe of Judah marked the fulfilment of Jacob's prophetic blessing upon Judah, for Jesus, Himself, is the Lion of the tribe of Judah. *"One of the elders said to me, "Do not weep. Look, the Lion who is of the tribe of Judah, the Root of David, has overcome so that he can open the scroll and loose its seven seals.""* (Revelations 5:5 NHEB.)

Judah and, indeed, Jacob himself might not have understood what the prophecy entailed, but we now understand. As we approach the end of times, the manifestation of Jacob's prophecy becomes clearer. Through the shedding of Jesus' blood, who is of the tribe of Judah, salvation came to the world. Jesus was crucified, buried, resurrected victoriously and ascended gloriously into heaven, where He now sits on the throne as the King of kings and reigns forever over all nations. *"The kingdom of the world now belongs to our Lord and to his Messiah, and he will reign forever and ever."* (Revelations 11:15 NHEB.)

As Jacob prophesied on his deathbed, his words resound through millennia and centuries. He said that the sceptre would not depart until it came to whom it rightly belonged. The physical rulership of Israel served its purpose, and the right person showed up. As Jacob prophesied, the obedience of the people would be to Him – His Kingship is universal and over the entire creation. *"Therefore God also highly exalted him, and gave to him the name which is above every name; ¹⁰that at the name of Jesus every knee should bow, of those in heaven, those on earth, and those under the earth"* (Philippians 2:9–10 NHEB).

Christ came with one singular purpose: to save the world, not from physical kings and their tyrannical rule, but from the enslavement and clutches of the evil one. He came to return mankind to his original position before the fall in Eden. He came to reconcile us to God. Now we have a choice to make, just as Adam and Eve had. It is either we bow to Him humbly in worship and surrender to Him now as the Lamb who takes away the sin of the world, or bow to Him in dread as the Lion of the tribe of Judah, that will come to tread the winepress of God's anger against all those who refuse to accept His Lordship. *"Out of his mouth proceeds a sharp sword, that with it he should strike the nations. He will rule them with an iron scepter. He treads the winepress of the fierceness of the wrath of God, the Almighty. ¹⁶He has on his garment and on his thigh a name written, "King of kings, and Lord of lords.""* (Revelations 19:15–16 NHEB.)

CHAPTER 25

TOPIC 1: YOUR WORD, YOUR BOND

GENESIS 50:4–14

One of the most significant actions of people, that often measures a person's worth and generates expectations, is giving a word of commitment to do something for someone. Simple as it may sometimes seem, the weight of responsibility that comes with the commitment to keep our word is realised not with mere utterance but with responsibility. When responsibility is put into action, trust is built, and then our word becomes our bond.

"I will do as you have said." (Genesis 47:30 NHEB.) Those were Joseph's words to the wish of his father, Jacob. Before Jacob's death, he had one particular desire – a wish to have his corpse buried in the cave situated at the field of Machpelah in the land of Canaan. He desired to be buried there alongside his fathers, Abraham and Isaac. While Joseph was obligated with a promise, he endeavoured to fulfil it. By seeking permission from Pharaoh, Joseph proved he was willing to leave no stone unturned to keep the promise made to his father. Joseph demonstrated his integrity of character and this is a lesson for us believers.

(For more on Your Word, Your Bond, see Chapter 22, Topic 4)

TOPIC 2: GRANDIOSITY OF BURIAL

GENESIS 50:7–10

"All fingers are not equal", it is said. Sadly, many people sweep this concept under the rug by refusing to cut their coats according to their cloth. Many people measure the standard of their lives against the standards of others, and we see many times that they are lost in the sea of competition that leads to misery. A funeral ceremony is one such case and many believe that, just because a person throws a flamboyant funeral ceremony, they must use that as a standard when burying a loved one. In many people's reckless desire to raise their bar to other people's standards they fail to consider the difference in their financial strengths. In the end, they are left with huge debts and a financial sandstorm suppressing them into misery and poverty.

Some funerals could compete with big secular celebrations. Inside the classy coffin could be the deceased, expensively dressed, as though they would be wearing the attire into the afterlife. Event planners may spend considerable time, energy and budget on the actualisation of the funeral ceremony. For them and the family, the main aim of the ceremony is to be as grandiose, if not more grandiose, than the ones organised by others. But if one could eavesdrop into bedroom conversations after such funeral ceremonies, one might discover secret tensions, as suppliers of materials and service providers are still owed, weeks or months after the funeral. People tend to forget that the essential thing in a funeral is not splendour; the essence is that life is commemorated, friends and relations express their condolences, a grieving family is comforted, and, importantly, a good lesson about life and death is taught and learnt.

Like the flow of a misty morning breeze, sadness swept through the house of Israel and the lands of Egypt. The demise of Jacob rocked the nation like a fiery storm. It was a sad day for Joseph, the beloved. It was a gloomy day for the house of Israel. Egypt wept for him and for

70 days he was mourned. Finally, the mourning days passed and it was time to lay him to the dust from whence he came. The chariots that greeted the lands of Canaan were enormous. The number of people and dignitaries who arrived there was massive. It was an event rarely witnessed, and the people of Canaan named that place Abel-mizraim, which is translated as "the place where the Egyptians wept" to commemorate the events that transpired that day.

Looking at the person and position of Joseph, it is understandable why his father's burial would evoke such grandeur and prestige. Joseph was second-in-command to Pharaoh; his societal and financial levels was at the very apex. Today, many people have the social status and economic power to pull off funerals of such magnitude. On the other hand, many people do not share the financial strength or need to pull off similar ceremonies. But, distressingly, this second set of people tend to go the extra mile to produce flamboyant funeral ceremonies.

Performing a grandiose funeral for one's deceased is not a sin but it is improper to incur debts to fund funeral ceremonies just to keep up with the next person; a funeral is not supposed to be a competition. No matter how much money you put into the burial of a loved one, it is of zero value to the dead person. Instead, it can catapult you into debt and reduce your financial state to debris.

Every man must cut his coat according to his cloth. Knowing that all fingers are not equal produces a rationale that will prevent us from going over the top for the burial of a loved one just because another person threw a massive funeral. No one should coerce us into borrowing or spending above our means. When the burial is over, those who insisted we hold a lavish ceremony will withdraw to their nest and let us fend for ourselves. After the funeral, you will have to come back to reality. The bills will pile up and various things requiring financial attention will come knocking. If reality checks on you, and you are not ready, it may reduce you to the torments of financial struggle and poverty. When we die we return to dust. What matters at that point is not the lavishness of a burial ceremony but the destination of our souls. We can spend all the money in this world but that does not affect our souls. We must not allow the standard of some other person's burial to pressure us into unnecessary spending. Remember, funerals should be done out of respect and love for the memories of a loved one, not for social competition and public satisfaction.

While parents are alive, they must not compel their children to hold an elaborate funeral on the occasion of their demise. We should be careful not to leave a financial burden on the living. The most crucial thing to set in place before one dies is the welfare of one's family. We must endeavour to settle all grievances if there are any, give them parting words of wisdom, distribute properties as we deem fit and, most importantly, ensure the family is walking in the way of the Lord.

Sometimes, people can be pretty hypocritical. When their loved ones were alive they could not care less about their welfare. When that money would have been of good value to them they neglected them. But now that they are gone, and just because they want to satisfy the public eye and deceive people into believing that they care, a grand funeral ceremony is thrown. Do we ever stop to wonder what value money has for the dead? What value do lavish burials have on their souls? Let us stop being hypocrites and start caring for our loved ones when they are alive.

Another factor to consider during funeral ceremonies is the complexity of funerary customs and beliefs, which differ from one culture to another. As Christians, we must not observe any funerary customs and beliefs that do not align with God's word.

A good funeral is one full of lessons and reminders that we will leave this world someday, and such events should be solemn. The ceremony can take many forms, and as long as the word of God is not contravened, it is fine. There could be music and prayers, tears and laughter, but at its conclusion let everyone go home thinking about life, its transient nature and how to please the Giver of it. Ecclesiastes

7:2 says: *"It is better to go to the house of mourning than to go to the house of feasting: for that is the end of all men, and the living should take this to heart."* (NHEB.)

TOPIC 3: RIGHT ATTITUDE TOWARDS ADVERSARIES

GENESIS 50:15–20

It is an inherent tendency of people to retaliate against wrongs done to them; they see retaliation as a justifiable action. So, when someone chooses not to retaliate it seems absurd and illogical to many people. It is like breaking the status quo of how things are supposed to be. It is tempting to have the power to exact vengeance, but it is truly divine not to use it.

Joseph had the power to take revenge. He could enact any justice he deemed fit against his brothers. They knew this, and it scared them. Their father, their supposed shield, had passed away and now they were prisoners of their guilt. They resolved to send a message to Joseph, claiming that they had been instructed to do so by their father, asking for forgiveness. Joseph broke into tears on receiving this message; settling old scores was not in his thoughts. He had forgiven them long before they came to the point of requesting forgiveness. When his brothers approached him with the troubles that tormented their hearts, Joseph quickly brushed those troubles aside, stating that God used their inhumane treatment and wickedness to accomplish His purpose. Though Joseph existed when Christ was yet to be born, and laws were not given, he still employed the biblical principle of repaying evil with good as taught by Christ. He promised to take care of his brothers' families in his loving and forgiving way. He displayed forgiveness with empathy – forgiveness accompanied by stretching out a helping hand.

Many people feel forgiveness is a weakness, but the truth is that forgiveness is a great strength. To look above the hurt and choose to let go is a strength many people do not possess. It is not easy to do good to someone who hurts us. Likewise, it is humanly difficult to love somebody who hates us. But following the path of love and forgiveness and being ready to go the extra mile differentiates a Christian from the world. The Christian who is being transformed by renewing his mind through the study of and obedience to God's word will not think of repaying evil with evil but will show love and compassion by reciprocating evil with good. This kind of character is proof that we are becoming more like Christ, who is the embodiment of love and compassion. In 1 Peter 2:23, Peter talks about how Jesus reacted to the offences done against Him. He wrote: **"Who, when he was cursed, did not curse back. When he suffered, did not threaten…"** (NHEB.) Christ sets the standard of the right attitude we should demonstrate whenever we react to offences and offenders. If we chose retaliation over forgiveness, we have lost our worthiness as the salt of the earth.

As long as we are still in this world, it is unavoidable that people will step on our toes and do all manner of things against us. As followers of Christ, we must emulate His attitude towards adversaries and allow His teachings to guide the way we live our lives in a world in which retaliation has become a common practice. Each time we demonstrate a right and godly attitude towards our adversaries God's love is displayed, Christ is preached and God is glorified. On account of this, our adversaries today may become our brethren in Christ tomorrow through their souls' salvation.

Christ's teachings are so different from the world's concepts, theories and practices. Repaying evil with good is not something the world stands for, but it is a trait replicated by Christians. It reflects the marvellous light of Christ that beams through us for the world to see. Christians are the light of the world. But if we repay evil with evil what image are we portraying? Certainly not that of Christ. To have the right attitude towards our adversaries, we will do well to heed Jesus' teaching: **"You have heard that it was said, 'An eye for an eye, and a tooth for a tooth.' 39 But I tell you, do not set yourself against** *the one who is evil. But whoever strikes you on your right cheek, turn to him the other also.* (Matthew 5:38–39 NHEB.)

(For more on Right Attitude Towards Adversaries, see Chapter 20, Topic 2)

TOPIC 4: GUILTY CONSCIENCE

GENESIS 50:15–21

It had been a long time after the brothers conspired against Joseph and sold him into slavery. Regardless of that and of Joseph's reassuring words of forgiveness, his brothers were guilt-struck and terrified that Joseph would punish them for all their evil, now that their father was dead. They were scared because they knew that no matter how much good had come from their evil what they had done was evil and worthy of punishment. The point is simple but really important: God's turning of evil action for good does not make the act less evil.

Joseph's brothers threw themselves down before him and were willing to be slaves to the one they had sold into slavery. Not only does that show the height of their submission, but also the level of their fear due to guilt. They had reason to feel guilty but, ironically, Joseph held no grudge against them; nonetheless, they found themselves running when no one was pursuing. They had been ruthless even when their brother was pleading, and the memory of their deeds and their guilt brought fear. And so it is with every guilty person. Joseph was not bitter or resentful, nor did he show any sign of vengefulness against his brothers. He saw everything as God's way of bringing him to his present position to preserve lives.

A guilty conscience exposes people to continual fright. Proverbs 28:1 perfectly describes this fact: *"The wicked flee when no one pursues; but the righteous are as bold as a lion."* (NHEB.) The solution for dealing with guilt is not just finding a way to feel better but finding a way to be right with God and the people concerned. The best route to freedom from guilt is repentance and confession.

(For more on Guilty Conscience, see Chapter 7, Topic 1 and Chapter 17, Topic 2)

TOPIC 5: GOING BACK HOME

GENESIS 50:24–26

Heaven: what is this place? Even our most enlarged ideas of this future glory – the home that awaits us – are faint, incomplete and do not do justice to it. Heaven could be said to be God's dwelling, the Saviour's home, a paradise of happiness, a temple of worship and adulation, a residence of perfect peace, purity and felicity. There, we understand God's glory in a broader light, the Saviour in His majesty, the angels performing their service and the saints eternally happy and in harmony with God. In heaven, holiness is perfected and mortality is swallowed up in life. In heaven, all pain is banished and all causes of sorrow shut out. There is no reason for weeping or wailing and there is no trouble besetting our path. Yet these beautiful and glorious descriptions of heaven do not do justice to the reality in heaven that awaits all those who conquer the world.

Joseph, like Jacob, his father, understood the temporal nature of their present dwelling in Egypt and the hope of their return to the land of Canaan, not minding his position. Though they had things that made life comfortable in Egypt, they knew Egypt was not their home.

Like his father and his forefathers, Joseph believed and trusted in the power of God to fulfil His promises. He gave strong proof of his faith and it is credited to him. Hebrews 11:22 records: ***"By faith, Joseph, when his end was near, made mention of the departure of the children of Israel; and gave instructions concerning his bones."*** (NHEB.)

Joseph's choice of words is amazing: *""God will surely visit you, and bring you up out of this land to the land which he swore to Abraham, to Isaac, and to Jacob." ²⁵ and you shall carry up my bones from here."* (Genesis 50:24–25 NHEB.) There was no atom of doubt in Joseph's mind; he fully trusted and believed that one day he and his family would return home. Joshua 24:32 depicts how Joseph's request was fulfilled. *"They buried the bones of Joseph, which the sons of Israel brought up out of Egypt, in Shechem, in the parcel of ground which Jacob bought of the sons of Hamor the father of Shechem for a hundred kesitahs. They became the inheritance of the children of Joseph."* (NHEB.) The Israelites also arrived in Canaan – to the home God promised them.

We can learn from Joseph's attitude towards his temporary home. As Joseph did not lose sight of the Promised Land we have to live as strangers here on earth anticipating our return to our heavenly Promised Land. Earth – its pleasures, its beauties and how so many cling to it; sadly, not only is it not the home of believers, it is nobody's home. At the close of the age there will be nothing left of this world. The entire world we see around us and everything in it will be destroyed without fail. *"But the heavens that now are, and the earth, by the same word have been stored up for fire, being reserved against the day of judgment and destruction of ungodly people."* (2 Peter 3:7 NHEB.) At the end of life, those living for the pleasures and the glory of this present world will realise that they were chasing shadows. They will fully understand the vanity and emptiness of all they were pursuing and fighting for and the futility of seeking hope and security in a fleeting world.

The world is filled with many attractions, distracting the heart of many from what is most essential – their soul's salvation. It creates comfort for many, and believers are not exempted from its lure. The negligence of preparedness by some believers about returning to their true home shows their contentment and attachment to this temporal residence. 1 Peter 2:11 warns us on this: *"Beloved, I urge you as foreigners and temporary residents, to abstain from fleshly lusts, which war against the soul"* (NHEB).

Since we are strangers and pilgrims in this world, our thoughts, desires and actions must be geared towards returning to our heavenly home. The words of Paul should further build the anticipation of this return. *"For our citizenship is in heaven, from where we also wait for a Savior, the Lord Jesus Christ"* (Philippians 3:20 NHEB). Let no comfort of this life ever make us forget the transient nature of this world. Many people are clouded by short-sightedness, stopping them from realising what awaits in paradise. How clearly the rich, young ruler exemplifies this. When Jesus told him to sell everything and follow Him, the young man could not bring himself to relinquish all his wealth for what was not tangible. His love for this world prevented him from seeing the glory that awaited him. We must learn not to be so attached to the things of this world. The more we grasp eternal realities, the less we will hold onto the momentary things of this world. The more we desire heavenly glory, the less we long for earthly toys and trifles.

What is this world or the glory of a thousand such perishing worlds compared to the heavenly home? We are travelling fast, unbeknown to most, and at every step we are nearing the day of our reckoning – when we will either spend eternity in the glorious abode of heaven or the wailing pit of damnation. How sad and how foolish it is for men to cleave dearly to the petty enjoyments of this present world, so much so that its lure overpowers us, hinders our heavenward course and make us carefree towards the things of God. What are the vanities of this world but shadows? In a short while, they will be no more. Solomon, after all his toil and enjoyment, penned this down, *"So I was great, and increased more than all who were before me in Jerusalem. My wisdom also remained with me. ¹⁰Whatever my eyes desired, I did not keep from them. I did not withhold my heart from any joy, for my heart rejoiced because of all my labor, and this was my portion from all my labor. ¹¹Then I looked at all the works that my hands had worked, and at the labor that I had labored to do; and look, all was vanity and a chasing after wind, and there was no profit under the sun."* (Ecclesiastes 2:9–11 NHEB.)

The world should hold no value to us; it is but vanity. We must endeavour to reflect a deep-rooted yearning for the place we actually belong to and want to be in – our heavenly home. Our lives should be a testament to how much we love God and love others during our stay here. They should be about the life of faith we have exhibited as pilgrims, the beauty of Christ we have reflected, and not holding the things of this earth so dearly. We are simply on transit to our home and we must represent what our real home stands for in our content of character and life of faith. What people think of Christ and Christianity is, in most cases, based on what they see in us during our stay in the world. So we should walk worthy of our eternal home – heaven.

Our departure from this world could be through the vehicle of death or through the rapture. How then should we handle the knowledge of our departure from this world? First, it should encourage us to go through earthly troubles with the joy and expectation that they will be replaced with the eternal bliss of heaven one day. Second, it should gear us up to living right so that we will spend eternity with Jesus. If it is only on earth that our hope lies, as Apostle Paul put it, we are the most miserable of all people. *"If we have only hoped in Christ in this life, we are of all people most to be pitied."* (1 Corinthians 15:19 NHEB.) Nevertheless, we have a hope that after all the toil of this earth, we are going home to meet our Lord.

We ought to keep reminding ourselves of the fact that Jesus is coming to take us home. The issue is not that many people do not know this fact, but that they do not live their lives in its anticipation. Some may be living under the illusion that they will be part of this home. But sadly, that day will be a reality check for them. The Master gives us an imagery of the fate of such. *"²¹Not everyone who says to me, 'Lord, Lord,' will enter into the kingdom of heaven; but he who does the will of my Father who is in heaven. ²³And then I will tell them, ' I never knew you. Depart from me, you who practice lawlessness.'"* (Matthew 7:21, 23 NHEB.) Our faith in Jesus' return will show in our level of obedience to God.

There is hope for all those not yet eligible for this home, as long as you are alive. But do not procrastinate, thinking you have all the time in the world. Life gives no guarantee of tomorrow. Today, make every effort to be an eligible member of this beautiful home and co-heir with Christ. The way to this home is the Saviour Himself, for He said, ***"I am the way, the truth, and the life. No one comes to the Father except through me."*** (John 14:6 NHEB.) You just have to believe and live in light of His gospel.

Here is the conclusion: we are strangers in this world, travelling through this wilderness with our faces lifted to Zion and in anticipation of that celestial city. Our path may be rough, but the Saviour sustains us by His grace. Our pilgrimage takes us through a valley of tears but faith cheers us with a view of the glorious rest. Let this consideration encourage us amid the troubles of this life. In a while, we shall obtain a joyous entrance into the glorious gates of our heavenly home. Therefore, let our hearts not be entangled with the cares and pleasures of this present life. Let us live in the world as those who are not of it, as those whose treasures are in heaven, and whose hearts are there also.

(For more on Going Back Home, see Chapter 23, Topic 3)

REFERENCES

Campbell, M. (1996) *Behind The Name*. Available at: www.behindthename.com (Assessed: 18 March, 2022).

Scriven, M. (1820-1886) *What a friend we have in Jesus*. Biblesoft Hymnal. PC Study Bible formatted electronic database, Biblesoft Inc. 2003. Available at: https://download.cnet.com/PC-Study-Bible-Limited-Edition/3000-2135_4-78001983.html

The Free Dictionary (2003-2022) Available at: https://www.thefreedictionary.com (Assessed: 18 March, 2022).